The Ultimate Ninja Foodi Cookbook

1000 Easy & Delicious Air Fry, Broil, Pressure Cook, Slow Cook, Dehydrate, and More Recipes for Beginners and Advanced Users

Beatrice S. Caba

Table of Contents

Tropical Fruits Steel-Cut Oats

Prep time: 5 minutes | Cook time: 10 minutes | Serves 4

el-cut oats
berries
on kosher salt
nole milk or your favorite
lternative
oons light brown sugar
opical fruit, such as kiwi,
o, pineapple, and toasted
nut, for garnish

1. Place the oats, allspice, salt, and 3 cups water into the Foodi's inner pot. Lock on the Pressure Lid, making sure the valve is set to Seal, and set to Pressure on High for 10 minutes. Turn off the Foodi and allow the pressure to release naturally for 15 minutes. Then quick-release any remaining pressure and carefully remove the lid.
2. Remove the allspice berries and stir in the milk and brown sugar. Divide among bowls and serve topped with fruit.

Sour Cream Scrambled Eggs

Prep time: 5 minutes | Cook time: 9 minutes | Serves 2

ggs, lightly beaten
oons cold butter, cut into
pieces
on kosher salt
spray
oon sour cream
wedges, for garnish
ground black pepper, for
sh
d chives, for garnish

1. Add the beaten eggs, butter, and salt to a medium bowl and stir to combine (the butter will stay in small pieces).
2. Generously coat the Foodi's inner pot with cooking spray. Drop the Crisping Lid and set the Foodi to Air Crisp at 390°F (199°C) for 9 minutes to preheat. After 1 minute, lift the lid and add the egg mixture. Drop the lid again and resume cooking, until eggs are fluffy and set.
3. When the timer reaches 0, lift the lid and stir in the sour cream. Serve the eggs with a lemon wedge, a sprinkle of pepper, and chives.

Eggs and Mushrooms Casserole

Prep time: 10 minutes | Cook time: 18 minutes | Serves 4

oon unsalted butter
m shallots, minced
s (227 g) button mushrooms,
d
on minced fresh thyme
s
by spinach leaves
oon kosher salt
ground black pepper, to taste
oon plus 1 teaspoon finely
ped fresh chives
ggs
Swiss cheese
baguette, sliced on a bias
spray
½ lemon

1. Add the butter to the Foodi's inner pot and set to Sear/Saute on High. When the butter has melted, use a silicone spatula to "paint" the bottom of the pot with the butter. When the butter starts to foam, after about 5 minutes, add the shallots and cook until they begin to soften, about 3 minutes, stirring occasionally. Stir in the mushrooms and thyme, and cook until mushrooms begin to soften, about 7 minutes.
2. Add the spinach, stir, and allow to cook until the spinach begins to wilt, about 1 minute; mix in the salt, pepper to taste, and 1 tablespoon of the chives. Turn off the heat, stir, and divide the mixture among four 8-ounce ramekins, tamping the mixture down into the bottom of each ramekin. Wash the inner pot.
3. Crack the eggs and add one to each of the ramekins, being careful not to break the yolks.
4. Add ½ cup water to the Foodi's inner pot, insert the reversible rack in the low position, and carefully set the ramekins on the rack. Lock on the Pressure Lid, making sure the valve is set to Seal, and set to Pressure on Low for 3 minutes. When the timer reaches 0, quick-release the pressure and carefully remove the lid. Lay 1 slice of cheese on top of each egg.
5. Spray the baguette slices on both sides with cooking spray and arrange on top of the cheese in each ramekin. Drop the Crisping Lid and set to Broil for 5 minutes, or until the cheese is melted.
6. Combine the lemon zest with the remaining teaspoon of chives. Lift the lid and carefully remove the rack and ramekins. Sprinkle with the zest and chives. Serve warm.

Chapter 1: 4-Week Ninja Foodi Plan

Plan for Week 1

	BREAKFAST	A.M SNACK	LUNCH	P.M SNACK	DINNER
Day 1	Tropical Fruits Steel-Cut Oats	Apple Pies	Hearty Korean Ribs	Cookie Pizza	Brisket with Onion
Day 2	Eggs and Mushrooms Casserole	Apple Pies	Hearty Korean Ribs	Cookie Pizza	Brisket with Onion
Day 3	Tropical Fruits Steel-Cut Oats	Apple Pies	Hearty Korean Ribs	Cookie Pizza	Brisket with Onion
Day 4	Tropical Fruits Steel-Cut Oats	Apple Pies	Lime Steak Tacos	Apple Pies	Brisket with Onion
Day 5	Tropical Fruits Steel-Cut Oats	Cookie Pizza	Lime Steak Tacos	Apple Pies	Hearty Korean Ribs
Day 6	Eggs and Mushrooms Casserole	Cookie Pizza	Lime Steak Tacos	Apple Pies	Hearty Korean Ribs
Day 7	Eggs and Mushrooms Casserole	Cookie Pizza	Lime Steak Tacos	Apple Pies	Hearty Korean Ribs

Plan for Week 2

	BREAKFAST	A.M SNACK	LUNCH	P.M SNACK	DINNER
Day 1	Japanese Pancake	Garlicky Bread	Heartfelt Sesame Fish	Baked Zucchini Bread	Bruschetta Chicken Meal
Day 2	Japanese Pancake	Garlicky Bread	Heartfelt Sesame Fish	Baked Zucchini Bread	Bruschetta Chicken Meal
Day 3	Japanese Pancake	Garlicky Bread	Heartfelt Sesame Fish	Baked Zucchini Bread	Bruschetta Chicken Meal
Day 4	Japanese Pancake	Garlicky Bread	Heartfelt Sesame Fish	Garlicky Bread	Bruschetta Chicken Meal
Day 5	Puffy Dutch Baby	Baked Zucchini Bread	Awesome Veggie Hash	Garlicky Bread	Apricot Salmon with Potatoes
Day 6	Puffy Dutch Baby	Baked Zucchini Bread	Awesome Veggie Hash	Garlicky Bread	Apricot Salmon with Potatoes
Day 7	Puffy Dutch Baby	Baked Zucchini Bread	Awesome Veggie Hash	Garlicky Bread	Apricot Salmon with Potatoes

Plan for Week 3

	BREAKFAST	A.M SNACK	LUNCH	P.M SNACK	DINNER
Day 1	Chinese Ginger Chicken Congee	Breakfast Cinnamon Monkey Bread	Chicken Korma	Breakfast Cinnamon Monkey Bread	Chicken Korma
Day 2	Chinese Ginger Chicken Congee	Breakfast Cinnamon Monkey Bread	Chicken Korma	Breakfast Cinnamon Monkey Bread	Chicken Korma
Day 3	Chinese Ginger Chicken Congee	Breakfast Cinnamon Monkey Bread	Chicken Korma	Breakfast Cinnamon Monkey Bread	Chicken Korma
Day 4	Chinese Ginger Chicken Congee	Breakfast Cinnamon Monkey Bread	Tuscan Chicken and Spinach Penne	Breakfast Cinnamon Monkey Bread	Tuscan Chicken and Spinach Penne
Day 5	Chinese Ginger Chicken Congee	Arborio Rice and Coconut Milk Pudding	Tuscan Chicken and Spinach Penne	Arborio Rice and Coconut Milk Pudding	Tuscan Chicken and Spinach Penne
Day 6	Chinese Ginger Chicken Congee	Arborio Rice and Coconut Milk Pudding	Tuscan Chicken and Spinach Penne	Arborio Rice and Coconut Milk Pudding	Tuscan Chicken and Spinach Penne
Day 7	Chinese Ginger Chicken Congee	Arborio Rice and Coconut Milk Pudding	Tuscan Chicken and Spinach Penne	Arborio Rice and Coconut Milk Pudding	Tuscan Chicken and Spinach Penne

Plan for Week 4

	BREAKFAST	A.M SNACK	LUNCH	P.M SNACK	DINNER
Day 1	Hash Browns	Spicy Ranch Chicken Wings	Thai Beef Rice Bowl	Turkey With Garlic Sauce	Thai Beef Rice Bowl
Day 2	Hash Browns	Spicy Ranch Chicken Wings	Thai Beef Rice Bowl	Turkey With Garlic Sauce	Thai Beef Rice Bowl
Day 3	Hash Browns	Spicy Ranch Chicken Wings	Thai Beef Rice Bowl	Turkey With Garlic Sauce	Thai Beef Rice Bowl
Day 4	Hash Browns	Spicy Ranch Chicken Wings	Thai Beef Rice Bowl	Hot And Spicy Paprika Chicken	Thai Beef Rice Bowl
Day 5	Hash Browns	Turkey With Garlic Sauce	Pork and Peanut Lettuce Wraps	Hot And Spicy Paprika Chicken	Pork and Peanut Lettuce Wraps
Day 6	Hash Browns	Turkey With Garlic Sauce	Pork and Peanut Lettuce Wraps	Hot And Spicy Paprika Chicken	Pork and Peanut Lettuce Wraps
Day 7	Hash Browns	Turkey With Garlic Sauce	Pork and Peanut Lettuce Wraps	Hot And Spicy Paprika Chicken	Pork and Peanut Lettuce Wraps

Chapter 2: Breakfast

Butter Cookies

Prep time: 5 minutes | Cook time: 15 minutes | Makes 6 biscuits

2 cups self-rising flour, plus extra as needed
½ cup (1 stick) cold unsalted butter, cut into small cubes, plus 3 tablespoons, melted
¾ cup buttermilk
Cooking spray
¼ teaspoon kosher salt

1. Remove the inner pot from the Foodi and add the flour and cold b[...] coated potato masher (so you don't scuff or scratch the pot) to m[...] together until there aren't any pieces of butter larger than a small p[...] the butter off the potato masher occasionally).
2. Add the buttermilk to the flour-butter mixture and use a silicone sp[...] sticky dough.
3. Coat your hands in some flour and work the dough in the Foodi po[...] needed to prevent sticking to the pot, until the dough is just barely [...] the dough out onto a lightly floured work surface, lightly flour the t[...] the underside of the Foodi pot to flatten the dough into a ¾-inch-t[...] hands to press the dough until it is about ½ inch thick. Wipe off the [...] the pot, and lightly coat the inside of the pot with cooking spray. In[...] Foodi.
4. Dip the rim of a drinking glass or biscuit cutter into a bit of flour an[...] the dough, flouring the cutter after each cut. (You can gather the s[...] and cut out 1 more biscuit.) Arrange the biscuits in the pot (it's tota[...] brush with the melted butter, and sprinkle with salt.
5. Drop the Crisping Lid and set the Foodi to Broil for 15 minutes, or u[...] brown. Let the biscuits cool for 5 minutes before lifting the lid and [...] pot.

Raspberry Jam

Prep time: 5 minutes | Cook time: 8 minutes | Makes 3 cups

12 ounces (340 g) frozen raspberries
1 cup sugar
Juice of 1 lemon
1 tablespoon cornstarch

1. Add the raspberries, sugar, and 1 cup water to the Foodi's inner pot[...] making sure the valve is set to Seal, and set the Foodi to Pressure o[...] the timer reaches 0, quick-release the pressure and carefully remov[...]
2. In a small bowl, whisk together the lemon juice and cornstarch and [...] the Crisping Lid and set the Foodi to Sear/Saute on High for 6 minu[...] mixture until bubbling and thickened and coats the back of a spoon[...]
3. Transfer the jam to a container and refrigerate uncovered until coo[...] hours. Once cool, cover the container and store in the refrigerator [...]

Chapter 1: 4-Week Ninja Foodi Plan

Plan for Week 1

	BREAKFAST	A.M SNACK	LUNCH	P.M SNACK	DINNER
Day 1	Tropical Fruits Steel-Cut Oats	Apple Pies	Hearty Korean Ribs	Cookie Pizza	Brisket with Onion
Day 2	Eggs and Mushrooms Casserole	Apple Pies	Hearty Korean Ribs	Cookie Pizza	Brisket with Onion
Day 3	Tropical Fruits Steel-Cut Oats	Apple Pies	Hearty Korean Ribs	Cookie Pizza	Brisket with Onion
Day 4	Tropical Fruits Steel-Cut Oats	Apple Pies	Lime Steak Tacos	Apple Pies	Brisket with Onion
Day 5	Tropical Fruits Steel-Cut Oats	Cookie Pizza	Lime Steak Tacos	Apple Pies	Hearty Korean Ribs
Day 6	Eggs and Mushrooms Casserole	Cookie Pizza	Lime Steak Tacos	Apple Pies	Hearty Korean Ribs
Day 7	Eggs and Mushrooms Casserole	Cookie Pizza	Lime Steak Tacos	Apple Pies	Hearty Korean Ribs

Plan for Week 2

	BREAKFAST	A.M SNACK	LUNCH	P.M SNACK	DINNER
Day 1	Japanese Pancake	Garlicky Bread	Heartfelt Sesame Fish	Baked Zucchini Bread	Bruschetta Chicken Meal
Day 2	Japanese Pancake	Garlicky Bread	Heartfelt Sesame Fish	Baked Zucchini Bread	Bruschetta Chicken Meal
Day 3	Japanese Pancake	Garlicky Bread	Heartfelt Sesame Fish	Baked Zucchini Bread	Bruschetta Chicken Meal
Day 4	Japanese Pancake	Garlicky Bread	Heartfelt Sesame Fish	Garlicky Bread	Bruschetta Chicken Meal
Day 5	Puffy Dutch Baby	Baked Zucchini Bread	Awesome Veggie Hash	Garlicky Bread	Apricot Salmon with Potatoes
Day 6	Puffy Dutch Baby	Baked Zucchini Bread	Awesome Veggie Hash	Garlicky Bread	Apricot Salmon with Potatoes
Day 7	Puffy Dutch Baby	Baked Zucchini Bread	Awesome Veggie Hash	Garlicky Bread	Apricot Salmon with Potatoes

Plan for Week 3

	BREAKFAST	A.M SNACK	LUNCH	P.M SNACK	DINNER
Day 1	Chinese Ginger Chicken Congee	Breakfast Cinnamon Monkey Bread	Chicken Korma	Breakfast Cinnamon Monkey Bread	Chicken Korma
Day 2	Chinese Ginger Chicken Congee	Breakfast Cinnamon Monkey Bread	Chicken Korma	Breakfast Cinnamon Monkey Bread	Chicken Korma
Day 3	Chinese Ginger Chicken Congee	Breakfast Cinnamon Monkey Bread	Chicken Korma	Breakfast Cinnamon Monkey Bread	Chicken Korma
Day 4	Chinese Ginger Chicken Congee	Breakfast Cinnamon Monkey Bread	Tuscan Chicken and Spinach Penne	Breakfast Cinnamon Monkey Bread	Tuscan Chicken and Spinach Penne
Day 5	Chinese Ginger Chicken Congee	Arborio Rice and Coconut Milk Pudding	Tuscan Chicken and Spinach Penne	Arborio Rice and Coconut Milk Pudding	Tuscan Chicken and Spinach Penne
Day 6	Chinese Ginger Chicken Congee	Arborio Rice and Coconut Milk Pudding	Tuscan Chicken and Spinach Penne	Arborio Rice and Coconut Milk Pudding	Tuscan Chicken and Spinach Penne
Day 7	Chinese Ginger Chicken Congee	Arborio Rice and Coconut Milk Pudding	Tuscan Chicken and Spinach Penne	Arborio Rice and Coconut Milk Pudding	Tuscan Chicken and Spinach Penne

Plan for Week 4

	BREAKFAST	A.M SNACK	LUNCH	P.M SNACK	DINNER
Day 1	Hash Browns	Spicy Ranch Chicken Wings	Thai Beef Rice Bowl	Turkey With Garlic Sauce	Thai Beef Rice Bowl
Day 2	Hash Browns	Spicy Ranch Chicken Wings	Thai Beef Rice Bowl	Turkey With Garlic Sauce	Thai Beef Rice Bowl
Day 3	Hash Browns	Spicy Ranch Chicken Wings	Thai Beef Rice Bowl	Turkey With Garlic Sauce	Thai Beef Rice Bowl
Day 4	Hash Browns	Spicy Ranch Chicken Wings	Thai Beef Rice Bowl	Hot And Spicy Paprika Chicken	Thai Beef Rice Bowl
Day 5	Hash Browns	Turkey With Garlic Sauce	Pork and Peanut Lettuce Wraps	Hot And Spicy Paprika Chicken	Pork and Peanut Lettuce Wraps
Day 6	Hash Browns	Turkey With Garlic Sauce	Pork and Peanut Lettuce Wraps	Hot And Spicy Paprika Chicken	Pork and Peanut Lettuce Wraps
Day 7	Hash Browns	Turkey With Garlic Sauce	Pork and Peanut Lettuce Wraps	Hot And Spicy Paprika Chicken	Pork and Peanut Lettuce Wraps

Chapter 2: Breakfast

Butter Cookies

Prep time: 5 minutes | Cook time: 15 minutes | Makes 6 biscuits

2 cups self-rising flour, plus extra as needed
½ cup (1 stick) cold unsalted butter, cut into small cubes, plus 3 tablespoons, melted
¾ cup buttermilk
Cooking spray
¼ teaspoon kosher salt

1. Remove the inner pot from the Foodi and add the flour and cold butter cubes. Use a silicone-coated potato masher (so you don't scuff or scratch the pot) to mash the butter and flour together until there aren't any pieces of butter larger than a small pea (you may have to push the butter off the potato masher occasionally).
2. Add the buttermilk to the flour-butter mixture and use a silicone spatula to stir until it makes a sticky dough.
3. Coat your hands in some flour and work the dough in the Foodi pot, adding more flour as needed to prevent sticking to the pot, until the dough is just barely holding together. Turn the dough out onto a lightly floured work surface, lightly flour the top of the dough, and use the underside of the Foodi pot to flatten the dough into a ¾-inch-thick disk. Then use your hands to press the dough until it is about ½ inch thick. Wipe off the bottom and the inside of the pot, and lightly coat the inside of the pot with cooking spray. Insert the pot back into the Foodi.
4. Dip the rim of a drinking glass or biscuit cutter into a bit of flour and then cut 6 biscuits from the dough, flouring the cutter after each cut. (You can gather the scraps, press them together, and cut out 1 more biscuit.) Arrange the biscuits in the pot (it's totally fine if they touch), brush with the melted butter, and sprinkle with salt.
5. Drop the Crisping Lid and set the Foodi to Broil for 15 minutes, or until the biscuits are golden brown. Let the biscuits cool for 5 minutes before lifting the lid and removing them from the pot.

Raspberry Jam

Prep time: 5 minutes | Cook time: 8 minutes | Makes 3 cups

12 ounces (340 g) frozen raspberries
1 cup sugar
Juice of 1 lemon
1 tablespoon cornstarch

1. Add the raspberries, sugar, and 1 cup water to the Foodi's inner pot. Lock on the Pressure Lid, making sure the valve is set to Seal, and set the Foodi to Pressure on High for 2 minutes. When the timer reaches 0, quick-release the pressure and carefully remove the lid.
2. In a small bowl, whisk together the lemon juice and cornstarch and add it to the pot. Drop the Crisping Lid and set the Foodi to Sear/Saute on High for 6 minutes, cooking the raspberry mixture until bubbling and thickened and coats the back of a spoon, lifting the lid to stir often.
3. Transfer the jam to a container and refrigerate uncovered until cool and thickened, about 3 hours. Once cool, cover the container and store in the refrigerator for up to 1 month.

Tropical Fruits Steel-Cut Oats

Prep time: 5 minutes | Cook time: 10 minutes | Serves 4

1 cup steel-cut oats
4 allspice berries
½ teaspoon kosher salt
½ cup whole milk or your favorite
    milk alternative
2 tablespoons light brown sugar
Sliced tropical fruit, such as kiwi,
    mango, pineapple, and toasted
    coconut, for garnish

1. Place the oats, allspice, salt, and 3 cups water into the Foodi's inner pot. Lock on the Pressure Lid, making sure the valve is set to Seal, and set to Pressure on High for 10 minutes. Turn off the Foodi and allow the pressure to release naturally for 15 minutes. Then quick-release any remaining pressure and carefully remove the lid.
2. Remove the allspice berries and stir in the milk and brown sugar. Divide among bowls and serve topped with fruit.

Sour Cream Scrambled Eggs

Prep time: 5 minutes | Cook time: 9 minutes | Serves 2

6 large eggs, lightly beaten
3 tablespoons cold butter, cut into
    small pieces
½ teaspoon kosher salt
Cooking spray
1 tablespoon sour cream
Lemon wedges, for garnish
Freshly ground black pepper, for
    garnish
Chopped chives, for garnish

1. Add the beaten eggs, butter, and salt to a medium bowl and stir to combine (the butter will stay in small pieces).
2. Generously coat the Foodi's inner pot with cooking spray. Drop the Crisping Lid and set the Foodi to Air Crisp at 390°F (199°C) for 9 minutes to preheat. After 1 minute, lift the lid and add the egg mixture. Drop the lid again and resume cooking, until eggs are fluffy and set.
3. When the timer reaches 0, lift the lid and stir in the sour cream. Serve the eggs with a lemon wedge, a sprinkle of pepper, and chives.

Eggs and Mushrooms Casserole

Prep time: 10 minutes | Cook time: 18 minutes | Serves 4

1 tablespoon unsalted butter
2 medium shallots, minced
8 ounces (227 g) button mushrooms,
    sliced
1 teaspoon minced fresh thyme
    leaves
1 cup baby spinach leaves
½ teaspoon kosher salt
Freshly ground black pepper, to taste
1 tablespoon plus 1 teaspoon finely
    chopped fresh chives
4 large eggs
4 slices Swiss cheese
4 pieces baguette, sliced on a bias
Cooking spray
Zest of ½ lemon

1. Add the butter to the Foodi's inner pot and set to Sear/Saute on High. When the butter has melted, use a silicone spatula to "paint" the bottom of the pot with the butter. When the butter starts to foam, after about 5 minutes, add the shallots and cook until they begin to soften, about 3 minutes, stirring occasionally. Stir in the mushrooms and thyme, and cook until mushrooms begin to soften, about 7 minutes.
2. Add the spinach, stir, and allow to cook until the spinach begins to wilt, about 1 minute; mix in the salt, pepper to taste, and 1 tablespoon of the chives. Turn off the heat, stir, and divide the mixture among four 8-ounce ramekins, tamping the mixture down into the bottom of each ramekin. Wash the inner pot.
3. Crack the eggs and add one to each of the ramekins, being careful not to break the yolks.
4. Add ½ cup water to the Foodi's inner pot, insert the reversible rack in the low position, and carefully set the ramekins on the rack. Lock on the Pressure Lid, making sure the valve is set to Seal, and set to Pressure on Low for 3 minutes. When the timer reaches 0, quick-release the pressure and carefully remove the lid. Lay 1 slice of cheese on top of each egg.
5. Spray the baguette slices on both sides with cooking spray and arrange on top of the cheese in each ramekin. Drop the Crisping Lid and set to Broil for 5 minutes, or until the cheese is melted.
6. Combine the lemon zest with the remaining teaspoon of chives. Lift the lid and carefully remove the rack and ramekins. Sprinkle with the zest and chives. Serve warm.

Giant Omelet

Prep time: 5 minutes | Cook time: 5 minutes | Serves 2

1 tablespoon unsalted butter
6 large eggs
½ teaspoon kosher salt
½ cup Chives, for garnish (optional)
Freshly ground black pepper, to taste

1. Add the butter to the Foodi's inner pot and set the Foodi to Sear/Saute on Medium. Use a silicone spatula to "paint" the bottom of the pot with the butter as it melts.
2. In a medium bowl, whisk together the eggs and salt until well combined and uniform in texture. Once the butter has completely melted, add the egg mixture to the inner pot and cook without stirring until just set, about 2 minutes.
3. After 2 minutes, stir the omelet once clockwise to create folds, then drop the Crisping Lid and set the Foodi to Air Crisp at 390°F (199°C) for 3 minutes, or until the omelet is just set.
4. Turn off the Foodi and allow the omelet to rest for 2 minutes. At this point, sprinkle any fillings you like over the omelet (the omelet is still hot enough to melt grated cheese, for example).
5. Lift the lid and remove the inner pot from the Foodi. Run a silicone spatula around the edge of the pot and shake the pot gently to slide the omelet out onto a plate. Fold the omelet over, garnish with chives, if desired, sprinkle with pepper, and enjoy.

Bacon and Gruyère Cheese Quiche

Prep time: 5 minutes | Cook time: 40 minutes | Makes 1 quiche

1 (9-inch) frozen piecrust (the kind that comes fitted into a tin pan)
6 large eggs
½ cup heavy cream
Kosher salt, to taste
Freshly ground black pepper to taste
8 ounces (227 g) Gruyère cheese, grated (about 1 cup)
1 cup cooked and crumbled bacon

1. Let the piecrust thaw for 15 minutes at room temperature. Prick the piecrust all over with the tines of a fork. Place the crust on the Foodi's reversible rack in the low position, then set the rack into the inner pot, drop the Crisping Lid, and set to Bake/Roast at 375°F (190°C) for 10 minutes, or until golden brown. Lift the lid and carefully remove the rack and piecrust from the Foodi; the crust won't be cooked all the way through—just slightly browned.
2. In a large bowl, whisk together the eggs and cream. Add a few pinches of salt and pepper, the grated cheese, and the bacon, and stir to combine.
3. Place the parbaked crust on the rack as before, place the rack in the Foodi's inner pot, and then carefully pour the egg filling into the crust. Drop the Crisping Lid and set the Foodi to Bake/Roast at 325°F (163°C) for 30 minutes, or until the center is set and the top is golden brown.
4. Lift the lid and carefully remove the rack and quiche, then set aside to cool. Serve warm or at room temperature. (The quiche can be refrigerated for up to 3 days and rewarmed before serving.)

Puffy Dutch Baby

Prep time: 10 minutes | Cook time: 16 minutes | Serves 4

¾ cup whole milk
3 large eggs
1 teaspoon vanilla extract
4 tablespoons unsalted butter, melted
½ cup all-purpose flour
2 tablespoons cornstarch
1 tablespoon granulated sugar
Whipped cream, for garnish
Assorted berries, for garnish
Confectioners' sugar, for garnish

1. In a medium bowl, vigorously whisk together the milk and eggs until frothy, about 1 minute. Add the vanilla and 2 tablespoons of the butter, whisk, then add the flour, cornstarch, and granulated sugar, whisking until well combined, about 1 minute more.
2. Set the Foodi to Sear/Saute on High and preheat the Foodi for 5 minutes. Add the remaining 2 tablespoons butter and stir it constantly, until browned, about 6 minutes. Add the batter—it should puff immediately—and cook until it begins to set, about 5 minutes. Drop the Crisping Lid and set to Bake/Roast at 375°F (190°C) for 5 minutes. At this point, the pancake will be set.
3. Lift the lid and carefully remove the inner pot from the Foodi. Run a silicone spatula around the edges of the pancake. Slide the Dutch Baby onto a plate and serve warm, topped with whipped cream, berries, and confectioners' sugar.

Japanese Pancake

Prep time: 10 minutes | Cook time: 22 minutes | Serves 4

2 cups all-purpose flour
3 tablespoons granulated sugar
2 teaspoons baking powder
½ teaspoon baking soda
½ teaspoon kosher salt
1½ cups whole milk
1 large egg
1 tablespoon fresh lemon juice
4 tablespoons unsalted butter, melted, plus extra for serving
Cooking spray
Confectioners' sugar or cocoa powder, for garnish
Warm maple syrup, for garnish

1. In a medium bowl, whisk together the flour, granulated sugar, baking powder, baking soda, and salt. In another medium bowl, whisk together the milk, egg, and lemon juice, and then whisk the melted butter into the milk mixture. Pour the wet ingredients into the dry ingredients, and whisk until completely combined and there aren't any flour streaks remaining in the batter (be cautious not to overmix or you'll end up with a less fluffy pancake).
2. Thoroughly spray the Foodi's inner pot with cooking spray. Add the batter. Lock on the Pressure Lid, making sure the valve is set to Seal, and set to Pressure on Low for 7 minutes. When the timer reaches 0, quick-release the pressure (if any) and carefully remove the lid.
3. Drop the Crisping Lid and set the Foodi to Air Crisp at 390°F (199°C) for 15 minutes, or until the pancake is golden brown and a toothpick inserted into the center comes out clean. While it cooks, open the lid and spray the top with cooking spray every 5 minutes. Use a silicone spatula to remove the pancake from the pot and place it on a platter. Dust with confectioners' sugar and serve in wedges like a pie, with butter and warm maple syrup.

Asparagus with Soft Boiled Eggs

Prep time: 5 minutes | Cook time: 4 minutes | Serves 6

1 pound (454 g) thick asparagus, ends trimmed
6 large eggs
Kosher salt, to taste
Freshly ground black pepper, to taste

1. Place the asparagus on the rack in the low position and set the whole, uncracked eggs directly on top of the asparagus. Add ½ cup water to the pot.
2. Lock on the Pressure Lid, making sure the valve is set to Seal, and set to Pressure on Low for 2 minutes. Fill a medium bowl with cold water and set aside.
3. When the timer reaches 0, quick-release the pressure and keep the lid on. Set the Foodi to Keep Warm for 2 minutes before removing the eggs.
4. Use tongs to transfer the eggs to the cold water and set aside until the eggs are cool enough to handle, about 3 minutes.
5. When the eggs are cool enough to handle and just before peeling them, divide the asparagus among the plates and season with salt and pepper. Lightly tap an egg against a flat work surface and peel away the shell. Repeat with the remaining eggs. Set 1 egg on top of each portion of asparagus, sprinkle with salt and pepper, and serve.

Scramble Tofu with Turmeric

Prep time: 15 minutes | Cook time: 8 minutes | Serves 4

3 tablespoons peanut oil or vegetable oil
½ medium yellow onion, diced
1 garlic clove, minced
8 ounces(227 g) sliced button or cremini mushrooms
1 cup finely chopped cauliflower
2 teaspoons ground cumin
2 teaspoons ground turmeric
1 cup drained canned diced fire-roasted tomatoes
1 (14- to 16-ounce / 397- to 454-g) block firm tofu, drained
1 cup baby spinach leaves
1 cup drained canned chickpeas
2 teaspoons kosher salt
Freshly ground black pepper, to taste

1. Pour the oil into the Foodi's inner pot and set the Foodi to Sear/Saute on High to preheat for 4 minutes. Drop a piece of onion, when it sizzles in the oil, add all the onion and the garlic and cook until they begin to soften, about 3 minutes, stirring occasionally.
2. Add the mushrooms and cook until they begin to soften, about 3 more minutes, stirring occasionally.
3. Mix in the cauliflower, cumin, and turmeric and cook until aromatic, about 2 minutes, stirring occasionally.
4. Add the tomatoes and crumble the tofu into the pot. Lock on the Pressure Lid, making sure the valve is set to Seal, and set to Pressure on High for 0 minutes. When the timer reaches 0, turn off the Foodi and quick-release the pressure. Carefully remove the lid.
5. Stir in the spinach leaves and the chickpeas, vigorously mixing to break up the tofu even more. Add the salt and pepper to taste. Use a silicone slotted spoon to serve.

Chinese Ginger Chicken Congee

Prep time: 5 minutes | Cook time: 15 minutes | Serves 8

2 cups medium-grain white rice
2 pounds (907 g) boneless, skinless chicken thighs
1 (2-inch) piece fresh ginger, peeled and minced
2 tablespoons kosher salt
Sliced scallions, for garnish (optional)
Soy sauce, for serving (optional)
Hot sauce or Chile oil, for serving (optional)
Cooked vegetables (optional)
Chopped fresh cilantro, for garnish (optional)
Soft-boiled egg, for serving (optional)

1. Place the rice, chicken, and ginger in the Foodi's inner pot and add enough water to come up to the fill line. Lock on the Pressure Lid, making sure the valve is set to Seal, and set the Foodi to Pressure on High for 15 minutes.
2. When the timer reaches 0, let the pressure release naturally for 40 minutes, then quick-release any remaining pressure. Carefully remove the lid and stir in the salt. Allow the congee to cool and thicken in the pot, stirring often, for about 10 minutes. Ladle into bowls and serve warm with your chosen garnishes.

Hanging Bacon

Prep time: 5 minutes | Cook time: 12 minutes | Makes 24 half-strips

1 pound (454 g) bacon strips
Cooking spray

1. Cut the bacon in half crosswise to make shorter strips. Coat the reversible rack with cooking spray and fold the bacon strips over every other rung of the rack.
2. Add ½ cup water to the Foodi's inner pot, then set the rack in the inner pot in the high position. Lock on the Pressure Lid, making sure the valve is set to Seal, and set to Pressure on High for 2 minutes. When timer reaches 0, quick-release the pressure and carefully remove the lid.
3. Drop the Crisping Lid and set the Foodi to Air Crisp at 390°F (199°C) for 10 to 15 minutes, depending on your preferred crispness. The bacon is actually fully cooked at this point—all you are doing now is crisping it up; I like my bacon crisp with a little chew here and there, so 13 minutes is my sweet spot.

Gooey Candied Bacon

Prep time: 5 minutes | Cook time: 22 minutes | Serves 6

1 pound (454 g) bacon strips
1 cup packed light brown sugar
1 teaspoon freshly ground black pepper

1. Place all the bacon in the Foodi's inner pot along with 1 cup water. Lock on the Pressure Lid, making sure the valve is set to Seal, and set to Pressure on High for 2 minutes. When the timer reaches 0, quick-release the pressure and carefully remove the lid.
2. Add the brown sugar and the pepper and stir to dissolve the brown sugar.
3. Drop the Crisping Lid and set the Foodi to Air Crisp at 390°F (199°C) for 20 minutes, lifting the lid every 5 minutes to stir the bacon, until it is crisp and sticky.
4. Lift the lid and use tongs to remove the bacon. Separate it into strips on a rack and allow the bacon to cool to room temperature, about 10 minutes to achieve maximum stickiness.

Pork Sausage Patties

Prep time: 5 minutes | Cook time: 20 minutes | Makes 6 patties

1 pound (454 g) ground pork
2 garlic cloves, minced
2 teaspoons finely minced fresh sage leaves
1 teaspoon maple syrup
1 teaspoon red pepper flakes
1 teaspoon kosher salt
¼ teaspoon freshly ground black pepper
Cooking spray

1. Add the pork, garlic, sage, maple syrup, red pepper flakes, salt, and pepper to a medium bowl and mix with your hands until all the ingredients are uniformly combined and sticking together. Lightly wet your hands (that helps the mixture from sticking to your hands) and form the mixture into 6 ½-inch-thick equal patties.
2. Insert the crisping basket into the Foodi's inner pot and generously spray it with cooking spray. Arrange the patties vertically, so that they lean against the walls of the crisping basket.
3. Drop the Crisping Lid and set the Foodi to Air Crisp at 390°F (199°C) for 15 minutes. Halfway through cooking, lift the lid and lay the patties down flat in a ring, slightly overlapping, drop the Crisping Lid again, and continue to cook for the remaining time, until the sausage patties begin to brown. Again, lift the lid and flip the patties, then drop the lid again and set the Foodi to Broil for 5 minutes, or until they are crisp. Use tongs to remove the patties and serve hot.

Spicy Red Shakshuka

Prep time: 10 minutes | Cook time: 18 minutes | Serves 6

2 red bell peppers, seeded, ribbed, and diced
½ medium yellow onion, diced
2 garlic cloves, minced
1 tablespoon tomato paste
1 (28-ounce / 794-g) can crushed tomatoes
2 tablespoons harissa
2 teaspoons ground cumin
¼ cup olive oil
½ teaspoon kosher salt
6 large eggs
Pita or good-quality bread, for serving

1. Place the bell peppers, onion, garlic, tomato paste, crushed tomatoes, harissa, cumin, olive oil, and ½ cup water in the Foodi's inner pot, stirring to combine. Lock on the Pressure Lid, making sure the valve is set to Seal, and set to Pressure on High for 5 minutes. When the timer reaches 0, quick-release the pressure and carefully remove the lid.
2. Set the Foodi to Sear/Sauté on High, and cook until the vegetables have broken down and are kind of saucy, about 5 minutes. Turn off the Foodi and stir in the salt.
3. Crack 1 egg into a measuring cup, being careful not to break the yolk. Carefully pour the egg on top of the shakshuka. Repeat with the remaining eggs, spacing them evenly around the top.
4. Drop the Crisping Lid and set to Broil for 8 minutes, or until the whites are set. Serve immediately with pita or bread.

Green Veggies Shakshuka

Prep time: 15 minutes | Cook time: 27 minutes | Serves 6

3 tablespoons peanut oil or vegetable oil
1 medium yellow onion, diced
4 garlic cloves, minced
1 green bell pepper, ribbed, seeded, and diced
2 serrano chiles, ribbed, seeded, and diced
1 jalapeño, ribbed, seeded, and diced
1 tablespoon ground cumin
1 tablespoon ground coriander
8 ounces (227 g) kale, tough stems and ribs removed, leaves finely chopped
1 teaspoon kosher salt
Juice of ½ lemon
1 bunch cilantro leaves, stems removed and leaves finely chopped
6 large eggs
Crumbled feta cheese, for serving
Finely chopped fresh dill, for garnish
Pita or good-quality bread, for serving

1. Pour the oil into the Foodi's inner pot and set to Sear/Sauté on High for 5 minutes to heat. Add the onion, garlic, bell pepper, chiles, and jalapeño and cook until they begin to soften, about 6 minutes more, stirring often.
2. Stir in the cumin and coriander and continue to cook until aromatic, about 3 minutes.
3. Add the kale to the inner pot. Lock on the Pressure Lid, making sure the valve is set to Seal, and set the Foodi to Pressure on High for 5 minutes. When the timer reaches 0, quick-release the pressure and carefully remove the lid. Stir in the salt and lemon juice, then add the cilantro.
4. Crack 1 egg into a measuring cup, being careful not to break the yolk. Carefully pour the egg on top of the shakshuka. Repeat with the remaining eggs, spacing them evenly around the top.
5. Drop the Crisping Lid and set to Air Crisp at 390°F (199°C) for 8 minutes, or until the whites are set. Sprinkle with feta and dill and serve hot with pita or bread.

Hash Browns

Prep time: 5 minutes | Cook time: 30 minutes | Serves 10 hash brown patties

4 medium russet
  potatoes, peeled and
  then grated on the
  medium holes of a
  box grater
2 tablespoons unsalted
  butter
¼ cup instant flour
1 tablespoon kosher salt
Freshly ground black
  pepper, to taste
Cooking spray

1. Place the grated potatoes in a large bowl and cover with water. Set aside for 1 hour.
2. Drain off the water and then, using cheesecloth, a clean towel, or a nut milk bag, squeeze the excess moisture from the potatoes.
3. Set the Foodi to Sear/Saute on High. Add the potatoes and the butter, and cook, stirring often, until potatoes are softened, about 10 minutes. Turn off the Foodi and add the instant flour, salt, and pepper, stirring until combined.
4. Line a sheet pan with parchment paper. Scoop about 1 cup of the potato mixture onto a piece of plastic wrap and use another piece of plastic wrap to press and shape the potato mixture into a somewhat rectangular patty that is a little larger than a credit card. Transfer the patty to the baking sheet and repeat with the remaining potato mixture; you should have about 10 patties. Freeze for at least 3 hours and up to 8 hours.
5. When you are ready to eat the hash browns, unwrap them, place them in the crisping basket (in a single layer so they cook evenly or vertically), and set the basket in the Foodi's inner pot. Spray all sides of the hash browns with cooking spray. Drop the Crisping Lid and set the Foodi to Air Crisp at 390°F (199°C) for 20 minutes, or until the hash browns are browned and crisp. Serve hot.

Tex-Mex Red Potatoes

Prep time: 5 minutes | Cook time: 29 minutes | Serves 6

3 pounds (1.4kg) baby red
  potatoes
1 tablespoon plus 1 teaspoon
  kosher salt
Cooking spray
1 tablespoon sweet paprika
Freshly ground black pepper

1. Place the potatoes into the crisping basket and set the basket into the Foodi's inner pot. Add 1 tablespoon of the salt and 1 cup water to the pot. Lock on the Pressure Lid, making sure the valve is set to Seal, and set to Pressure on High for 4 minutes. When the timer reaches 0, quick-release the pressure and carefully remove the lid.
2. Remove the crisping basket and remove the inner pot from the Foodi. Discard the water remaining in the inner pot. Return the crisping basket to the inner pot and place the pot in the Foodi. Spray the potatoes heavily with cooking spray, gently tossing to make sure they are thoroughly coated. Season the potatoes with the remaining teaspoon salt, the paprika, and the pepper.
3. Drop the Crisping Lid and set the Foodi to Air Crisp at 390°F (199°C) for 25 minutes. Lift the lid and stir potatoes every 5 minutes with a silicone spoon or spatula, breaking them open slightly; spray them with more cooking spray so the interiors are also well coated. Cook until the potato skins are crisp and browned. Serve hot.

Cheddar Shrimp and Grits

Prep time: 10 minutes | Cook time: 22 minutes | Serves 4

3 tablespoons unsalted butter
1 cup Quaker Oats Quick 5-Minute Grits
2 garlic cloves, minced
1 teaspoon kosher salt, plus more as
  needed
Freshly ground black pepper, to taste
2 cups whole milk
½ cup shredded cheddar cheese
2 tablespoons minced pickled jalapeño
12 ounces (340 g) frozen, peeled, and
  deveined raw extra jumbo shrimp
  (16–20 count)
Cooking spray
Chopped fresh chives, for garnish

1. Set the Foodi to Sear/Saute on High. Add the butter to the inner pot and cook until melted, stirring the butter occasionally with a silicone spatula, about 4 minutes.
2. Add the grits, garlic, 1 teaspoon salt, and the pepper and allow to cook until the garlic begins to soften, about 3 minutes, stirring occasionally. Add 2 cups water and stir the grits once. Lock on the Pressure Lid, making sure the valve is set to Seal, and set to Pressure on High for 0 minutes. When the timer reaches 0, quick-release the pressure and carefully remove the lid.
3. Stir in the milk, cheese, and jalapeño. Insert the reversible rack in the high position.
4. In a bowl, spray both sides of the shrimp with cooking spray. Season with salt and pepper, then place the shrimp on the rack. Drop the Crisping Lid and set the Foodi to Broil for 10 minutes. After 5 minutes, lift the lid and flip the shrimp. Drop the lid and continue to cook until the shrimp are pink, about another 5 minutes. Set the shrimp aside.
5. Stir the grits and divide among 4 bowls. Top each bowl with a few shrimp, then sprinkle with chives and serve immediately.

Korean Casserole with Chile Sauce

Prep time: 20 minutes | Cook time: 45 minutes | Serves 4

For the Chile Sauce:

½ cup gochujang paste
¼ cup hard apple cider (not cider vinegar)
1 tablespoon maple syrup
2 teaspoons apple cider vinegar
1 teaspoon toasted sesame oil
½ teaspoon ground cinnamon

For the Casserole:

6 tablespoons peanut oil or vegetable oil
4 large eggs
1 teaspoon toasted sesame seeds
5 ounces (142 g) fresh shiitake mushrooms, stems removed and caps sliced
1 tablespoon apple cider vinegar
2 cups diced butternut squash
2 cups fresh baby spinach leaves
4 ounces (113 g) snow peas, ends trimmed
Cooking spray
1 (20-ounce / 567-g) bag frozen sweet potato fries
Kosher salt, to taste
1 teaspoon toasted sesame oil

1. Make the chile sauce: In a small bowl, combine the gochujang, cider, maple syrup, vinegar, sesame oil, and cinnamon. Set aside.
2. Make the casserole: Add 3 tablespoons of the oil to the Foodi's inner pot. Set the Foodi to Sear/Saute on High, and heat the oil for 4 minutes. (We are adding a fair amount of liquid to the pot, so I like to let the oil heat up a little extra.)
3. Crack the eggs into a medium bowl, being careful not to break the yolks. Carefully pour the eggs into the inner pot and sprinkle with the sesame seeds. Cook until the bottoms of the whites are set, about 2 minutes. Drop the Crisping Lid, and set the Foodi to Broil for 1 minute, or until the top of the whites are set.
4. Lift the lid and use a silicone spatula to carefully loosen the eggs from the Foodi pot. Remove the inner pot and slide the eggs out onto a sheet pan.
5. Put the inner pot back in the Foodi and set to Sear/Saute on High for 3 minutes. Add the mushrooms and cook, stirring once, until they are softened, about 4 minutes. Add the vinegar, stir, and continue to cook until most of the vinegar is absorbed, about 1 more minute. Transfer the mushrooms to the sheet pan with the eggs, placing them in a separate area.
6. Add the remaining 3 tablespoons oil to the inner pot and set the Foodi to Sear/Saute for 1 minute. Add the butternut squash and cook until it begins to soften, about 3 minutes, stirring every minute or so.
7. Push the butternut squash to one side of the pot and add the spinach to the open space. Clear some room on the bottom of the inner pot and insert the reversible rack in the high position. Add the snow peas to the rack in a single layer, then spray the snow peas generously with cooking spray. Drop the Crisping Lid and set the Foodi to Air Crisp at 390°F (199°C) for 6 minutes. The snow peas will be crisp yet blistered.
8. Lift the lid and carefully remove the rack. Transfer the snow peas to the sheet pan with the eggs and mushrooms and then spoon the spinach and butternut squash onto it, as well.
9. Insert the crisping basket into the inner pot again and spray it liberally with cooking spray. Add the sweet potato fries, spraying them with more cooking spray. Drop the lid and set the Foodi to Air Crisp at 390°F (199°C) for 20 minutes, or until the potatoes are crisp, shaking the basket halfway through the cooking.
10. Lift the lid and remove the crisping basket. Pour the frozen fries directly into the inner pot and season with salt to taste. Carefully arrange the other veggies on top of the sweet potato fries. Drizzle the sesame oil over the veggies and fries, then carefully place the eggs on top.
11. Drop the Crisping Lid and set the Foodi to Air Crisp at 390°F (199°C) for 2 minutes, or until the eggs and veggies are reheated. Lift the lid and drizzle with the chile sauce to taste. Mix lightly, scoop out, and serve.

Chapter 3: Delightful Beef, Pork and Lamb Dishes

Tantalizing Beef Jerky

Prepping time: 10 minutes | Cooking time: 20 minutes | For 4 servings

½ pound beef, sliced into 1/8 inch thick strips
½ cup of soy sauce
2 tablespoons Worcestershire sauce
2 teaspoons ground black pepper
1 teaspoon onion powder
½ teaspoon garlic powder
1 teaspoon salt

1. Add listed ingredient to a large-sized Ziploc bag, seal it shut
2. Shake well, leave it in the fridge overnight
3. Lay strips on dehydrator trays, making sure not to overlap them
4. Lock Air Crisping Lid and set the temperature to 135 degrees F, cook for 7 hours
5. Store in airtight container, enjoy!

Beefed Up Spaghetti Squash

Prepping time: 5 minutes | Cooking time: 10-15 minutes | For 4 servings

2 pounds ground beef
1 medium spaghetti squash
32 ounces marinara sauce
3 tablespoons olive oil

1. Slice squash in half lengthwise and dispose of seeds
2. Add trivet to your Ninja Foodi. Add 1 cup water
3. Arrange squash on the rack and lock lid, cook on HIGH pressure for 8 minutes
4. Quick release pressure.Remove from pot. Clean pot and set your Ninja Foodi to Saute mode
5. Add ground beef and add olive oil, let it heat up
6. Add ground beef and cook until slightly browned and cooked
7. Separate strands from cooked squash and transfer to a bowl
8. Add cooked beef, and mix with marinara sauce. Serve and enjoy!

Adobo Cubed Steak

Prepping time: 5 minutes | Cooking time: 25 minutes | For 4 servings

2 cups of water
8 steaks, cubed, 28 ounces pack
Pepper to taste
1 and ¾ teaspoons adobo seasoning
1 can (8 ounces tomato sauce
1/3 cup green pitted olives
2 tablespoons brine
1 small red pepper
½ a medium onion, sliced

1. Chop peppers, onions into ¼ inch strips
2. Prepare beef by seasoning with adobo and pepper . Add into Ninja Foodi
3. Add remaining and Lock lid, cook on HIGH pressure for 25 minutes
4. Release pressure naturally. Serve and enjoy!

Cool Beef Bourguignon

Prepping time: 10 minutes | Cooking time: 30 minutes | For 4 servings

1 pound stewing steak
½ pound bacon
5 medium carrots, diced
1 large red onion, peeled and sliced
2 garlic cloves, minced
2 teaspoons salt
2 tablespoons fresh thyme
2 tablespoons fresh parsley
2 teaspoons ground pepper
½ cup beef broth
1 tablespoon olive oil
1 tablespoon sugar-free maple syrup (Keto friendly)

1. Set your Ninja Foodi to Saute mode and add 1 tablespoon of oil, allow the oil to heat up
2. Pat your beef dry and season it well
3. Add beef into the Ninja Foodi (in batches and Saute them until nicely browned up
4. Slice up the cooked bacon into strips and add the strips to the pot
5. Add onions as well and brown them. Add the rest of the listed and lock up the lid
6. Cook for 30 minutes on HIGH pressure
7. Allow the pressure to release naturally over 10 minutes . Enjoy!

A Keto-Friendly Philly Willy Steak And Cheese

Prepping time: 10 minutes | Cooking time: 40 minutes | For 4 servings

2 tablespoons olive oil
2 large onion, sliced
8 ounces mushrooms, sliced
1-2 teaspoons Keto friendly steak seasoning
1 tablespoon butter
2 pounds beef chuck roast
12 cup beef stock

1. Set your Ninja Foodi to Saute mode and add oil, let it heat up
2. Rub seasoning over roast and Saute for 1-2 minutes per side
3. Remove and add butter, onion. Add mushrooms, pepper, stock, and roast
4. Lock lid and cook on HIGH pressure for 35 minutes. Naturally, release pressure over 10 minutes
5. Shred meat and sprinkle cheese if using, enjoy!

Beef Stew

Prepping time: 10 minutes | Cooking time: 10 minutes | For 4 servings

1 pound beef roast
4 cups beef broth
3 garlic cloves, chopped
1 carrot, chopped
2 celery stalks, chopped
2 tomatoes, chopped
½ white onion, chopped
¼ teaspoon salt
1/8 teaspoon ground black pepper

1. Add listed to your Ninja Foodi and lock lid, cook on HIGH pressure for 10 minutes
2. Quick release pressure. Open the lid and shred the bee using forks, serve and enjoy!

Juiciest Keto Bacon Strips

Prepping time: 5 minutes | Cooking time: 7 minutes | For 2 servings

10 bacon strips
¼ teaspoon chili flakes
1/3 teaspoon salt
¼ teaspoon basil, dried

1. Rub the bacon strips with chili flakes, dried basil, and salt
2. Turn on your air fryer and place the bacon on the rack
3. Lower the air fryer lid. Cook the bacon at 400F for 5 minutes
4. Cook for 3 minutes more if the bacon is not fully cooked. Serve and enjoy!

Quick Picadillo Dish

Prepping time: 10 minutes | Cooking time: 15-20 minutes | For 4 servings

½ pound lean ground beef
2 garlic cloves, minced
½ large onion, chopped
1 teaspoon salt
1 tomato, chopped
½ red bell pepper, chopped
1 tablespoon cilantro

½ can (4 ounces tomato sauce
1 teaspoon ground cumin
1-2 bay leaves
2 tablespoons green olives, capers
2 tablespoons brine
3 tablespoons water

1. Set your Ninja Foodi to Saute mode and add meat, salt, and pepper, slightly brown
2. Add garlic, tomato, onion, cilantro and Saute for 1 minute
3. Add olives, brine, leaf, cumin, and mix. Pour in sauce, water, and stir
4. Lock lid and cook on HIGH pressure for 15 minutes. Quick release pressure

Simple/Aromatic Meatballs

Prepping time: 8 minutes | Cooking time: 11 minutes | For 4 servings

2 cups ground beef
1 egg, beaten
1 teaspoon Taco seasoning
1tablespoon sugar-free marinara sauce
1 teaspoon garlic, minced
½ teaspoon salt

1. Take a big mixing bowl and place all the into the bowl
2. Add all the into the bowl. Mix together all the by using a spoon or fingertips. Then make the small size meatballs and put them in a layer in the air fryer rack
3. Lower the air fryer lid. Cook the meatballs for 11 minutes at 350 F. Serve immediately and enjoy!

Generous Shepherd's Pie

Prepping time: 10 minutes | Cooking time: 10-15 minutes | For 4 servings

2 cups of water
4 tablespoons butter
4 ounces cream cheese
1 cup mozzarella
1 whole egg
Salt and pepper to taste
1 tablespoon garlic powder
2-3 pounds ground beef
1 cup frozen carrots
8 ounces mushrooms, sliced
1 cup beef broth

1. Add water to Ninja Foodi, arrange cauliflower on top, lock lid and cook for 5 minutes on HIGH pressure
2. Quick release and transfer to a blender, add cream cheese, butter, mozzarella cheese, egg, pepper, and salt. Blend well. Drain water from Ninja Foodi and add beef
3. Add carrots, garlic powder, broth and pepper, and salt
4. Add in cauliflower mix and lock lid, cook for 10 minutes on HIGH pressure
5. Release pressure naturally over 10 minutes. Serve and enjoy!

Hybrid Beef Prime Roast

Prepping time: 10 minutes | Cooking time: 45 minutes | For 4 servings

2 pounds chuck roast
1 tablespoon olive oil
1 teaspoon salt
1 teaspoon ground black pepper
1 teaspoon onion powder
1 teaspoon garlic powder
4 cups beef stock

1. Place roast in Ninja Food pot and season it well with salt and pepper
2. Add oil and set the pot to Saute mode, sear each side of roast for 3 minutes until slightly browned . Add beef broth, onion powder, garlic powder, and stir
3. Lock lid and cook on HIGH pressure for 40 minutes
4. Once the timer goes off, naturally release pressure over 10 minutes
5. Open the lid and serve hot. Enjoy!

The Epic Carne Guisada

Prepping time: 10 minutes | Cooking time: 45 minutes | For 4 servings

3 pounds beef stew
3 tablespoon seasoned salt
1 tablespoon oregano chili powder
1 tablespoon organic cumin
1 pinch crushed red pepper
2 tablespoons olive oil
½ medium lime, juiced
1 cup beef bone broth
3 ounces tomato paste
1 large onion, sliced

1. Trim the beef stew as needed into small bite-sized portions
2. Toss the beef stew pieces with dry seasoning
3. Set your Ninja Foodi to Saute mode and add oil, allow the oil to heat up
4. Add seasoned beef pieces and brown them
5. Combine the browned beef pieces with rest of the
6. Lock up the lid and cook on HIGH pressure for 3 minutes. Release the pressure naturally . Enjoy!

No-Noodle Pure Lasagna

Prepping time: 10 minutes | Cooking time: 10-15 minutes | For 4 servings

2 small onions
2 garlic cloves, minced
1 pound ground beef
1 large egg
1 and ½ cups ricotta cheese
½ cup parmesan cheese
1 jar (25 ounceso marinara sauce
8 ounces mozzarella cheese, sliced

1. Set your Ninja Foodi to Saute mode add beef, brown the beef
2. Add onion and garlic
3. Add parmesan, ricotta, egg in a small dish and keep it on the side
4. Add sauce to browned meat, reserve half for later
5. Sprinkle mozzarella and half of ricotta cheese to the browned meat
6. Top with remaining meat sauce
7. For the final layer, add more mozzarella cheese and remaining ricotta
8. Stir well . Cover with foil transfer to Ninja Foodi
9. Lock lid and cook on HIGH pressure for 8-10 minutes
10. Quick release pressure. Drizzle parmesan cheese on top. Enjoy!

The Wisdom Worthy Corned Beef

Prepping time: 10 minutes | Cooking time: 60 minutes | For 4 servings

4 pounds beef brisket
2 garlic cloves, peeled and minced
2 yellow onions, peeled and sliced
11 ounces celery, thinly sliced
1 tablespoon dried dill
3 bay leaves
4 cinnamon sticks, cut into halves
Salt and pepper to taste
17 ounces of water

1. Take a bowl and add beef, add water and cover, let it soak for 2-3 hours
2. Drain and transfer to the Ninja Foodi
3. Add celery, onions, garlic, bay leaves, dill, cinnamon, dill, salt, pepper and rest of the water to the Ninja Foodi
4. Stir and combine it well. Lock lid and cook on HIGH pressure for 50 minutes
5. Release pressure naturally over 10 minutes
6. Transfer meat to cutting board and slice, divide amongst plates and pour the cooking liquid (alongside veggies over the servings. Enjoy!

Hearty Korean Ribs

Prepping time: 10 minutes | Cooking time: 45 minutes | For 6 servings

1 teaspoon olive oil
2 green onions, cut into 1-inch length
3 garlic cloves, smashed
3 quarter sized ginger slices
4 pounds beef short ribs, 3 inches thick, cut into 3 rib portions
½ cup of water
½ cup coconut aminos
¼ cup dry white wine
2 teaspoons sesame oil
Mince green onions for serving

1. Set your Ninja Foodi to "SAUTE" mode and add oil, let it shimmer
2. Add green onions, garlic, ginger, Saute for 1 minute
3. Add short ribs, water, amines, wine, sesame oil, and stir until the ribs are coated well
4. Lock lid and cook on HIGH pressure for 45 minutes . Release pressure naturally over 10 minutes
5. Remove short ribs from pot and serve with the cooking liquid. Enjoy!

Traditional Beef Sirloin Steak

Prepping time: 5 minutes | Cooking time: 17 minutes | For 4 servings

3 tablespoons butter
½ teaspoon garlic powder
1-2 pounds beef sirloin steaks
Salt and pepper to taste
1 garlic clove, minced

1. Set your Ninja Foodi to sauté mode and add butter, let the butter melt
2. Add beef sirloin steaks . Saute for 2 minutes on each side
3. Add garlic powder, garlic clove, salt, and pepper
4. Lock lid and cook on Medium-HIGH pressure for 15 minutes
5. Release pressure naturally over 10 minutes
6. Transfer prepare Steaks to a serving platter, enjoy!

Pork and Orecchiette Ragu

Prep time: 10 minutes | Cook time: 25 minutes | Serves 6

3 tablespoons extra-virgin olive oil, divided
1 pound (454 g) pork shoulder, cut into large pieces
1 small onion, diced
1 carrot, diced
1 celery stalk, diced
1 garlic clove, minced
1 (28-ounce / 794-g) can crushed tomatoes
1 (28-ounce / 794-g) can tomato purée
1 cup red wine
2 cups beef stock
1 (16-ounce / 454-g) box orecchiette pasta
1 teaspoon sea salt
1 teaspoon Italian seasoning
1 bunch Tuscan kale, ribs and stems removed, torn
¼ cup unsalted butter, cubed
½ cup grated Parmesan cheese

1. Select SEAR/SAUTÉ and set to HI. Select START/STOP to begin. Let preheat for 5 minutes.
2. Place 2 tablespoons of oil in the pot. Once hot, add the pork pieces and sear on all sides, turning until brown, about 10 minutes in total. Transfer the pork to a large plate and set aside.
3. Add onion, carrot, and celery and cook for about 5 minutes. Add the garlic and cook for 1 minute.
4. Add the crushed tomatoes, tomato purée, red wine, beef stock, pasta, salt, and Italian seasoning. Place the pork back in the pot. Assemble pressure lid, making sure the pressure release valve is in the SEAL position.
5. Select PRESSURE and set to LO. Set time to 0 minutes. Select START/STOP to begin.
6. When pressure cooking is complete, allow pressure to naturally release for 10 minutes. After 10 minutes, quick release remaining pressure by moving the pressure release valve to the VENT position. Carefully remove lid when unit has finished releasing pressure.
7. Pull the pork pieces apart using two forks. Add the remaining 1 tablespoon of olive oil, kale, butter, and Parmesan cheese and stir until the butter melts and the kale is wilted. Serve.

Dogs in Blankets

Prep time: 15 minutes | Cook time: 15 minutes | Serves 4

4 beef hot dogs
4 bacon strips
Cooking spray
4 bakery hot dog buns, split and toasted
½ red onion, chopped
1 cup sauerkraut, rinsed and drained

1. Place Cook & Crisp Basket in pot. Close crisping lid. Select AIR CRISP, set temperature to 360°F (182°C), and set time to 5 minutes. Select START/STOP to begin preheating.
2. Wrap each hot dog with 1 strip of bacon, securing it with toothpicks as needed.
3. Once unit has preheated, open lid and coat the basket with cooking spray. Place the hot dogs in the basket in a single layer. Close crisping lid.
4. Select AIR CRISP, set temperature to 360°F (182°C), and set time to 15 minutes. Select START/STOP to begin.
5. After 10 minutes, open lid and check doneness. If needed, continue cooking until it reaches your desired doneness.
6. When cooking is complete, place the hot dog in the buns with the onion and sauerkraut. Top, if desired, with condiments of your choice, such as yellow mustard, ketchup, or mayonnaise.

Pork and Peanut Lettuce Wraps

Prep time: 10 minutes | Cook time: 30 minutes | Serves 6

3 pounds (1.4 kg) boneless pork shoulder, cut into 1- to 2-inch cubes
2 cups light beer
1 cup brown sugar
1 teaspoon chipotle chiles in adobo sauce
1 cup barbecue sauce
1 head iceberg lettuce, quartered and leaves separated
1 cup roasted peanuts, chopped or ground
Cilantro leaves

1. Place the pork, beer, brown sugar, chipotle, and barbecue sauce in the pot. Assemble pressure lid, making sure the pressure release valve is in the SEAL position.
2. Select PRESSURE and set to HI. Set the timer to 30 minutes. Select START/STOP to begin.
3. When pressure cooking is complete, quick release the pressure by turning the pressure release valve to the VENT position. Carefully remove lid when unit has finished releasing pressure.
4. Using a silicone-tipped utensil, shred the pork in the pot. Stir to mix the meat in with the sauce.
5. Place a small amount of pork in a piece of lettuce. Top with peanuts and cilantro to serve.

Baked Taco Elbow Pasta

Prep time: 10 minutes | Cook time: 20 minutes | Serves 6

1 tablespoon extra-virgin olive oil
1 small onion, diced
1 pound (454 g) ground beef
1 packet taco seasoning
1 (14½-ounce / 411-g) can diced tomatoes
1 (4-ounce / 113-g) can diced green chiles
1 (16-ounce / 454-g) box dry elbow pasta
4 cups beef broth
2 ounces (57 g) cream cheese, cut into pieces
3 cups shredded Mexican blend cheese, divided
Optional toppings:
Sour cream, for garnish
Red onion, for garnish
Chopped cilantro, for garnish

1. Select SEAR/SAUTÉ and set to MD:HI. Select START/STOP to begin. Let preheat for 5 minutes.
2. Place the oil, onion, and beef in the pot and cook for about 5 minutes, using a wooden spoon to break apart the beef as it cooks. Add the taco seasoning and mix until the beef is coated.
3. Add the tomatoes, green chiles, pasta, and beef broth. Assemble pressure lid, making sure the pressure release valve is in the SEAL position.
4. Select PRESSURE and set to LO. Set time to 0 minutes. Select START/STOP to begin.
5. When pressure cooking is complete, allow pressure to naturally release for 10 minutes. After 10 minutes, quick release remaining pressure by moving the pressure release valve to the VENT position. Carefully remove lid when unit has finished releasing pressure.
6. Add the cream cheese and 2 cups of cheese. Stir well to melt cheese and ensure all ingredients are combined. Cover the pasta evenly with the remaining 1 cup of cheese. Close crisping lid.
7. Select BROIL and set time to 5 minutes. Select START/STOP to begin.
8. When cooking is complete, serve immediately.

Kielbasa Sausage with Cabbage

Prep time: 10 minutes | Cook time: 1 hour | Serves 6

1½ pounds (680 g) fresh kielbasa sausage links
½ stick (¼ cup) unsalted butter
½ medium onion, thinly sliced
2 garlic cloves, minced
1 large head red cabbage, cut into ¼-inch slices
¼ cup granulated sugar
⅓ cup apple cider vinegar
½ cup water
2 teaspoons caraway seeds
Kosher salt
Freshly ground black pepper

1. Insert Cook & Crisp Basket into pot and close crisping lid. Select AIR CRISP, set temperature to 390°F (199°C), and set time to 15 minutes. Select START/STOP to begin. Let preheat for 5 minutes.
2. Add the sausage to the basket. Close lid and cook for 10 minutes.
3. When cooking is complete, open lid and remove basket and sausage. Set aside.
4. Select SEAR/SAUTÉ and set to HI. Select START/STOP to begin.
5. Add the butter and let it heat for 5 minutes. Add the onion and garlic and cook for 3 minutes.
6. Add the cabbage, sugar, vinegar, water, and caraway seeds, and season with salt and pepper. Assemble pressure lid, making sure the pressure release valve is in the SEAL position.
7. Select PRESSURE and set to HI. Set time to 10 minutes. Select START/STOP to begin.
8. When pressure cooking is complete, quick release the pressure by moving the pressure release valve to the VENT position.
9. Select SEAR/SAUTÉ and set to HI. Set time to 10 minutes. Select START/STOP to begin.
10. After 5 minutes, open lid and add the sausage to the top of cabbage. Close lid and continue cooking.
11. When cooking is complete, open lid and serve.

Mac and Cheese with Bacon

Prep time: 10 minutes | Cook time: 30 minutes | Serves 6

4 strips bacon, chopped
5 cups water
1 (16-ounce / 454-g) box elbow pasta
2 tablespoons unsalted butter
1 tablespoon ground mustard
1 (5-ounce / 142-g) can evaporated milk
8 ounces (227 g) Cheddar cheese, shredded
8 ounces (227 g) Gouda, shredded
Sea salt
Freshly ground black pepper
2 cups panko or Italian bread crumbs
1 stick (½ cup) butter, melted

1. Select SEAR/SAUTÉ and set temperature to HI. Select START/STOP to begin. Let preheat for 5 minutes.
2. Add the bacon and cook, stirring frequently, for about 6 minutes or until crispy. Using a slotted spoon, transfer the bacon to a paper towel-lined plate to drain.
3. Add the water, pasta, 2 tablespoons of butter, and mustard. Assemble pressure lid, making sure the pressure release valve is in the SEAL position.
4. Select PRESSURE and set to LO. Set time to 0 minutes. Select START/STOP to begin.
5. When pressure cooking is complete, allow pressure to naturally release for 10 minutes. After 10 minutes, quick release remaining pressure by moving the pressure release valve to the VENT position. Carefully remove lid when unit has finished releasing pressure.
6. Add the evaporated milk, Cheddar cheese, Gouda cheese and the bacon. Season with salt and pepper. Stir well to melt the cheeses and ensure all ingredients are combined.
7. In a medium bowl, stir together the bread crumbs and melted butter. Cover the pasta evenly with the mixture. Close crisping lid.
8. Select AIR CRISP, set temperature to 360°F (182°C), and set time to 7 minutes. Select START/STOP to begin.
9. When cooking is complete, serve immediately.

Italian Rigatoni, Sausage, and Meatball Potpie

Prep time: 20 minutes | Cook time: 55 minutes | Serves 8

5 cups, plus 1 teaspoon water, divided
1 (16-ounce / 454-g) box rigatoni pasta
4 (4-ounce / 113-g) fresh Italian sausage links
1 (12-ounce / 340-g) bag frozen cooked meatballs
16 ounces (454 g) whole milk Ricotta cheese
1 (25½-ounce / 723-g) jar marinara sauce
2 cups shredded Mozzarella cheese
1 refrigerated store-bought pie crust, room temperature
1 large egg

1. Pour 5 cups of water and the rigatoni in the pot. Assemble pressure lid, making sure the pressure release valve is in the SEAL position.
2. Select PRESSURE and set to LO. Set time to 0 minutes. Select START/STOP to begin.
3. When pressure cooking is complete, quick release the pressure by turning the pressure release valve to the VENT position. Carefully remove lid when unit has finished releasing pressure.
4. Drain the pasta and set it aside, keeping warm. Wipe out pot and return it to base. Insert Cook & Crisp Basket into pot. Close crisping lid.
5. Select AIR CRISP, set temperature to 390°F (199°C), and set time to 15 minutes. Select START/STOP to begin. Let preheat for 5 minutes.
6. Open lid and place the sausages in the basket. Close lid and cook for 10 minutes.
7. When cooking is complete, remove sausages to a cutting board. Add the meatballs to the basket. Close crisping lid.
8. Select AIR CRISP, set temperature to 390°F (199°C), and set time to 10 minutes. Select START/STOP to begin.
9. Slice sausages into very thin rounds.
10. When cooking is complete, transfer the meatballs to the cutting board and slice them in half.
11. In the pot, in this order, add a layer of Ricotta, marinara sauce, sausage, Mozzarella cheese, pasta, marinara sauce, meatballs, Mozzarella cheese, pasta, Ricotta, and marinara sauce. Place the pie crust on top of the filling.
12. In a small bowl, whisk together the egg and remaining 1 teaspoon of water. Brush this on top of the pie crust. With a knife, slice a couple of small holes in the middle of crust to vent it. Close crisping lid.
13. Select BAKE/ROAST, set temperature to 350°F (177°C), and set time to 30 minutes. Select START/STOP to begin.
14. When cooking is complete, open lid. Let sit for 10 minutes before serving.

BBQ Burnt Ends

Prep time: 5 minutes | Cook time: 1 hour 50 minutes | Serves 6

3 pounds (1.4 kg) beef brisket, some (but not all) fat trimmed
¼ cup barbecue spice rub
1 cup water
2 cups barbecue sauce

1. Season the brisket liberally and evenly with the barbecue spice rub.
2. Add the water, then place the brisket in the pot. Assemble pressure lid, making sure the pressure release valve is in the SEAL position.
3. Select PRESSURE and set to HI. Set time to 1 hour, 30 minutes. Select START/STOP to begin.
4. When pressure cooking is complete, quick release the pressure by moving the pressure release valve to the VENT position. Carefully remove lid when unit has finished releasing pressure.
5. Carefully remove the brisket from the pot and place on a cutting board. Let cool at room temperature for 10 minutes, or until brisket can be easily handled.
6. Cut the brisket into 2-inch chunks. Drain the cooking liquid from the pot. Place the brisket chunks in the pot. Add the barbecue sauce and stir gently so the brisket chunks are coated. Close crisping lid.
7. Select AIR CRISP, set temperature to 360°F (182°C), and set time to 20 minutes (for more charred-like results, set time to 23 minutes). Select START/STOP to begin.
8. When cooking is complete, open lid and serve.

Super Cheesy Pepperoni Calzones

Prep time: 10 minutes | Cook time: 18 minutes | Serves 4

All-purpose flour, for dusting
16 ounces (454 g) store-bought pizza dough
1 egg, beaten
2 cups shredded Mozzarella cheese
1 cup Ricotta cheese
½ cup grated Parmesan cheese
½ cup sliced pepperoni
Cooking spray
Pizza sauce, for dipping

1. Dust a clean work surface with the flour. Divide the pizza dough into four equal pieces. Place the dough on the floured surface and roll each piece into an 8-inch round of even thickness. Dust your rolling pin and work surface with additional flour, as needed, to ensure the dough does not stick. Brush egg wash around the edges of each round.
2. Place Cook & Crisp Basket in pot. Close crisping lid. Select AIR CRISP, set temperature to 390°F (199°C), and set time to 5 minutes. Select START/STOP to begin preheating.
3. In a medium bowl, combine the Mozzarella, Ricotta, and Parmesan cheese. Fold in the pepperoni.
4. Spoon one-quarter of the cheese mixture onto one side of each dough round. Fold the other half over the filling and press firmly to seal the edges together. Brush each calzone all over with the egg wash.
5. Once unit is preheated, open lid and coat the basket with cooking spray. Place two calzones in the basket in a single layer. Close crisping lid.
6. Select AIR CRISP, set temperature to 390°F (199°C), and set time to 9 minutes. Select START/STOP to begin.
7. After 7 minutes, open lid to check for doneness. If desired, cook for up to 2 minutes more, until golden brown.
8. When cooking is complete, remove calzone from basket. Repeat steps 5 and 6 with the remaining calzones. Serve warm.

Lime Steak Tacos

Prep time: 5 minutes | Cook time: 16 minutes | Serves 4

2 pounds (907 g) flank steak, cut into ¼-inch strips
¼ cup freshly squeezed lime juice
3 tablespoons grated garlic
3 tablespoons extra-virgin olive oil
2 teaspoons kosher salt
2 teaspoons freshly ground black pepper
2 tablespoons canola oil
12 (8-inch) flour tortillas

1. Place the steak, lime juice, garlic, olive oil, salt, and pepper in a large resealable plastic bag. Refrigerate and marinate for a minimum of 30 minutes or up to 3 hours.
2. Select SEAR/SAUTÉ and set to MD:HI. Select START/STOP to begin. Let preheat for 5 minutes.
3. Add the canola oil and heat for 1 minute. Working in batches, place the steak in the pot and cook, stirring frequently, until the steak is browned, about 8 minutes per batch.
4. Divide the steak slices evenly between the tortillas. Add desired toppings, such as guacamole or sliced avocado, sour cream, pineapple chunks, salsa, and cilantro, and serve immediately.

Thai Beef Rice Bowl

Prep time: 10 minutes | Cook time: 20 minutes | Serves 8

2 pounds (907 g) ground beef
2 tablespoons sriracha
4 tablespoons fish sauce
3 tablespoons soy sauce
Zest of 2 limes
Juice of 2 limes
3 tablespoons brown sugar
2 shallots, diced
2 tablespoons minced garlic
1 red bell pepper, diced
1 bunch Thai basil leaves
6 scallions, sliced
Basmati rice, for serving

1. Select SEAR/SAUTÉ and set temperature to HI. Select START/STOP to begin. Let preheat for 5 minutes.
2. Add the ground beef. Cook, stirring occasionally, until the beef is fully cooked, 3 to 5 minutes.
3. In a small bowl, whisk together the sriracha, fish sauce, soy sauce, lime zest and juice, and brown sugar.
4. Once the beef is cooked, add the shallot and garlic and cook until soft, about 2 minutes.
5. Add sauce mixture and stir. Let boil until reduced slightly, about 5 minutes.
6. Add the bell pepper and basil. Cook just until the basil wilts, about 1 minute.
7. When cooking is complete, garnish with the scallions and serve over rice.

Brisket with Onion

Prep time: 5 minutes | Cook time: 1 hour 10 minutes | Serves 4

---

3 pounds (1.4 kg) beef brisket, quartered
1 onion, cut into quarters
2 cups beef broth
Splash Worcestershire sauce
1 teaspoon kosher salt

1. Select SEAR/SAUTÉ and set temperature to MD:HI. Select START/STOP to begin and allow to preheat for 5 minutes.
2. Add the brisket (fat side down) into the cooking pot and sear for 5 minutes. Using tongs, carefully flip the brisket over and sear on the other side for an additional 5 minutes.
3. In the cooking pot, combine the onion, beef broth, Worcestershire sauce, and salt.
4. Assemble the pressure lid, making sure the pressure release valve is in the SEAL position.
5. Select PRESSURE and set to HI. Set the time to 60 minutes. Select START/STOP to begin.
6. When pressure cooking is complete, allow the pressure to naturally release for 20 minutes. After 20 minutes, quick release any remaining pressure by moving the pressure release valve to the VENT position. Carefully remove lid when unit has finished releasing pressure.
7. Shred or slice the meat, as desired for serving.

Pork Chop Quinoa Bowl

Prep time: 5 minutes | Cook time: 17 minutes | Serves 4

¼ cup smoked paprika
2 tablespoons ground cumin
½ teaspoon cayenne pepper
2 tablespoons dark brown sugar
3 tablespoons kosher salt, divided
2 teaspoons freshly ground black pepper
2 (6-ounce / 170-g) boneless pork chops
2 cups quinoa
3 cups chicken stock

1. In a small bowl, mix together the paprika, cumin, cayenne pepper, sugar, salt, and pepper.
2. Pat the pork chops dry with a paper towel, then rub the spice mixture over the meat ensuring that it's fully covered.
3. Place the quinoa, chicken stock, and salt into the pot. Assemble pressure lid, making sure the pressure release valve is in the SEAL position.
4. Select PRESSURE and set to HI. Set time to 2 minutes. Select START/STOP to begin.
5. When pressure cooking is complete, allow pressure to naturally release for 10 minutes. After 10 minutes, quick release remaining pressure by turning the pressure release valve to the VENT position. Carefully remove lid when unit has finished releasing pressure.
6. Place Reversible Rack in pot in the higher position. Place the pork on the rack. Close crisping lid.
7. Select AIR CRISP, set temperature to 375ºF (191ºC), and set time to 15 minutes. Select START/STOP to begin.
8. After 8 minutes, open lid, and using tongs, flip the pork chops. Close lid and continue cooking until the pork chops have reached an internal temperature of 165ºF (74ºC).
9. When cooking is complete, remove the pork and rice from the pot. Slice the pork and serve in bowls over the rice with desired toppings, such as mint, avocado, mango, blueberries, sprouts, or grape tomatoes.

Pineapple Rack Ribs

Prep time: 10 minutes | Cook time: 29 minutes | Serves 4

---

1 (3-pound / 1.4-kg) rack St. Louis ribs, cut in thirds
1 teaspoon sea salt
½ teaspoon freshly ground black pepper
½ cup water
¼ cup apple cider vinegar
½ cup tomato ketchup
1 (8-ounce / 227-g) can crushed pineapple
3 tablespoons brown sugar
2 tablespoons cornstarch
1 tablespoon soy sauce

1. Season the ribs with salt and pepper.
2. Pour the water into the pot. Place the ribs in the Cook & Crisp Basket and insert basket in pot. Assemble pressure lid, making sure the pressure release valve is in the SEAL position.
3. Select PRESSURE and set to HI. Set time to 19 minutes. Select START/STOP to begin.
4. Add the vinegar, ketchup, pineapple, brown sugar, cornstarch, and soy sauce to a blender and blend under high speed until well combined.
5. When pressure cooking is complete, quick release the pressure by turning the pressure release valve to the VENT position. Carefully remove pressure lid when unit has finished releasing pressure.
6. Liberally brush the ribs with the sauce. Close crisping lid.
7. Select AIR CRISP, set temperature to 400ºF (204ºC), and set time to 20 minutes. Select START/STOP to begin.
8. After 10 minutes, open lid and liberally brush ribs with additional sauce. Flip the ribs and brush the other side. Close lid and continue cooking. Add additional time and basting as desired for crispier results.
9. When cooking is complete, the internal temperature of the meat should read at least 185ºF (85ºC) on a meat thermometer. Remove basket and ribs and serve.

Garlic-Hosin Pork Shoulder and Broccoli

Prep time: 5 minutes | Cook time: 1 hour 5 minutes | Serves 4

1 boneless pork shoulder, between 2½ (1.1 kg) and 3 pounds (1.4 kg)
2½ cups garlic-hoisin sauce, divided, plus additional for glazing
¾ cups water
1 head broccoli, cut into 2-inch florets
1 tablespoon canola oil
Kosher salt
Freshly ground black pepper

1. Place the pork shoulder and 1½ cups of hoisin sauce in large, resealable plastic bag. Move contents to ensure that all pork has been coated with the sauce and seal bag. Refrigerate and let marinate for at least 10 minutes and up to 4 hours.
2. Place Cook & Crisp Basket in pot. Place the water in the pot. Place the pork in the basket. Assemble pressure lid, making sure the pressure release valve is in the SEAL position.
3. Select PRESSURE and set to HI. Set time to 45 minutes. Select START/STOP to begin.
4. Combine the broccoli, oil, ½ cup of hoisin sauce, and salt and pepper in a large bowl. Mix well to coat broccoli with sauce and seasonings.
5. When pressure cooking is complete, quick release the pressure by moving the pressure release valve to the VENT position. Carefully remove lid when unit has finished releasing pressure.
6. Move the pork to one side of the basket and place broccoli in the other side. Brush the remaining ½ cup of hoisin sauce over the pork. Close crisping lid.
7. Select AIR CRISP, set temperature to 390°F (199°C), and set time to 20 minutes. Select START/STOP to begin.
8. Every 5 minutes or so, open lid and glaze pork with additional hoisin sauce. Close lid and continue cooking. Begin checking pork for desired crispiness after 15 minutes, cooking for up to an additional 5 minutes if desired.
9. When cooking is complete, remove pork and broccoli and serve in a family-style dish. If desired, pour some of the cooking liquid over the top of pork and broccoli for even more flavor.

Korean Honey Back Ribs

Prep time: 10 minutes | Cook time: 25 minutes | Serves 4

½ cup soy sauce
2 tablespoons rice vinegar
2 tablespoons sesame oil
1 tablespoon cayenne pepper
8 garlic cloves, minced
1 tablespoon grated fresh ginger
1 small onion, minced
1 (3-pound / 1.4-kg) rack baby back ribs, cut into quarters
½ cup water
¼ cup honey
Sesame seeds, for garnish

1. In a mixing bowl, combine the soy sauce, rice vinegar, sesame oil, cayenne pepper, garlic, ginger, and onion. Pour the mixture over the ribs, cover, and let marinate in the refrigerator for 30 minutes.
2. Place the ribs in the Cook & Crisp Basket, reserving the remaining marinade. Pour the water in the pot and place basket in pot. Assemble pressure lid, making sure the pressure release valve is in the SEAL position.
3. Select PRESURE and set to HI. Set time to 10 minutes. Select START/STOP to begin.
4. When pressure cooking is complete, quick release the pressure by turning the pressure release valve to the VENT position. Carefully remove lid when pressure has finished releasing.
5. Pour the remaining marinade over the ribs. Close lid.
6. Select AIR CRISP, set temperature to 400°F (204°C), and set time to 15 minutes. Select START/STOP to begin.
7. After 10 minutes, open lid and liberally brush the ribs with the honey. Close lid and continue cooking.
8. When cooking is complete, open lid and remove the ribs. Cut them into individual ribs. Sprinkle with the sesame seeds and serve.

Green Bean Pork with Scalloped Potatoes

Prep time: 15 minutes | Cook time: 45 minutes | Serves 2

1½ cups chicken broth
2 cups half-and-half
¼ cup cornstarch
2 teaspoons garlic powder
Kosher salt
Freshly ground black pepper
4 Russet potatoes, sliced ¼-inch thick
4 cups shredded Cheddar cheese, divided
2 bone-in pork chops
½ pound (227 g) green beans, ends trimmed
1 teaspoon minced garlic
1 teaspoon extra-virgin olive oil

1. In a medium bowl, whisk together the chicken broth, half-and-half, cornstarch, garlic powder, salt, and pepper. Pour just enough broth mixture to cover the bottom of the pot.
2. Layer half of the sliced potatoes in the bottom of the pot. Cover the potatoes with 1 cup of cheese, then layer the remaining potatoes over the cheese. Cover the second layer of potatoes with 1 cup of cheese, then pour in the remaining broth mixture to cover potatoes. Assemble pressure lid, making sure the pressure release valve is in the SEAL position.
3. Select PRESSURE and set to HI. Set time to 25 minutes. Select START/STOP to begin.
4. When pressure cooking is complete, allow pressure to release naturally for 25 minutes. After 25 minutes, quick release remaining pressure by moving the pressure release valve to the VENT position. Carefully remove lid when unit has finished releasing pressure.
5. Cover the potatoes with remaining 2 cups of cheese. Place the Reversible Rack in the broil position in the pot. Close crisping lid.
6. Select BROIL and set time to 20 minutes. Select START/STOP to begin.
7. Season the pork chops with salt and pepper.
8. After 4 minutes, open lid. Place the pork chops on the rack. Close the lid and continue cooking for another 12 minutes.
9. In a large bowl, toss the green beans with the garlic and oil, and season with salt and pepper.
10. After 12 minutes, open lid and add the green beans to the rack with the pork chops. Close lid and continue cooking for the remaining 4 minutes.
11. When cooking is complete, open lid and serve.

Herbed Pork with Chutney

Prep time: 10 minutes | Cook time: 23 minutes | Serves 4

1 pound (454 g) pork tenderloin
2½ tablespoons minced rosemary, divided
2½ tablespoons minced thyme, divided
Kosher salt
Freshly ground black pepper
2 tablespoons extra-virgin olive oil
1 small white onion
1 tablespoon minced garlic
¾ cup apple juice
2 apples, cut into ½-inch cubes
2½ tablespoons balsamic vinegar
1 tablespoon honey
2½ teaspoons cornstarch
3 tablespoons unsalted butter, cubed

1. Select SEAR/SAUTÉ and set to HI. Select START/STOP to begin. Let preheat for 5 minutes.
2. Season the pork with 1 tablespoon of rosemary, 1 tablespoon of thyme, salt, and pepper.
3. Once unit is preheated, add the olive oil. Once hot, add the pork and sear for 3 minutes on each side. Once seared, place the pork on a plate and set aside.
4. Add the onion, garlic, and apple juice. Stir, scraping the bottom of the pot to remove any brown bits. Add apples and vinegar and stir. Return the pork to the pot, nestling it in the apple mixture. Assemble pressure lid, making sure the pressure release valve is in the SEAL position.
5. Select PRESSURE and set to HI. Set time to 7 minutes. Select START/STOP to begin.
6. When pressure cooking is complete, allow pressure to naturally release for 14 minutes. After 14 minutes, quick release the pressure by turning the pressure release valve to the VENT position. Carefully remove lid when unit has finished releasing pressure.
7. Remove the pork from the pot, place it on a plate, and cover with aluminum foil.
8. Slightly mash the apples with a potato masher. Stir the honey into the mixture.
9. Remove ¼ cup of cooking liquid from the pot and mix it with the cornstarch until smooth. Pour this mixture into the pot and stir until thickened. Add the butter, 1 tablespoon of rosemary, and 1 tablespoon of thyme and stir until the butter is melted.
10. Slice the pork and serve it with the chutney. Garnish with the remaining ½ tablespoon of rosemary and ½ tablespoon of thyme.

Asian Beef Meatballs in Lettuce

Prep time: 10 minutes | Cook time: 20 minutes | Serves 8

1 pound (454 g) frozen beef meatballs
1¼ cups garlic-hoisin sauce
¼ cup soy sauce
½ cup rice vinegar
2 tablespoons brown sugar
½ tablespoon sriracha
2 tablespoons freshly squeezed lime juice
2 tablespoons cornstarch
2 tablespoons water
1 head butter lettuce

1. Place the meatballs, hoisin sauce, soy sauce, rice vinegar, brown sugar, sriracha, and lime juice in the pot and stir. Assemble pressure lid, making sure the pressure release valve is in the SEAL position.
2. Select PRESSURE and set to HI. Set the time to 20 minutes. Select START/STOP to begin.
3. When pressure cooking is complete, quick release the pressure by turning the pressure release valve to the VENT position. Carefully remove the lid when the unit has finished releasing pressure.
4. Transfer the meatballs to a serving bowl.
5. In a small bowl, mix together the cornstarch and water until smooth. Pour this mixture into the pot, whisking it into the sauce. Once sauce has thickened, pour it over the meatballs.
6. Serve the meatballs in lettuce cups with the toppings of your choice, such as sesame seeds, sliced scallions, chopped peanuts, and julienned cucumber.

Hearty Korean Meatloaf

Prep time: 15 minutes | Cook time: 30 minutes | Serves 4

1 pound (454 g) beef, pork, and veal meatloaf mix
1 large egg
1 cup panko bread crumbs
½ cup whole milk
⅓ cup minced onion
¼ cup chopped cilantro
1 garlic clove, grated
1 tablespoon grated fresh ginger
½ tablespoon fish sauce
1½ teaspoons sesame oil
1 tablespoon, plus 1 teaspoon soy sauce
¼ cup, plus 1 tablespoon gochujang
1 cup water
1 tablespoon honey

1. In a large bowl, stir together the beef, egg, bread crumbs, milk, onion, cilantro, garlic, ginger, fish sauce, sesame oil, 1 teaspoon of soy sauce, and 1 tablespoon of gochujang.
2. Place the meat mixture in the Ninja Loaf Pan or an 8½-inch loaf pan and cover tightly with aluminum foil.
3. Pour the water into the pot. Place the loaf pan on the Reversible Rack, making sure the rack is in the lower position. Place the rack with pan in the pot. Assemble pressure lid, making sure the pressure release valve is in the SEAL position.
4. Select PRESSURE and set to HI. Set time to 15 minutes. Select START/STOP to begin.
5. When pressure cooking is complete, quick release the pressure by moving the pressure release valve to the VENT position. Carefully remove lid when unit has finished releasing pressure.
6. Carefully remove the foil from the pan. Close crisping lid.
7. Select BAKE/ROAST, set temperature to 360°F (182°C), and set time to 15 minutes. Select START/STOP to begin.
8. In a small bowl stir together the remaining ¼ cup of gochujang, 1 tablespoon of soy sauce, and honey.
9. After 7 minutes, open lid and top the meatloaf with the gochujang barbecue mixture. Close lid and continue cooking.
10. When cooking is complete, open lid and remove meatloaf from the pot. Let cool for 10 minutes before serving.

Ricotta Pork Meatballs with Grits

Prep time: 15 minutes | Cook time: 26 minutes | Serves 8 to 10

2 pounds (907 g) ground pork
1 cup whole milk Ricotta cheese
2 eggs
1 cup panko bread crumbs
4 garlic cloves, minced
¼ cup parsley, minced, plus more for garnishing
1½ cups grated Parmesan cheese, divided
2 tablespoons kosher salt, divided
1 teaspoon freshly ground black pepper
2 tablespoons canola oil
4 cups whole milk
1 cup coarse ground grits

1. In a large bowl, combine the pork, Ricotta, eggs, bread crumbs, garlic, parsley, ½ cup of Parmesan, 1 tablespoon of salt, and pepper. Use your hands or a sturdy spatula to mix well.
2. Use a 3-ounce (85-g) ice cream scoop to portion the mixture into individual meatballs. Use your hands to gently form them into balls.
3. Select SEAR/SAUTÉ and set to HI. Select START/STOP to begin. Let preheat for 5 minutes.
4. Add the oil. Add half the meatballs and sear for 6 minutes, flipping them after 3 minutes. Remove from the pot and repeat with the remaining meatballs. Remove the second batch of meatballs from the pot.
5. Add the milk, grits, and remaining 1 tablespoon of salt and stir. Gently place meatballs back in the pot. They will sink slightly when placed in the milk. Assemble pressure lid, making sure pressure release valve is in the SEAL position.
6. Select PRESSURE and set to HI. Set time to 6 minutes. Select START/STOP to begin.
7. When pressure cooking is complete, quick release the pressure by moving the pressure release valve to the VENT position. Carefully remove lid when unit has finished releasing pressure.
8. Sprinkle the remaining 1 cup of Parmesan cheese over the top of the grits and meatballs. Close crisping lid.
9. Select BROIL and set time to 8 minutes. Select START/STOP to begin.
10. When cooking is complete, serve immediately.

Brisket Green Chili Verde

Prep time: 10 minutes | Cook time: 19 minutes | Serves 4

1 tablespoon vegetable oil
½ white onion, diced
1 jalapeño pepper, diced
1 teaspoon garlic, minced
1 pound (454 g) brisket, cooked
1 (19-ounce / 539-g) can green chile enchilada sauce
1 (4-ounce / 113-g) can fire-roasted diced green chiles
Juice of 1 lime
1 teaspoon seasoning salt
½ teaspoon ground chipotle pepper

1. Select SEAR/SAUTÉ and set temperature to HI. Select START/STOP to begin and allow to preheat for 5 minutes.
2. Add oil to the pot and allow to heat for 1 minute. Add the onion, jalapeño, and garlic. Sauté for 3 minutes or until onion is translucent.
3. Add the brisket, enchilada sauce, green chiles, lime juice, salt, and chipotle powder. Mix well.
4. Assemble the pressure lid, making sure the pressure release valve is in the SEAL position.
5. Select PRESSURE and set to HI. Set the time to 15 minutes. Select START/STOP to begin.
6. When cooking is complete, quick release the pressure by turning the pressure release valve to the VENT position. Carefully remove the lid when the unit has finished releasing pressure.

Pork, Bean, and Chile Pie

Prep time: 10 minutes | Cook time: 45 minutes | Serves 8

2 tablespoons extra-virgin olive oil
1 pound (454 g) ground pork
1 yellow onion, diced
1 (12-ounce / 340-g) can black beans, drained
1 cup frozen corn kernels
1 (4-ounce / 113-g) can green chiles
2 tablespoons chili powder
1 box cornbread mix
1½ cups milk
1 cup shredded Cheddar cheese

1. Select SEAR/SAUTÉ and set temperature to MED. Select START/STOP to begin. Let preheat for 3 minutes.
2. Add the olive oil, pork, and onion. Brown the pork, stirring frequently to break the meat into smaller pieces, until cooked through, about 5 minutes.
3. Add the beans, corn, chiles, and chili powder and stir. Simmer, stirring frequently, about 10 minutes.
4. In a medium bowl, combine the cornbread mix, milk, and cheese. Pour it over simmering mixture in an even layer. Close crisping lid.
5. Select BAKE/ROAST, set temperature to 360ºF (182ºC), and set time for 25 minutes. Select START/STOP to begin.
6. After 20 minutes, use wooden toothpick to check if cornbread is done. If the toothpick inserted into the cornbread does not come out clean, close lid and cook for the remaining 5 minutes.
7. When cooking is complete, open lid. Let cool for 10 minutes before slicing and serving.

Chunk and Bell Pepper Ropa Vieja

Prep time: 15 minutes | Cook time: 1 hour 25 minutes | Serves 6

2 tablespoons canola oil, divided
1 red bell pepper, thinly sliced
1 yellow bell pepper, thinly sliced
1 green bell pepper, thinly sliced
1 large onion, thinly sliced
4 garlic cloves, minced
Kosher salt
Freshly ground black pepper
2½ pounds (1.1 kg) chuck roast, cut in half
1 cup beef stock
2 bay leaves
½ cup dry white wine
1 tablespoon white vinegar
1 (16-ounce / 454-g) can crushed tomatoes
1 (8-ounce / 227-g) can tomato paste
2 teaspoons dried oregano
1½ teaspoons ground cumin
1 teaspoon paprika
⅛ teaspoon ground allspice
1 cup green olives with pimentos
Cilantro, for garnish
Lime wedges, for garnish

1. Select SEAR/SAUTÉ and set to HI. Select START/STOP to begin. Let preheat for 5 minutes.
2. Add 1 tablespoon of oil, the bell peppers, onions, and garlic, and season with salt and pepper. Cook, stirring occasionally, for about 5 minutes, or until vegetables have softened and are fragrant.
3. Liberally season the chuck with salt and pepper.
4. When the vegetables are cooked, remove and set aside.
5. Add the remaining 1 tablespoon of oil and meat. Sear the roast on both sides so that a dark crust forms, about 5 minutes per side.
6. Add the beef stock and bay leaves. Scrape the bottom of the pot with a rubber or wooden spoon to release any browned bits stuck to it. Assemble pressure lid, making sure the pressure release valve is in the SEAL position.
7. Select PRESSURE and set to HI. Set time to 40 minutes. Select START/STOP to begin.
8. When pressure cooking is complete, quick release the pressure by turning the pressure release valve to the VENT position. Carefully remove lid when unit has finished releasing pressure.
9. Carefully shred the beef in the pot using two forks.
10. Select SEAR/SAUTÉ and set to MED. Select START/STOP to begin. Add the vegetables, wine, vinegar, crushed tomatoes, tomato paste, oregano, cumin, paprika, and allspice and stir with a rubber or wooden spoon, being sure to scrape the bottom of the pot. Simmer, stirring occasionally, for about 25 minutes or until sauce has reduced and thickened.
11. Add the olives and continue cooking for 2 minutes. Serve, garnished with cilantro and lime wedges.

Quinoa, Nut, and Chickpea Stuffed Butternut Squash

Prep time: 10 minutes | Cook time: 13 minutes | Serves 4

2 tablespoons extra-virgin olive oil

1 tablespoon minced garlic

1 small shallot, minced

Kosher salt

Freshly ground black pepper

½ cup dried cranberries

1 cup tri-colored quinoa

2¾ cups water, divided

2 cups roughly chopped kale

1 small butternut squash, top trimmed, halved lengthwise

1 tablespoon freshly squeezed orange juice

Zest of 1 orange

1 (2-ounce / 57-g) jar pine nuts

1 (15-ounce / 425-g) can chickpeas, rinsed and drained

1. Select SEAR/SAUTÉ and set to HI. Select START/STOP to begin. Let preheat for 5 minutes.
2. Add the olive oil, garlic, shallot, salt, and pepper. Cook until garlic and shallot have softened and turned golden brown, about 2 minutes.
3. Stir in the cranberries, quinoa, and 1¼ cups of water. Assemble pressure lid, making sure the pressure release valve is in the SEAL position.
4. Select PRESSURE and set to HI. Set time to 2 minutes. Select START/STOP to begin.
5. When pressure cooking is complete, allow pressure to naturally release for 10 minutes. After 10 minutes, quick release remaining pressure by turning the pressure release valve to the VENT position. Carefully remove lid when the unit has finished releasing pressure.
6. Place the quinoa in a large bowl. Stir in the kale. Cover the bowl with aluminum foil and set aside.
7. Pour the remaining 1½ cups of water into the pot. Place the butternut squash cut-side up on the Reversible Rack, then lower it into the pot. Assemble pressure lid, making sure the pressure release valve is in the SEAL position.
8. Select PRESSURE and set to HI. Set the time to 8 minutes. Select START/STOP to begin.
9. Mix the orange juice, orange zest, pine nuts, and chickpeas into the quinoa mixture.
10. When pressure cooking is complete, quick release the pressure by turning the pressure release valve to the VENT position. Carefully remove lid when unit has finished releasing pressure.
11. Carefully remove rack from pot. Using a spoon slightly hollow out the squash. Spoon the quinoa mixture into the squash. Cut in half and serve.

Cauliflower and Chickpea Green Salad

Prep time: 10 minutes | Cook time: 15 minutes | Serves 6

1 head cauliflower, cut into florets

1 (14-ounce / 397-g) can chickpeas, rinsed and drained

3 tablespoons, plus ¼ cup extra-virgin olive oil

1 tablespoon chili powder

2 teaspoons paprika

3 garlic cloves, minced

4 cups mixed baby greens

1 cucumber, sliced

3 tablespoons chopped fresh parsley

Juice of 1 lemon

2 tablespoons honey

2 tablespoons Dijon mustard

2 tablespoons apple cider vinegar

⅓ cup crumbled feta cheese

Sea salt

Freshly ground black pepper

1. Insert Cook & Crisp Basket in pot. Close crisping lid. Select AIR CRISP, set temperature to 390ºF (199ºC), and set the time to 5 minutes. Select START/STOP to begin preheating.
2. In a large bowl combine the cauliflower florets, chickpeas, 3 tablespoons of olive oil, chili powder, paprika, and garlic.
3. Once unit has preheated, open lid and add the cauliflower and chickpeas to the basket. Close lid.
4. Select AIR CRISP, set temperature to 390ºF (199ºC), and set time to 15 minutes. Select START/STOP to begin.
5. In another large bowl, combine the mixed greens, cucumber, and parsley.
6. In a small bowl, whisk together the lemon juice, honey, mustard, and vinegar.
7. When cooking is complete, carefully remove basket with cauliflower and chickpeas. Add them to the bowl of greens and toss well to combine. Top with feta cheese and dressing, season with salt and pepper, and serve.

Mushroom and Cheddar Poutine

Prep time: 10 minutes | Cook time: 46 minutes | Serves 4

2 tablespoons unsalted butter
1 small yellow onion, diced
1 garlic clove, minced
8 ounces (227 g) cremini mushrooms, sliced
¼ cup red wine
3 cups vegetable stock
¼ cup all-purpose flour
Kosher salt
Freshly ground black pepper
1 pound (454 g) frozen French fries
8 ounces (227 g) Cheddar cheese, cubed

1. Select SEAR/SAUTÉ and set to MED. Select START/STOP to begin. Let preheat for 3 minutes.
2. Add the butter, onion, and garlic. Cook, stirring occasionally, for 5 minutes. Add the mushrooms and sauté for 5 minutes. Add the wine and let it simmer and reduce for 3 minutes.
3. In large bowl, slowly whisk together the stock and flour. Whisk this mixture into the vegetables in the pot. Cook the gravy for 10 minutes. Season with salt and pepper. Transfer the gravy to a medium bowl and set aside. Clean out the pot and return to unit.
4. Insert Cook & Crisp Basket and add the French fries. Close crisping lid.
5. Select AIR CRISP, set temperature to 360°F (182°C), and set time to 18 minutes. Select START/STOP to begin.
6. Every 5 minutes, open lid and remove and shake basket to ensure even cooking.
7. Once cooking is complete, remove fries from basket and place in the pot. Add the cheese and stir. Cover with the gravy. Close crisping lid.
8. Select AIR CRISP, set temperature to 375°F (191°C), and set time 5 minutes. Select START/STOP to begin.
9. When cooking is complete, serve immediately.

Wine-Glazed Roasted Cabbage

Prep time: 5 minutes | Cook time: 32 minutes | Serves 8

1 head green cabbage
½ cup, plus 1 tablespoon water
1 tablespoon extra-virgin olive oil
Kosher salt
Freshly ground black pepper
2 cups white wine
¼ cup minced red onion
1 cup heavy (whipping) cream
¼ cup minced fresh dill
¼ cup minced fresh parsley
2 tablespoons whole-grain mustard
1 tablespoon cornstarch

1. Place the cabbage and ½ cup of water, stem-side down, in the pot.
2. With a knife cut an X into the top of the cabbage cutting all the way through to the bottom through the core. Assemble pressure lid, making sure the pressure release valve is in the SEAL position.
3. Select PRESSURE and set temperature to HI. Set time to 15 minutes. Select START/STOP to begin.
4. When pressure cooking is complete, quick release the pressure by turning the pressure release valve to the VENT position. Carefully remove lid when unit has finished releasing pressure.
5. Brush the cabbage with the olive oil and season with salt and pepper. Close crisping lid.
6. Select AIR CRISP, set temperature to 390°F (199°C), and set time to 12 minutes. Select START/STOP to begin.
7. Once cooking is complete, open lid, lift out the cabbage, wrap with foil, and set aside. Leave any remaining water in the pot.
8. Select SEAR/SAUTÉ. Set temperature to HI. Select START/STOP to begin.
9. Add the white wine and onion and stir, scraping any brown bits off the bottom of the pot. Stir in the cream, dill, parsley, and mustard. Let simmer for 5 minutes.
10. In a small bowl, whisk together the cornstarch and the remaining 1 tablespoon of water until smooth. Stir it into the mixture in the pot. Cook until the sauce has thickened and coats the back of a spoon, about 2 minutes.
11. Pour half of the sauce over the cabbage. Cut the cabbage into 8 pieces and serve with remaining sauce.

Lentils and Paneer Curry

Prep time: 15 minutes | Cook time: 35 minutes | Serves 8

1 tablespoon vegetable oil
1 small onion, diced
1 small bell pepper, diced
1 large potato, cut into 1-inch cubes
1 teaspoon ground turmeric
1 teaspoon cumin seeds
1 teaspoon ground cumin
1 teaspoon garam masala (optional)
1 teaspoon curry powder
1 (15-ounce / 425-g) jar curry sauce, plus 1 jar water
1 (14-ounce / 397-g) can diced tomatoes
1 cup dried red lentils
8 ounces (227 g) paneer, cubed (optional)
1 cup fresh cilantro, roughly chopped (optional)
Salt
Freshly ground black pepper

1. Select SEAR/SAUTÉ and set temperature to HI. Select START/STOP to begin and allow to preheat for 5 minutes.
2. Add the oil to the pot and allow to heat for 1 minute. Add the onion and bell pepper and sauté for 3 to 4 minutes.
3. Add the potato, turmeric, cumin seeds, cumin, garam masala, and curry powder. Stir and cook for 5 minutes.
4. Stir in the curry sauce, water, tomatoes, and lentils.
5. Assemble the pressure lid, making sure the pressure release valve is in the SEAL position.
6. Select PRESSURE and set to HI. Set the time to 15 minutes. Select START/STOP to begin.
7. When pressure cooking is complete, allow the pressure to naturally release for 10 minutes. After 10 minutes, quick release any remaining pressure by moving the pressure release valve to the VENT position. Carefully remove the lid when the unit has finished releasing pressure.
8. Stir in the paneer (if using) and cilantro. Taste and season with salt and pepper, as needed.

Harissa Broccoli and Bean Roast

Prep time: 10 minutes | Cook time: 30 minutes | Serves 4

2 cups water
2 small heads broccoli, cut in half
2 tablespoons unsalted butter
½ white onion, minced
2 garlic cloves, minced
1 (15½-ounce / 439-g) can cannellini beans, rinsed and drained
1 (10-ounce / 283-g) can fire-roasted tomatoes and peppers
1 tablespoon spicy harissa
Sea salt
Freshly ground black pepper
¼ cup tahini
¼ cup walnuts, toasted and chopped
Zest of 1 lemon
Juice of 1 lemon

1. Place Reversible Rack in pot, making sure it is in the lowest position. Pour the water into the pot and place the broccoli on the rack. Assemble the pressure lid, making sure the pressure release valve is in the SEAL position.
2. Select STEAM. Set time to 8 minutes. Select START/STOP to begin.
3. When steaming is complete, quick release the pressure by turning the pressure release valve to the VENT position. Carefully remove lid when unit has finished releasing pressure.
4. Remove rack and broccoli and set aside. Drain the remaining water from the pot and reinsert it in base.
5. Select SEAR/SAUTÉ and set to HI. Select START/STOP to begin. Let preheat for 5 minutes.
6. Add the butter to pot. Once melted, add the onions and garlic and cook for 3 minutes. Add the beans, tomatoes, harissa, and season with salt and pepper. Cook for 4 minutes.
7. Reinsert rack and broccoli. Close crisping lid.
8. Select AIR CRISP, set temperature to 390°F (199°C), and set time to 15 minutes. Select START/STOP to begin.
9. After 10 minutes, open lid and flip the broccoli. Close lid and continue cooking.
10. When cooking is complete, remove rack with broccoli from pot. Place the beans in serving dishes and top with the broccoli. Drizzle tahini over the broccoli and sprinkle with walnuts. Garnish with the lemon zest and juice and serve.

Tempeh Hash in Kale with Avocado

Prep time: 20 minutes | Cook time: 20 minutes | Serves 6

2 pounds (907 g) Red Bliss potatoes, diced
½ cup water
2 tablespoons coconut oil
8 ounces (227 g) tempeh, diced
1 yellow onion, diced
3 garlic cloves, minced
3 Roma tomatoes, diced
Kosher salt
Freshly ground black pepper
2 tablespoons soy sauce
1 tablespoon maple syrup
2 cups baby kale
1 ripe avocado, diced

1. Place the potatoes in the Cook & Crisp Basket. Add the water to the pot and insert basket into unit. Assemble pressure lid, making sure the pressure release valve is in the SEAL position.
2. Select PRESSURE and set to HI. Set time to 2 minutes. Select START/STOP to begin.
3. Once pressure cooking is complete, quick release the pressure by turning the pressure release valve to the VENT position. Carefully remove lid when unit has finished releasing pressure.
4. Remove basket. Drain any remaining water from the pot and reinsert it into base.
5. Select SEAR/SAUTÉ and set to MD:HI. Select START/STOP to begin. Let preheat for 3 minutes.
6. Add the coconut oil and tempeh. Crisp the tempeh for 5 minutes, stirring occasionally.
7. Transfer the tempeh to a plate and add the onion, garlic, and tomatoes. Season with salt and pepper. Stir to incorporate, then add the potatoes.
8. Press START/STOP to pause. Stir in the tempeh, soy sauce, and maple syrup. Fold in the kale. Close crisping lid.
9. Select AIR CRISP, set temperature to 375ºF (191ºC), and set time to 10 minutes. Select START/STOP to begin.
10. When cooking is complete, top with diced avocados and serve.

Tofu and Kimchi Fried Rice

Prep time: 10 minutes | Cook time: 30 minutes | Serves 6

1 cup Texmati brown rice
1¼ cups water
2 tablespoons canola oil
2 garlic cloves, minced
1 tablespoon minced fresh ginger
8 ounces (227 g) extra-firm tofu, cut into ½-inch squares
½ cup frozen peas and carrots
1 large egg, beaten
½ cup kimchi, chopped
2 scallions, sliced thin
¼ cup basil, coarsely chopped
1 tablespoon soy sauce
Kosher salt
Freshly ground black pepper

1. Rinse the rice under cold running water in a fine-mesh strainer.
2. Place the rice and water in the pot. Assemble pressure lid, making sure the pressure release valve is in the SEAL position.
3. Select PRESSURE and set to HI. Set time to 2 minutes. Select START/STOP to begin.
4. When pressure cooking is complete, allow pressure to naturally release for 10 minutes. After 10 minutes, quick release remaining pressure by moving the pressure release valve to the VENT position. Carefully remove lid when unit has finished releasing pressure.
5. Evenly layer the rice on a sheet pan and refrigerate until cool, preferably overnight.
6. Select SEAR/SAUTÉ and set to HI. Select START/STOP to begin. Add the canola oil and let heat for 5 minutes.
7. Add the garlic and ginger and cook for 1 minute. Add the tofu, rice, and peas and carrots, and cook for 5 minutes, stirring occasionally.
8. Move the rice to one side and add the egg to empty side of pot. Cook 30 seconds, stirring occasionally to scramble it. Add the kimchi, scallions, basil, and soy sauce, and stir. Cook for 5 minutes, stirring frequently.
9. Season with salt, pepper, and more soy sauce, if needed. Serve.

Avocado and Spinach Pasta

Prep time: 15 minutes | Cook time: 2 minutes | Serves 8

1 (16-ounce / 454-g) box dry pasta, such as rigatoni or penne
4 cups water
2 tablespoons extra-virgin olive oil, divided
2 teaspoons kosher salt, divided
3 avocados
Juice of 2 limes
2 tablespoons minced cilantro
1 red onion, chopped
1 cup cherry tomatoes, halved
4 heaping cups spinach, half an 11-ounce (312-g) container
¼ cup shredded Parmesan cheese, divided
Freshly ground black pepper, for serving

1. Place the pasta, water, 1 tablespoon of olive oil, and 1 teaspoon of salt in the pot. Stir to incorporate. Assemble pressure lid, making sure the pressure release valve is in the SEAL position.
2. Select PRESSURE and set to LO. Set time to 2 minutes. Select START/STOP to begin.
3. While pasta is cooking, place the avocados in a medium-sized mixing bowl and mash well with a wooden spatula until a thick paste forms. Add all remaining ingredients to the bowl and mix well to combine.
4. When pressure cooking is complete, allow pressure to naturally release for 10 minutes. After 10 minutes, quick release remaining pressure by moving the pressure release valve to the VENT position. Carefully remove lid when unit has finished releasing pressure.
5. If necessary, strain pasta to remove any residual water and return pasta to pot. Add avocado mixture to pot and stir.
6. Garnish pasta with Parmesan cheese and black pepper, as desired, then serve.

Cauliflower and Tomato Enchiladas

Prep time: 15 minutes | Cook time: 25 minutes | Serves 5

2 tablespoons canola oil
1 large head cauliflower, cut into 1-inch florets
2 teaspoons ground cumin
1 teaspoon ground chili pepper
2 teaspoons kosher salt
½ teaspoon freshly ground black pepper
1 (14½-ounce / 411-g) can diced tomatoes, drained
5 (6-inch) flour tortillas
1 (10-ounce / 283-g) can red enchilada sauce
1½ cups shredded Mexican blend cheese
½ cup chopped cilantro, for garnish

1. In a medium bowl, toss together the oil, cauliflower, cumin, chili pepper, salt, and black pepper. Place the cauliflower in the Cook & Crisp Basket and place the basket in pot. Close crisping lid.
2. Select AIR CRISP, set temperature to 390°F (199°C), and set time to 15 minutes. Select START/STOP to begin.
3. After 8 minutes, open lid, then lift the basket and shake the cauliflower. Lower basket back into pot and close lid. Continue cooking, until the cauliflower reaches your desired crispiness.
4. When cooking is complete, remove basket from pot. Place the cauliflower in a bowl and mix with the tomatoes.
5. Lay the tortillas on a work surface. Divide the cauliflower-
6. tomato mixture between the tortillas and roll them up. Place the filled tortillas seam-side down in the pot. Pour the enchilada sauce on top.
7. Close crisping lid. Select BROIL and set time to 10 minutes. Select START/STOP to begin.
8. After 5 minutes, open lid and add the cheese on top. Close lid and continue cooking until cheese is golden brown.
9. When cooking is complete, add cilantro and serve.

Italian Caprese Elbow Salad

Prep time: 10 minutes | Cook time: 3 minutes | Serves 8

1 (16-ounce / 454-g) box elbow pasta
4 cups water
1 tablespoon sea salt
2 tablespoons extra-virgin olive oil
½ cup red bell pepper, diced
1 cup cherry tomatoes, sliced
¼ cup black olives, sliced
½ pound (227 g) fresh Mozzarella, diced
½ cup chopped fresh basil
½ cup Italian dressing

1. Place the pasta, water, and salt in the pot. Assemble pressure lid, making sure the pressure release valve is in the SEAL position.
2. Select PRESSURE and set to HI. Set time to 3 minutes. Select START/STOP to begin.
3. When pressure cooking is complete, allow pressure to naturally release for 10 minutes. After 10 minutes, quick release remaining pressure by moving the pressure release valve to the VENT position. Carefully remove lid when unit has finished releasing pressure.
4. Drain the pasta in a colander. Place the pasta in a large bowl and toss with the olive oil. Set aside to cool for 20 minutes.
5. Stir in the bell pepper, cherry tomatoes, olives, Mozzarella, and basil. Gently fold in the Italian seasoning.
6. Serve immediately or cover and refrigerate for later.

Sumptuous Vegetable and Penne Primavera

Prep time: 10 minutes | Cook time: 18 minutes | Serves 6

½ red onion, sliced

1 carrot, thinly sliced

1 head broccoli, cut into florets

1 red bell pepper, thinly sliced

1 yellow squash, halved lengthwise and sliced into half moons

1 zucchini, halved lengthwise and sliced into half moons

¼ cup extra-virgin olive oil

½ teaspoon dried basil

½ teaspoon dried oregano

½ teaspoon dried parsley

¼ teaspoon dried rosemary

¼ teaspoon crushed red pepper flakes

1 (16-ounce / 454-g) box penne pasta

4 cups water

2 tablespoons freshly squeezed lemon juice

½ cup grated Parmesan cheese, divided

1. Place Cook & Crisp Basket in pot. Close crisping lid. Select AIR CRISP, set temperature to 390°F (199°C), and set time to 5 minutes. Select START/STOP to begin preheating.
2. In a large bowl, combine the red onion, carrot, broccoli, bell pepper, yellow squash, zucchini, olive oil, basil, oregano, parsley, rosemary, and red pepper flakes, and toss to combine.
3. Once unit has preheated, add the vegetable mixture to the basket. Close lid.
4. Select AIR CRISP, set temperature to 390°F (199°C), and set time to 15 minutes. Select START/STOP to begin.
5. When cooking is complete, remove the vegetables and basket, and set aside.
6. Add the pasta and water. Assemble pressure lid, making sure the pressure release valve is in the SEAL position.
7. Select PRESSURE and set to HI. Set time to 3 minutes. Select START/STOP to begin.
8. When pressure cooking is complete, allow pressure to naturally release for 10 minutes. After 10 minutes, quick release remaining pressure by moving the pressure release valve to the VENT position. Carefully remove lid when unit has finished releasing pressure.
9. Add vegetables to pasta. Add the lemon juice and ¼ cup of Parmesan cheese and stir. Serve and top with remaining cheese.

Carrot and Celery Potpie

Prep time: 10 minutes | Cook time: 22 minutes | Serves 6

4 tablespoons unsalted butter

½ large onion, diced

1½ cups diced carrot (about 2 large carrots)

1½ cups diced celery (about 3 celery stalks)

2 garlic cloves, minced

3 cups red potatoes, diced

1 cup vegetable broth

½ cup frozen peas

½ cup frozen corn

1 tablespoon chopped fresh Italian parsley

2 teaspoons fresh thyme leaves

¼ cup all-purpose flour

½ cup heavy (whipping) cream

Salt

Freshly ground black pepper

1 prepared piecrust

1. Select SEAR/SAUTÉ and set temperature to MD:HI. Set the time to 5 minutes to preheat. Select START/STOP to begin.
2. Add the butter to the pot to melt. Add the onion, carrot, and celery to the melted butter. Sauté for about 3 minutes until softened.
3. Stir in the garlic and cook, stirring constantly, for about 30 seconds until fragrant. Select START/STOP to end the function.
4. Add the potatoes and vegetable broth to pot and stir to combine.
5. Assemble the pressure lid, making sure the pressure release valve is in the SEAL position.
6. Select PRESSURE and set to HI. Set the time to 5 minutes. Select START/STOP to begin.
7. When pressure cooking is complete, quick release the pressure by turning the pressure release valve to the VENT position. Carefully remove the lid when the unit has finished releasing pressure.
8. Add the peas, corn, parsley, and thyme to the pot. Season with salt and pepper. Sprinkle the flour over the top and stir to mix well. Stir in the heavy cream.
9. Select SEAR/SAUTÉ and set temperature to MD:HI. Select START/STOP to begin. Cook for 2 to 3 minutes, stirring constantly, until the sauce thickens and is hot. Select START/STOP to end the function.
10. Place the piecrust over the vegetable mixture. Fold over the edges of the crust to fit the pot. Make a small slit in the center of the crust for steam to release. Close the crisping lid.
11. Select BROIL. Set the time to 10 minutes. Select START/STOP to begin.
12. After the cooking is complete, carefully transfer the inner pot to a heat-proof surface. Let the potpie sit for 10 minutes before serving.

Tomato and Leek Galette

Prep time: 15 minutes | Cook time: 40 minutes | Serves 4

½ pound (227 g) mixed tomatoes, cut into ¼-inch slices
3 inches of leek, thinly sliced
2 garlic cloves, diced
Kosher salt
1 store-bought refrigerated pie crust
2 tablespoons bread crumbs
4 tablespoons shredded Parmesan cheese, divided
4 tablespoons shredded Mozzarella, divided
1 egg, beaten
Freshly ground black pepper

1. Place the tomatoes, leeks, and garlic into large bowl. Sprinkle with salt and set aside for at least 5 minutes to draw out the juices from the vegetables.
2. Strain the excess juice off the tomato mixture and pat down the vegetables with paper towels.
3. Unroll the pie crust and place it in the Ninja Multi-Purpose Pan or a 1½-quart round ceramic baking dish and form it to the bottom of the pan. Lay the extra dough loosely on the sides of the pan.
4. Sprinkle the bread crumbs in a thin layer on the pie crust bottom, then scatter 3 tablespoons each of Parmesan and Mozzarella cheese on top. Place the tomato mixture in a heap in the middle of the dough and top with the remaining 1 tablespoon each of Parmesan and Mozzarella cheese.
5. Fold the edges of the crust over the tomatoes and brush with the egg.
6. Close crisping lid. Select BAKE/ROAST, set temperature to 350°F (177°C), and set time to 45 minutes. Select START/STOP to begin. Let preheat for 5 minutes.
7. Place pan on the Reversible Rack, making sure the rack is in the lower position. Cover galette loosely with aluminum foil (do not seal the pan).
8. Once unit has preheated, open lid and carefully place the rack with pan in the pot. Close crisping lid.
9. After 20 minutes, open lid and remove the foil. Close lid and continue cooking.
10. When cooking is complete, remove rack with pan and set aside to let cool. Cut into slices, season with pepper, and serve.

Bell Pepper and Mushroom Pizza

Prep time: 10 minutes | Cook time: 8 minutes | Makes 1 pizza

1 (7-ounce / 198-g) store-bought pizza dough, rolled into an 8-inch circle
¼ cup traditional pizza sauce
1 teaspoon minced garlic
⅔ cup shredded Mozzarella cheese
¼ cup chopped green bell pepper
¼ cup sliced mushrooms
Crushed red pepper flakes, for garnish

1. Select BAKE/ROAST, set the temperature to 400°F (204°C), and set time to 5 minutes to preheat. Select START/STOP to begin.
2. Place the rolled dough in the Ninja Cook & Crisp Basket. Spread the pizza sauce over the crust, leaving about a 1-inch border uncovered. Sprinkle on the garlic, top with the Mozzarella cheese, and evenly distribute the green bell pepper and mushrooms over the pizza.
3. Place the Cook & Crisp Basket into the pot and close the crisping lid.
4. Select BAKE/ROAST, set the temperature to 400°F (204°C), and set the time to 8 minutes. Select START/STOP to begin.
5. When cooking is complete, carefully open the lid and remove the pizza. Serve, garnished with red pepper flakes, if using.

Tomato-Basil Bread Pizza

Prep time: 2 minutes | Cook time: 10 minutes | Serves 6

6 slices frozen garlic bread or Texas Toast
¾ cup tomato-basil sauce or your favorite tomato sauce
6 slices Mozzarella cheese

1. Insert Cook & Crisp Basket in pot. Close crisping lid. Select AIR CRISP, set temperature to 390°F (199°C), and set time to 5 minutes. Select START/STOP to begin preheating.
2. Once unit has preheated, place three of the garlic bread slices in the basket, and top with half the sauce and 3 slices of cheese. Close crisping lid.
3. Select AIR CRISP, set temperature to 375°F (191°C), and set time to 5 minutes. Select START/STOP to begin.
4. When cooking is complete, remove the pizzas from the basket. Repeat steps 2 and 3 with the remaining slices of garlic bread, sauce, and cheese.

Black Bean and Sweet Potato Tacos

Prep time: 15 minutes | Cook time: 1 hour | Serves 8

For the Black Beans:

1 pound (454 g) dried black beans, rinsed and picked through for debris

2 chipotle chiles from a can of chipotles in adobo sauce

2 garlic cloves, smashed

1 teaspoon ground cumin

1 teaspoon kosher salt

½ teaspoon ground coriander

For the Sweet Potatoes:

3 tablespoons peanut oil or vegetable oil

1 tablespoon sauce from a can of chipotles in adobo sauce

2 teaspoons ground cumin

1 teaspoon kosher salt

3 medium sweet potatoes, peeled and diced

16 to 20 (6-inch) corn tortillas, warmed

Sour cream, for serving (optional)

Salsa or pico de gallo, for serving (optional)

Shredded Mexican-style cheese, for serving (optional)

Chopped fresh cilantro, for serving (optional)

1. Make the black beans: Place the beans, chipotle chiles, garlic, cumin, salt, and coriander along with 6 cups water into the Foodi's inner pot. Lock on the Pressure Lid, making sure the valve is set to Seal, and set to Pressure on High for 25 minutes. When the timer reaches 0, allow the pressure to naturally release for 20 minutes, then quick-release the remaining pressure. Carefully remove the lid. Let the beans cool to room temperature. (If desired, transfer beans to an airtight container along with the cooking liquid and refrigerate for up to 1 week.)
2. Make the sweet potatoes: Clean and dry the inner pot. Place the oil, adobo sauce, cumin, and salt in the pot. Add the sweet potatoes and stir to coat until the potatoes glisten.
3. Transfer the potatoes to the crisping basket and place the basket in the inner pot. Drop the Crisping Lid and set to Air Crisp at 390ºF (199ºC) for 35 to 45 minutes, depending on how browned and crisp you want the potatoes. While they are cooking, lift the lid and shake the basket periodically to move them about. When cooked and tender, lift the lid and transfer the potatoes to a plate.
4. To serve, place some beans and sweet potatoes onto a tortilla, add the toppings of your choice, and serve.

Cauliflower Steaks

Prep time: 5 minutes | Cook time: 20 minutes | Serves 2

1 large cauliflower

2 tablespoons peanut oil or vegetable oil

Kosher salt, to taste

Freshly ground black pepper, to taste

Grated zest of 1 lemon

1. Place the cauliflower on a cutting board and trim off any leaves. Get a good look at where the stem is connected—that area is going to be the steaks. Trim a ¾-inch slice from each side of the cauliflower (save the trimmed bits for another use) and then cut the cauliflower in half to make two steaks. Rub the oil and a liberal amount of salt and pepper onto both sides of the steaks.
2. Insert the crisping basket into the Foodi's inner pot and arrange the steaks in the basket so they are propped up by the basket sides—they should fit snugly in a vertical position. Drop the Crisping Lid and set the Foodi to Air Crisp at 390**º**F (199**º**C) for 20 minutes, until the steaks brown.
3. Lift the lid and remove the basket from the Foodi. Transfer the cauliflower steaks to a platter or individual plates. Sprinkle with the lemon zest and serve.

Parmesan Broccoli Florets

Prep time: 5 minutes | Cook time: 8 minutes | Serves 4

12 ounces (340 g) fresh broccoli florets

1 tablespoon peanut oil or vegetable oil

¼ teaspoon kosher salt

Pinch of freshly ground black pepper

½ cup freshly shredded Parmesan cheese

1. Place the broccoli florets in the crisping basket and set the basket into the Foodi's inner pot along with ½ cup water. Lock on the Pressure Lid, making sure the valve is set to Seal, and set to Pressure on High for 0 minutes. When the timer reaches 0, quick-release the pressure and carefully remove the lid. Transfer the broccoli to a medium bowl. Drain the liquid from the inner pot, wash, and dry it.
2. Add the oil, salt, pepper, and Parmesan to the broccoli in the bowl. Stir to combine. Place the crisping basket back into the inner pot and transfer the broccoli mixture to the basket, scraping any cheese left in the bowl on top of the broccoli. Drop the Crisping Lid and set the Foodi to Air Crisp at 390**º**F (199**º**C) for 8 minutes, or until the broccoli is crisped and the cheese is browned. Lift the lid and serve hot.

Refried Black Beans

Prep time: 5 minutes | Cook time: 40 minutes | Serves 6

1 pound (454 g) dried black beans, rinsed and picked through for debris
½ medium yellow onion, diced
2 garlic cloves, minced
1 teaspoon ground cumin
1 teaspoon kosher salt, plus more as needed
2 tablespoons peanut oil or vegetable oil

1. Place the beans, onion, garlic, cumin, salt, and 4 cups water into the Foodi's inner pot. Lock on the Pressure Lid, making sure the valve is set to Seal, and set to Pressure on High for 30 minutes. When the timer reaches 0, allow the Foodi to naturally release for 20 minutes, then quick-release any remaining pressure and carefully remove the lid.
2. Add the oil and mash the beans with a silicone potato masher until they are smooth. Set the Foodi to Sear/Saute on High and cook for 10 minutes, or until very thick and shiny, stirring and mashing every couple of minutes. Season with salt to taste before serving.

Maple-Glazed Carrots

Prep time: 5 minutes | Cook time: 29 minutes | Serves 6

2 tablespoons unsalted butter
1 tablespoon ground cumin
2 pounds (907 g) carrots, cut into 2-inch pieces
½ cup orange juice
¼ cup maple syrup
1 teaspoon kosher salt

1. Place the butter and cumin in the Foodi's inner pot and set the Foodi to Sear/Saute until the butter is bubbling and aromatic, about 6 minutes.
2. Add the carrots and orange juice, then lock on the Pressure Lid, making sure the valve is set to Seal, and set to Pressure on High for 3 minutes. When the timer reaches 0, quick-release the pressure and carefully remove the lid.
3. Stir in the maple syrup and salt. Set the Foodi to Air Crisp at 390°F (199°C) for 20 minutes, or until the carrots are nicely browned. Lift the lid and transfer the carrots to a platter. Serve warm or at room temperature if you want them to be a little stickier.

Ham Hock Braised Collard Greens

Prep time: 10 minutes | Cook time: 13 minutes | Serves 6

2 tablespoons unsalted butter
1 medium yellow onion, diced
2 garlic cloves, minced
1 smoked ham hock
2 cups chicken stock
2 pounds (907 g) collard greens, tough stems and ribs removed, leaves thinly sliced
Juice of 1 lemon
2 teaspoons kosher salt

1. Add the butter to the Foodi's inner pot and set the Foodi to Sear/Saute on High until melted, about 4 minutes. Add the onion and garlic and cook until beginning to soften, about 6 minutes more, stirring occasionally.
2. Add the ham hock and stock and stir once, then add the collard greens (you may really have to jam them in!). Lock on the Pressure Lid, making sure the valve is set to Seal, and set to Pressure on High for 3 minutes. When the timer reaches 0, quick-release the pressure and carefully remove the lid. (If you plan on eating the greens soon after cooking them, turn the Foodi to the Keep Warm setting.)
3. Use tongs to remove the ham hock and set it aside to cool slightly before cutting the meat into chunks (discard the bone). Stir the ham back into the greens, then stir in the lemon juice and salt and serve.

Homemade Ratatouille

Prep time: 15 minutes | Cook time: 22 minutes | Serves 6

For the Sauce:
2 (14½-ounce / 411-g) cans diced tomatoes with juice
1 medium yellow onion, diced
1 red bell pepper, seeded, ribbed, and diced
4 garlic cloves, minced
7 fresh basil leaves
3 tablespoons extra-virgin olive oil
½ teaspoon kosher salt
¼ teaspoon freshly ground black pepper

For the Vegetables:
½ medium Italian eggplant, sliced as thin as possible into rounds
3 vine-ripened tomatoes, sliced as thin as possible into rounds
1 medium yellow squash, sliced as thin as possible into rounds
1 medium zucchini, sliced as thin as possible into rounds
Cooking spray
Kosher salt, to taste
Freshly ground black pepper, to taste
6 sprigs fresh thyme
1 tablespoon fresh torn basil leaves
1 tablespoon finely chopped fresh flat-leaf parsley

Make the Sauce
1. Add the diced tomatoes, onion, bell pepper, garlic, basil, olive oil, salt, pepper, and ½ cup water to the Foodi's inner pot. Lock on the Pressure Lid, making sure the valve is set to Seal, and set to Pressure on High for 2 minutes. When the timer reaches 0, quick-release the pressure and carefully remove the lid.

Make the Vegetables
2. Starting from the center of the Foodi pot, arrange the veggie slices by overlapping them in a spiral, alternating among the different vegetables. The vegetables will shrink as they cook, so really pack them in. It's okay if they are placed vertically once you get near the edge of the pot.
3. Spray the top of the vegetables heavily with cooking spray and season with salt and pepper. Lay the thyme sprigs on top and drop the Crisping Lid. Set the Foodi to Air Crisp at 390°F (199°C) for 20 minutes, or until the veggies begin to brown.
4. Lift the lid and carefully remove the thyme. Shake the dried leaves off the stems, then sprinkle the dried thyme onto the ratatouille along with the fresh basil and parsley. Let the ratatouille cool at least 5 minutes before scooping from the pot and serving.

Twice-Baked Cheese Potatoes

Prep time: 10 minutes | Cook time: 33 minutes | Serves 4

2 medium russet potatoes, poked a few times with a fork
½ teaspoon kosher salt
Cooking spray
1 cup shredded mild Cheddar cheese
2 tablespoons sour cream
1 garlic clove, minced
½ teaspoon smoked paprika
Chopped fresh chives, for garnish
Smoked paprika, for garnish

1. Add ½ cup water and salt to the Foodi's inner pot. Place the reversible rack in the pot in the low position and set the potatoes on the rack. Lock on the Pressure Lid, making sure the valve is set to Seal, and set to Pressure on High for 20 minutes. When the timer reaches 0, allow the pressure to release naturally for 10 minutes, then quick-release the remaining pressure and carefully remove the lid.
2. Use tongs to remove the potatoes from the Foodi and set aside to cool enough to pick up and hold—about 5 minutes for my iron hands (but letting them cool longer won't hurt). Remove the rack from the inner pot but leave the cooking liquid in the pot.
3. Spray a knife with cooking spray and slice the potatoes in half lengthwise. Use a fork to lightly rake and fluff the insides of the potato halves and then use a small spoon to carefully remove the flesh of each, keeping as much of the skin intact as possible. Set the skins aside to stuff later.
4. Add the scooped-out potato flesh to the Foodi's inner pot and combine with the cooking liquid. Add the cheese, sour cream, and garlic to the pot and set the Foodi to Sear/Saute on High. Mash everything together and cook, stirring often, until the cheese is melted, about 3 minutes.
5. Carefully spoon the potato mixture into the potato skins. Place the reversible rack in the Foodi in the high position, and arrange the stuffed potatoes on the rack (it's okay if they are touching). Spray the potatoes with cooking spray, drop the Crisping Lid, and set the Foodi to Broil for 10 minutes, or until the cheesy mixture is browned on top. Lift the lid and sprinkle the potatoes with the smoked paprika, then let cool for 5 minutes before transferring them to plates. Serve sprinkled with chives and paprika.

Bread Stuffing

Prep time: 10 minutes | Cook time: 48 minutes | Serves 6

1 loaf French bread, cut into 1-inch cubes
4 tablespoons unsalted butter
1 medium yellow onion, diced
3 celery ribs, diced
1½ cups chicken stock
1 large egg, lightly beaten
2 teaspoons kosher salt
1 teaspoon freshly ground black pepper
1 tablespoon minced fresh thyme leaves
4 fresh sage leaves, minced
Minced fresh parsley, for garnish
Fresh thyme leaves, for garnish

1. Place the bread cubes in the crisping basket and set the crisping basket in the Foodi's inner pot. Drop the Crisping Lid and set the Foodi to Dehydrate at 195°F (91°C) for 15 minutes, or until the bread is dried out. Lift the lid, carefully remove the basket with the bread, and set aside. Use a damp paper towel to wipe out any crumbs that might have fallen into the pot.
2. Add the butter to the inner pot and set the Foodi to Sear/Saute on High until the butter is melted and quite warm (you want the vegetables to sizzle when they are added to the pot), about 5 minutes. Add the onion and celery and cook until they begin to soften, about 8 minutes, stirring often.
3. Meanwhile, in a medium bowl, whisk together the stock, egg, salt, and pepper.
4. Add the dried bread cubes and the fresh thyme and sage to the onion mixture in the inner pot, then stir in the egg mixture, making sure all the bread is moistened. Flatten out the stuffing so the top layer is somewhat even. Drop the Crisping Lid and set the Foodi to Bake/Roast at 375°F (190°C) for 20 minutes, or until browned yet moist, stirring halfway through. Transfer the stuffing to a serving dish and garnish with fresh parsley and thyme.

Roasted Zucchini and Summer Squash

Prep time: 10 minutes | Cook time: 25 minutes | Serves 4

2 medium zucchini, cut into ¼-inch-thick rounds
2 medium yellow summer squash, cut into ¼-inch-thick rounds
½ cup fresh flat-leaf parsley leaves
3 tablespoons peanut oil or vegetable oil
Zest of 1 lemon
2 teaspoons kosher salt
½ teaspoon freshly ground black pepper

1. Place the zucchini, yellow squash, parsley, oil, lemon zest, salt, and pepper into the Foodi's inner pot and stir to evenly coat the squash with the oil. Transfer the squash mixture to the crisping basket and place it in the inner pot. Set the Foodi to Air Crisp at 390°F (199°C) for 25 minutes, stirring occasionally, or until browned.
2. Serve warm.

Brown Sugar-Glazed Brussels Sprouts

Prep time: 10 minutes | Cook time: 23 minutes | Serves 6

3 tablespoons peanut oil or vegetable oil
2 pounds (907 g) Brussels sprouts, stem ends trimmed and scored with an "x"
2 teaspoons kosher salt
½ teaspoon freshly ground black pepper
3 tablespoons light brown sugar
2 tablespoons fish sauce
¼ cup pickled jalapeños, plus ¼ cup pickling liquid
Juice of 1 lime

1. Place the oil, Brussels sprouts, salt, and pepper into the Foodi's inner pot, stirring to fully coat the Brussels sprouts with the oil. Transfer the sprouts to the crisping basket, place the basket in the Foodi pot, and set the Foodi to Air Crisp at 390°F (199°C) for 20 minutes, or until browned. Lift the lid and remove the basket with the sprouts.
2. Add the brown sugar, fish sauce, and jalapeños and pickling liquid to the inner pot. Set the Foodi to Sear/Saute and cook until the brown sugar has melted, about 3 minutes.
3. Add the lime juice to the pot and then return the sprouts to the pot. Toss to coat in the sauce and serve immediately.

Green Beans with Dill

Prep time: 5 minutes | Cook time: 18 minutes | Serves 4

12 ounces (340 g) fresh green beans,
   ends trimmed
1 tablespoon peanut oil or vegetable
   oil
¼ teaspoon kosher salt
Zest of 1 lemon
1 tablespoon finely chopped fresh
   dill, plus more for garnish

1. Place the beans, oil, and salt into the Foodi's inner pot, stirring to coat the beans with the oil. Transfer the beans to the crisping basket and place the basket in the inner pot. Drop the Crisping Lid and set the Foodi to Air Crisp at 390°F (199°C) for 15 minutes. After 12 minutes, lift the lid, add the lemon zest and dill, and shake the basket to coat the beans. Drop the lid again and continue to cook until the beans are blistered, about 3 minutes more.
2. Serve warm.

Canned Pickled Beets

Prep time: 10 minutes | Cook time: 1 minute | Makes 4 pints

8 (2-pound / 907-g) medium beets,
   scrubbed, trimmed, peeled, and
   cut into eighths
2 cups apple cider vinegar
1 cup sugar
12 whole cloves
6 allspice berries
6 cardamom pods
1 cinnamon stick
2 tablespoons kosher salt
1 teaspoon black peppercorns

1. Place the beets, vinegar, sugar, cloves, allspice, cardamom, cinnamon stick, salt, and peppercorns in the Foodi's inner pot. Add enough water to just barely cover the beets. Lock on the Pressure Lid, making sure the valve is set to Seal, and set the Foodi to Pressure on High for 1 minute. When the timer reaches 0, quick-release the pressure and carefully remove the lid. Allow the beets to cool in the pickling liquid for 2 to 3 hours.
2. Transfer the beets and the liquid, spices and all, to an airtight container or 4 pint-size glass jars and refrigerate for up to 1 month.

Saffron and Orange Rice Pilaf

Prep time: 10 minutes | Cook time: 20 minutes | Serves 4

3 tablespoons peanut oil or
   vegetable oil
½ medium yellow onion, diced
1 garlic clove, minced
Pinch of saffron threads
½ teaspoon dried orange peel
2 cups basmati rice
2 cups chicken stock
1 (10-ounce / 283-g) package frozen
   mixed vegetables
½ teaspoon kosher salt
Thinly sliced scallions, for garnish
Sweet paprika, for garnish
Flat-leaf parsley or mint, for garnish

1. Add the oil to the Foodi's inner pot and set the Foodi to Sear/Saute on High, heating for 5 minutes. Add the onion, garlic, saffron, and orange peel to the pot and cook until aromatic, about 4 minutes, stirring frequently.
2. Stir in the rice and cook until slightly toasted, about 4 minutes, stirring often. Add the stock. Lock on the Pressure Lid, making sure the valve is set to Seal, and set the Foodi to Pressure on High for 3 minutes. When the time reaches 0, allow the pressure to naturally release for 6 minutes, then quick-release the remaining pressure and carefully remove the lid.
3. Add the mixed vegetables. Drop the Crisping Lid and set the Foodi to Air Crisp at 390°F (199°C) for 8 minutes, or until the vegetables are warmed through. Lift the lid and stir in the salt. Serve sprinkled with the scallions, paprika, and parsley.

Fried Rice with Vegetable

Prep time: 10 minutes | Cook time: 18 minutes | Serves 6

2 cups short-grain white rice, rinsed well

2 tablespoons soy sauce

1 tablespoon oyster sauce

1 teaspoon sugar

1 teaspoon freshly ground black pepper

½ teaspoon kosher salt

¼ cup peanut oil or vegetable oil

2 large eggs, lightly beaten

4 garlic cloves, minced

1 (10-ounce / 283-g) package mixed frozen vegetables

3 scallions, trimmed and thinly sliced

1. Place the rice and 2 cups water into the Foodi's inner pot. Lock on the Pressure Lid, making sure the valve is set to Seal, and set to Pressure on High for 3 minutes. When the timer reaches 0, allow the pressure to naturally release for 11 minutes, then quick-release any remaining pressure. Carefully remove the lid. Scoop out the rice from the Foodi and transfer to a bowl to cool. Wash and dry the inner pot.
2. In a small bowl, combine the soy sauce, oyster sauce, sugar, pepper, and salt.
3. Set the Foodi to Sear/Sauté on High, add the oil to the Foodi's inner pot, and allow to heat for 2 minutes. Add the eggs to the pot and stir, cooking until just set, about 3 minutes. Stir in the garlic and cook until aromatic, about 3 minutes.
4. Return the rice to the pot and use a silicone spatula to stir and break it up. Cook the rice until it toasts slightly, about 3 minutes, stirring often. Add the soy sauce mixture and cook until the sauce is absorbed, about 2 minutes, continuing to stir often.
5. Make a large well in the center of the rice, pushing the rice to the sides of the pot. Add the vegetables. Drop the Crisping Lid and set the Foodi to Air Crisp at 390°F (199°C) for 5 minutes, or until the vegetables are tender. Lift the lid and give the rice a good stir, then add the scallions and stir again before serving.

Spanish White Quinoa

Prep time: 10 minutes | Cook time: 2 minutes | Serves 6

1 cup white quinoa, rinsed

1 (14-ounce / 397-g) can diced tomatoes with juice

2 garlic cloves, minced

1 teaspoon ground cumin

½ teaspoon chili powder

½ teaspoon kosher salt

1 tablespoon unsalted butter

1. Place the quinoa, tomatoes and juice, garlic, cumin, chili powder, salt, butter, and ½ cup water into the Foodi's inner pot and stir to combine. Lock on the Pressure Lid, set the valve to Seal, and set the Foodi to Pressure on High for 2 minutes. When the timer reaches 0, allow the pressure to naturally release for 10 minutes, then quick-release any remaining pressure and carefully remove the lid.
2. Fluff with a silicone spatula and serve.

Moroccan-Style Couscous

Prep time: 5 minutes | Cook time: 1 minutes | Serves 4

Cooking spray

1 cup Moroccan-style couscous (not Israeli couscous)

2 tablespoons unsalted butter

1. Spray the Foodi's inner pot with cooking spray. Add the couscous, butter, and 1½ cups water. Lock on the Pressure Lid, making sure the valve is set to Seal, and set to Pressure on High for 1 minute. When the timer reaches 0, allow pressure to naturally release, then carefully remove the lid.
2. Fluff the couscous with a fork and serve.

Farro, Fennel and Arugula Salad

Prep time: 5 minutes | Cook time: 10 minutes | Serves 6

1 cup farro
2 fennel bulbs, fronds separated and reserved (optional), bulbs halved, cored, and diced
1 tablespoon fennel seeds
Zest and juice of 1 lemon
1 teaspoon kosher salt, plus more as needed
2 tablespoons extra-virgin olive oil
5 ounces (142 g) arugula leaves

1. Place the farro, half the fennel, the fennel seeds, lemon zest, and salt into the Foodi's inner pot. Add 1¾ cups water, lock on the Pressure Lid, making sure the valve is set to Seal, and set to Pressure on High for 10 minutes. When the timer reaches 0, allow the pressure to naturally release for 5 minutes, then quick-release any remaining pressure and carefully remove the lid. Allow the farro to cool completely.
2. Chop the fennel fronds, if using, and add them to the cooled farro along with the remaining chopped fennel, the lemon juice, and the olive oil. Toss to coat. Add the arugula and toss once more. Season with salt and serve.

Persian Crunch Rice Tahdig

Prep time: minutes | Cook time: 23 minutes | Serves 4 to 6

2 cups basmati rice
1 teaspoon ground turmeric
1 teaspoon kosher salt
4 tablespoons unsalted butter, at room temperature

1. Place the rice, 2 cups water, turmeric, and salt in the Foodi's inner pot. Lock on the Pressure Lid, making sure the valve is set to Seal, and set to Pressure on High for 3 minutes. When the timer reaches 0, allow the pressure to naturally release for 6 minutes, then quick-release any remaining pressure and carefully remove the lid.
2. Make a well in the center of the rice and add 2 tablespoons of the butter. Use a silicone spatula to draw spokes out of the well that extend to the pot sides (so the butter has a route to disperse). Set the Foodi to Sear/Saute on High, and allow the butter to melt—this should take about 2 minutes. Once melted, use the spatula to smooth over the rice, covering the well, then continue to cook the rice until the bottom has crisped (you can slide a silicone spatula under the rice to get a sense of its texture), about 8 minutes more.
3. Use the spatula again to smear the remaining 2 tablespoons of butter over the top of the rice, smoothing and pressing it down on the surface of the rice. Drop the Crisping Lid and set the Foodi to Broil for 10 minutes, or until the top of the rice is crisp. Lift the lid and carefully remove the pot from the Foodi. Run the spatula around the edge of the rice to loosen it before inverting it onto a plate. Serve hot.

Lebanese Tabbouleh

Prep time: 10 minutes | Cook time: 9 minutes | Serves 6

4 tablespoons extra-virgin olive oil
½ teaspoon ground cumin
1 cup whole-grain red bulgur
1 teaspoon kosher salt
Zest and juice of ½ lemon
2 ripe plum tomatoes, halved, seeded, and diced
1 English cucumber, seeded and diced
1 tablespoon chopped fresh mint
1 tablespoon chopped fresh flat-leaf parsley
Ground sumac, for garnish
Flat-leaf parsley, for garnish

1. Add 3 tablespoons of the olive oil to the Foodi's inner pot and set the Foodi to Sear/Saute on High. Allow the oil to heat for 3 minutes, then add the cumin and the bulgur and cook until aromatic, about 3 minutes more, stirring often.
2. Add ½ teaspoon of the salt and 2 cups water. Lock on the Pressure Lid, making sure the valve is set to Seal, and set to Pressure on High for 3 minutes. When the timer reaches 0, allow the pressure to release naturally, then carefully remove the lid.
3. Stir the bulgur to fluff it up and then stir in the remaining tablespoon olive oil and half the lemon juice. Transfer to a bowl and allow to cool completely.
4. When ready to serve, add the tomatoes, cucumber, mint, parsley, remaining ½ teaspoon salt, and remaining lemon juice plus the zest. Stir and serve with sumac and parsley.

Parmesan Risotto with Herbs

Prep time: 10 minutes | Cook time: 26 minutes | Serves 4

4 tablespoons unsalted butter
½ medium yellow onion, diced
2 garlic cloves, minced
1 shallot, minced
1 cup arborio rice
1 cup dry white wine
2 cups chicken stock
2 teaspoons kosher salt
1 cup finely grated Parmesan cheese, plus
  more for serving
Finely chopped fresh chives, for garnish
Flat-leaf parsley or fresh basil, for garnish

1. Add the butter to the Foodi's inner pot, set the Foodi to Sear/Saute on High, and allow the butter to melt, about 5 minutes. Add the onion, garlic, and shallot to the pot and cook until slightly softened, about 4 minutes.
2. Stir in the rice, making sure all the grains get coated with butter. Continue cooking until the rice is looking a little translucent, about 4 minutes. Pour in the wine, stir, and cook until the alcohol smell has diminished, about 2 minutes.
3. Add the stock and the salt. Lock on the Pressure Lid, making sure the valve is set to Seal, and set the Foodi to Pressure on Low for 6 minutes. When the timer reaches 0, quick-release the pressure and carefully remove the lid.
4. Set the Foodi to Sear/Saute on High. Stir in the Parmesan cheese and cook until the liquid is absorbed and a starchy texture develops, about 5 minutes, stirring often. Serve immediately with extra cheese and garnished with fresh herbs.

Cajun Red Beans and Rice

Prep time: 15 minutes | Cook time: 47 minutes | Serves 4

For the Rice:
2 cups short-grain white rice, rinsed well
½ teaspoon kosher salt
For the Beans:
3 tablespoons peanut oil or vegetable oil
3 celery stalks, chopped
1 medium yellow onion, diced
1 green bell pepper, seeded, ribbed, and
  diced
3 garlic cloves, minced
5 sprigs fresh thyme
2 dried bay leaves, or 1 fresh
3 tablespoons Cajun seasoning
1 smoked ham hock
1 pound (454 g) dried red kidney beans
1 teaspoon kosher salt
Fresh thyme leaves, for garnish
Black pepper, for garnish

Make the Rice
1. Add the rice, 2 cups water, and the salt to the Foodi's inner pot. Lock on the Pressure Lid, making sure the valve is set to Seal, and set to Pressure on High for 3 minutes. When the timer reaches 0, allow the pressure to naturally release for 11 minutes, then quick-release any remaining pressure and carefully remove the lid. Transfer the rice to a large bowl. Wash and dry the inner pot.

Make the Beans
2. Add the oil to the inner pot, set the Foodi to Sear/Saute on High, and heat the oil for 5 minutes. Add the celery, onion, and bell pepper and cook until beginning to soften, about 6 minutes, stirring often.
3. Add the garlic, thyme, bay leaves, and Cajun seasoning and cook until aromatic, about 3 minutes, stirring occasionally.
4. Add the ham hock, kidney beans, and 4 cups water and stir. Lock on the Pressure Lid, making sure the valve is set to Seal, and set the Foodi to Pressure on High for 30 minutes. When the timer reaches 0, allow the pressure to naturally release for 15 minutes, then quick-release any remaining pressure and carefully remove the lid. Stir in the salt. Add a ladleful of beans and broth to a bowl, top with a small scoop of rice, and serve with extra thyme and pepper.

Creamy Potato Soup with Crispy Leek

Prep time: 15 minutes | Cook time: 20 minutes | Serves 6

2 tablespoons extra-virgin olive oil, divided
4 leeks, cleaned and thinly sliced, divided
4 garlic cloves, minced
5 Yukon Gold potatoes, peeled and diced
3 thyme sprigs, stems removed
2 bay leaves
5 cups vegetable broth

¾ cup white wine
1½ teaspoons dried oregano
1 teaspoon sea salt
½ teaspoon freshly ground black pepper
1½ cups light cream
½ cup grated Cheddar cheese

1. Select Sear/Sauté and set to Medium High. Select Start/Stop to begin. Allow the pot to preheat for 5 minutes.
2. Put 1 tablespoon of oil and three-quarters of the sliced leeks in the pot. Cook until soft, about 5 minutes. Add the garlic and cook for 1 minute more.
3. Add the potatoes, thyme, bay leaves, vegetable broth, white wine, oregano, salt, and black pepper to the pot. Assemble the Pressure Lid, making sure the pressure release valve is in the Seal position.
4. Select Pressure and set to High. Set the time to 10 minutes, then select Start/Stop to begin.
5. When pressure cooking is complete, quick release the pressure by moving the pressure release valve to the Vent position. Carefully remove the lid when the unit has finished releasing pressure.
6. Remove and discard the bay leaves. Add the cream and use a potato masher to mash the soup to your desired consistency. Evenly top with the cheese.
7. In a small bowl, toss the remaining sliced leeks with the remaining 1 tablespoon of oil. Place the Reversible Rack in the pot in the higher position. Place a sheet of aluminum foil on top of the rack and arrange the leeks on top.
8. Close the Crisping Lid. Select Broil and set the time to 5 minutes. Select Start/Stop to begin.
9. When cooking is complete, check to see if the leeks have reached your desired crispiness. Remove the rack from the pot and serve the crispy leeks over the soup.

Awesome Korean Pork Lettuce Wraps

Prepping time: 10 minutes | Cooking time: 60 minutes | For 8 servings

¼ cup of miso
¼ cup of soy sauce (Low Sodium)/
    Coconut Aminos
3 tablespoon of Korean red paste
1 teaspoon of ground sesame oil
1 teaspoon of ground black pepper
1 pork shoulder trimmed of excess fat

Serving

Lettuce leaves
Radishes
Cucumbers
Green onion

1. Take a small bowl and add miso, soy sauce, ¼ cup of water Korean red paste, black pepper, and sesame oil. Mix well until smooth
2. Pour half of the sauce into your Ninja Foodi . Add pork and pour the rest of the sauce on top
3. Lock up the lid and cook on HIGH pressure for 1 hour. Release the pressure naturally
4. Shred the pork and serve in lettuce wraps with cucumbers, radish, green onion etc.

Spicy "Faux" Pork Belly

Prepping time: 10 minutes | Cooking time: 15 minutes | For 4 servings

1 pound of pork belly, chopped
4 cups cauliflower, riced
½ a cup of bone broth
½ red onion, sliced
½ a cup of cilantro
2 green onion, sliced
1 tablespoon of lime juice
3 cloves garlic cloves, sliced
1 teaspoon turmeric
1 tablespoon oregano
1 tablespoon cumin
½ a teaspoon salt

1. Add all of the to your Instant Pot except ¼ cup of cilantro
2. Lock up the lid and cook on HIGH pressure for 15 minutes
3. Release the pressure naturally over 10 minutes
4. Open the lid and serve with sprinkled cilantro leaves
5. Enjoy!

Spiced Up Chipotle Pork Roast

Prepping time: 5 minutes| Cooking time:605 minutes | For 4 servings

6 ounces bone broth
7 and ¼ ounces tomatoes, diced
2 ounces green chilies, diced
2 pounds pork roast
½ teaspoon cumin, onion powder each
1 teaspoon chipotle powder

1. Add listed to your Ninja Foodi. Lock lid and cook on HIGH pressure for 60 minutes
2. Release pressure naturally over 10 minutes. Serve and enjoy!

Happy Burrito Bowl Pork

Prepping time: 10 minutes | Cooking time: 5 minutes | For 4 servings

1 and ½ tablespoons pork lard
1 onion, sliced
2 bell peppers, sliced
1 garlic clove, chopped
Salt and pepper to taste
1 pound pulled pork
½ cup of chicken pork
½ cup chicken broth
6 cups lettuce, chopped
6 cups cabbage, chopped
¼ cup guacamole

1. Set your Ninja Foodi to Saute mode and add lard, let it melt and add onion and bell pepper
2. Cook for 2 minutes, stirring for 2 minutes. Add garlic, salt, and pepper
3. Stir well. Add pulled pork and chicken pork
4. Lock lid and cook on HIGH pressure for 1 minute. Quick release pressure
5. Arrange lettuce and green cabbage in serving bowls and add pulled pork on top
6. Top with guacamole and serve. Enjoy!

Awesome Sauerkraut Pork

Prepping time: 10 minutes | Cooking time: 35 minutes | For 4 servings

3 pounds of pork shoulder
Salt and pepper to taste
3 tablespoons butter
2 onions, chopped
3 cloves garlic, sliced
6 cups sauerkraut, divided
1 pound hot dog, sliced and cooked
½ pound kielbasa, sliced and cooked

1. Season pork roast with salt and pepper
2. Set your Ninja Foodi to Saute mode and add butter, let the butter melt
3. Add pork roast and brown. Pour 2 cups water, onion and garlic
4. Season with salt and pepper and lock lid. Cook on HIGH pressure for 35 minutes
5. Release pressure naturally over 10 minutes
6. Shred pork and stir in sauerkraut, hotdog, and kielbasa. Serve and enjoy!

Spice Lover's Jalapeno Hash

Prepping time: 5 minutes | Cooking time: 10 minutes | For 4 servings

4 jalapeno peppers, chopped
½ cup chicken stock
3 ounces bacon, chopped and cooked
6 ounces zucchini, chopped
1 teaspoon ground black pepper
1 teaspoon butter

1. Add jalapeno peppers and zucchini into the Ninja Foodi pot
2. Put bacon, ground black pepper, butter, and chicken stock
3. Seal the lid. Set Pressure High. Cook the meat for 5 minutes
4. Then make natural pressure release for 10 minutes
5. Once cooked, let the meal chill for a few minutes. Serve with chicken stock and enjoy!

The Premium Red Pork

Prepping time: 10 minutes | Cooking time: 40 minutes | For 6 servings

2 pounds of pork belly
2 tablespoons maple syrup
3 tablespoons sherry
1 tablespoon blackstrap molasses
2 tablespoons coconut amino
1 teaspoon salt
1/3 cup water
1 piece ginger, peeled and smashed
Few sprigs of cilantro, garnish

1. Add the pork cubes to a pot and place it over medium heat
2. Add enough water to submerge them. Allow the water to come to a boil
3. Boil the cubes for 3 minutes and drain and rinse the cubes to remove any impurities
4. Keep them on the side. Set your Ninja Foodi to Saute mode and add maple syrup
5. Add cooked cubes and cook them for 1 minute until browned
6. After 10 minutes, add the remaining into the mix and bring the whole mixture to a boil. Lock up the lid and cook for 25 minutes at HIGH pressure
7. Allow the pressure to release naturally.
8. Open up the lid and set your Ninja Foodi to Saute mode again
9. Allow the contents to simmer for a while until the liquid has been reduced sufficiently enough to just coat the cubes. Serve with a garnish of cilantro. Enjoy!

Cool Spicy Pork Salad Bowl

Prepping time: 10 minutes | Cooking time: 90 minutes | For 6 servings

4 pounds pork shoulder butter
2 teaspoons salt
2 cups chicken stock
1 teaspoon smoked paprika powder
1 teaspoon garlic powder
1 teaspoon black pepper
1 pinch dried oregano leaves
4 tablespoons coconut oil
6 garlic cloves

1. Remove rind from pork and cut meat from the bone, slice into large chunks
2. Trim fat off met
3. Set your Foodi to Saute mode and add oil, let it heat up
4. Once the oil is hot, layer chunks of meat in the bottom of the pot and Saute for around 30 minutes until browned
5. While the meat is being browned, peel garlic cloves and cut into small chunks
6. Once the meat is browned, transfer it to a large-sized bowl
7. Add a few tablespoons of chicken stock to the pot a deglaze it, scraping off browned bits
8. Transfer browned bits to the bowl with meat chunks. Repeat if any more meat is left
9. Once done, add garlic, oregano leaves, smoked paprika, Garlic powder, pepper, and salt to the meat owl and mix it up. Add all chicken stock to the pot and bring to a simmer over Saute mode
10. Once done, return seasoned meat to the pot and lock lid, cook on HIGH pressure for 45 minutes. Release pressure naturally over 10 minutes
11. Open the lid and shred the meat using a fork, transfer shredded meat to a bowl and pour cooking liquid through a mesh to separate fat into the bowl with shredded meat
12. Serve with lime and enjoy!

Dill And Butter Pork Chops

Prepping time: 10 minutes | Cooking time: 20 minutes | For 4 servings

2 tablespoons unsalted butter
4 pieces ½ inch thick pork loin chops
½ teaspoon salt
½ teaspoon pepper
16 baby carrots
½ cup white wine vinegar
½ cup chicken broth

1. Set your Ninja Foodi to Saute mode. Season the chops with pepper and salt
2. Toss your chops into your pot and cook for 4 minutes
3. Transfer the chops to a plate and repeat to cook and brown the rest
4. Pour in 1 tablespoon of butter and Toss in your carrots, dill to the cooker and let it cook for about 1 minute
5. Pour in the wine and scrape off any browned bits in your cooker while the liquid comes to a boil
6. Stir in the broth. return the chops to your pot
7. Lock up the lid and let it cook for about 18 minutes at high pressure
8. Naturally, release the pressure by keeping it aside for 8 minutes
9. Unlock and serve with some sauce poured over

Cranberry Pork BBQ Dish

Prepping time: 10 minutes | Cooking time: 45 minutes | For 4 servings

3-4 pounds pork shoulder, boneless, fat trimmed
For Sauce

3 tablespoons of liquid smoke
2 tablespoons tomato paste
2 cups fresh cranberries
¼ cup hot sauce (Keto-Friendly)
1/3 cup blackstrap molasses
½ cup of water
½ cup apple cider vinegar
1 teaspoon salt
1 tablespoon adobo sauce (Keto Friendly and Sugar-Free)
1 cup tomato puree (Keto-Friendly and Sugar-Free)
1 chipotle pepper in adobo sauce, diced

1. Cut pork against halves/thirds and keep it on the side
2. Set your Ninja Foodi to "SAUTE" mode and let it heat up. Add cranberries and water to the pot
3. Let them simmer for 4-5 minutes until cranberries start to pop, add rest of the sauce and simmer for 5 minutes more. Add pork to the pot and lock lid
4. Cook on HIGH pressure for 40 minutes. Quick release pressure
5. Use a fork to shred the pork and serve on your favorite greens

Definitive Pork Carnita

Prepping time: 10 minutes | Cooking time: 25 minutes | For 4 servings

2 pounds pork butt, chopped into 2-inch pieces
1 teaspoon salt
½ teaspoon oregano
½ teaspoon cumin
1 yellow onion, cut into half
6 garlic cloves, peeled and crushed
½ cup chicken broth

1. Insert a pan into your Ninja Foodi and add pork
2. Season with salt, cumin, oregano and mix well, making sure that the pork is well seasoned
3. Take the orange and squeeze the orange juice all over
4. Add squeezed orange to into the insert pan as well
5. Add garlic cloves and onions. Pour ½ cup chicken broth into the pan
6. Lock the lid of the Ninja Foodi, making sure that the valve is sealed well
7. Set pressure to HIGH and let it cook for 20 minutes
8. Once the timer beeps, quick release the pressure
9. Open the lid and take out orange, garlic cloves, and onions
10. Set your Nina Foodi to Sauté mode and adjust the temperature to medium-high
11. Let the liquid simmer for 10-15 minutes
12. After most of the liquid has been reduced, press the stop button
13. Close the Ninja Foodi with "Air Crisp" lid. Pressure broil option and set timer to 8 minutes
14. Take the meat and put it in wraps. Garnish with cilantro and enjoy!

Technical Keto Pork Belly

Prepping time: 10 minutes | Cooking time: 40 minutes | For 4 servings

1 pound pork belly
½-1 cup white wine vinegar
1 garlic clove
1 tablespoon olive oil
Salt and pepper to taste

1. Set your Ninja Foodi to "SAUTE" mode and add oil, let it heat up
2. Add pork and sear for 2-3 minutes until both sides are golden and crispy
3. Add vinegar until about a quarter inch, season with salt, pepper, and garlic
4. Add garlic clove and Saute until the liquid comes to a boil
5. Lock lid and cook on HIGH pressure for 40 minutes
6. Once done, quick release pressure. Slice the meat and serve with the sauce. Enjoy!

Jamaican Pork Pot

Prepping time: 10 minutes | Cooking time: 45 minutes | For 4 servings

½ cup beef stock
1 tablespoon olive oil
¼ cup Jamaican jerk spice blend
4 ounces of pork shoulder

1. Rub roast with olive oil and spice blend
2. Set your Ninja Foodi to Saute mode and add meat, brown all sides
3. Pour beef broth. Lock lid and cook on HIGH pressure for 45 minutes
4. Quick release pressure. Shred pork and serve!

The Mexican Pulled Pork Ala Lettuce

Prepping time: 10 minutes | Cooking time: 60 minutes | For 4 servings

4 pounds pork roast
1 head butter lettuce, washed and dried
2 carrots, grated
2 tablespoons olive oil
2 lime wedges
1 onion, chopped
1 tablespoon salt
2-3 cups water

For Spice Mix

1 tablespoon unsweetened cocoa powder
2 teaspoons oregano
1 teaspoon red pepper flakes
1 teaspoon garlic powder
1 teaspoon white pepper
1 teaspoon cumin
1/8 teaspoon cayenne
1/8 teaspoon coriander

1. Marinate pork overnight by transferring the meat to a bowl and mixing in all of the spices
2. Set your Ninja Foodi to "SAUTE" mode and add roast, let it brown
3. Add 2-3 cups water to fully submerge the roast
4. Lock lid and cook on HIGH pressure for 55 minutes
5. Release pressure naturally over 10 minutes
6. Set your pot to "SAUTE" mode again and take out the meat, shred the meat and keep it on the side. Reduce the liquid by half and strain/skim any excess fat
7. Mix pork with cooking liquid and serve with lettuce, grated carrots, squire of lime and any other topping you desire. Enjoy!

Pork With Cranberries And Pecan

Prepping time: 10 minutes | Cooking time: 45 minutes | For 4 servings

¼ cup of spicy brown mustard
½ a teaspoon of garlic powder
½ a teaspoon of stevia
½ a teaspoon of salt
¼ teaspoon of pepper freshly ground
3 and a ½ pound of pork shoulder, boneless and trimmed of excess fat
2 cups onion, chopped
1 cup of fresh cranberries
3 cups of cabbage, finely shredded
½ a cup of toasted pecans
½ a cup of dried cranberries

1. Take a small bowl and add mustard, stevia, garlic powder, pepper, and salt and mix them well
2. Rub the mix all over the pork
3. Add pork to the Ninja Foodi
4. Top with cranberries and onion
5. Lock up the lid and cook on HIGH pressure for 45 minutes
6. Release the pressure naturally
7. Transfer the pork to cutting board and shred using two forks
8. Strain the liquid making sure to discard the cranberries and onion
9. Pour the strained liquid over pork
10. Serve over shredded cabbage topped with pecans and cranberries
11. Enjoy!

Cuban And Garlic Pork Meal

Prepping time: 10 minutes | Cooking time: 80 minutes | For 4 servings

3 pounds boneless pork shoulder blade roast, fat trimmed and removed
6 garlic cloves, minced
2/3 cup grapefruit juice
½ tablespoon fresh oregano
½ tablespoon cumin
1 lime, juiced
1 tablespoon salt
1 bay leaf
Lime wedges as needed
Cilantro, chopped, for garnish
Hot sauce as needed
Salsa as needed

1. Cut the pork chops in 4 individual pieces and add them to a bowl
2. Take a small sized blender and add garlic, grapefruit juice, lime, oregano, cumin, salt, and blend well. Pour the marinade over your pork and allow it to sit for 60 minutes
3. Transfer the mix to your Ninja Foodi and add bay leaf
4. Cover and cook on HIGH pressure for 80 minutes. Release the pressure naturally
5. Remove the pork and shred it up. Return the pork back to the Foodi and add 1 cup of liquid
6. Season with some salt and allow it warm for a while (over Saute mode)
7. Enjoy!

Mean Cream Mushroom Garlic Chicken

Prepping time: 10 minutes | Cooking time: 15 minutes | For 4 servings

2 pounds chicken thighs
7 ounces Cremini mushrooms
2 teaspoons garlic, minced
½ cup chicken broth
½ cup whipping cream
1 teaspoon cayenne pepper
1 tablespoon lemon juice
1 tablespoon parsley, chopped
1 tablespoon olive oil
Salt and pepper to taste

1. Trim the stems of mushrooms. Wash and rinse chicken thighs under cold water
2. Pat dry with paper towels
3. Use kitchen scissors to trim excess skin and d fat from chicken thighs
4. Season both sides with salt and pepper, keep them on the side (covered)
5. Set your Ninja Foodi to Saute mode and add olive oil, let it heat up
6. Add chicken thighs and brown both sides. Scoop out excess fat and discard
7. Add garlic, whipping cream, mushrooms, broth, salt and pepper
8. Lock lid and cook on HIGH pressure for 10 minutes. Release pressure naturally over 10 minutes
9. Open the lid and set your pot to Saute mode. Add lemon juice and parsley. Serve and enjoy!

Pork Roast And Cauliflower Gravy

Prepping time: 10 minutes | Cooking time: 90 minutes | For 4 servings

2-3 pounds pork roast
1 teaspoon salt
½ teaspoon pepper
4 cups cauliflower, chopped
1 medium onion, chopped
4 garlic cloves
2 ribs celery
8 ounces portabella mushrooms, sliced
2 tablespoons organic coconut oil
2 cups of filtered water

1. Pre-heat your oven to 400 degrees Fahrenheit
2. Add cauliflower, celery, garlic, onion, and water to your Ninja Foodi
3. Top them up with the roast . Season with a bit of pepper and salt
4. Lock up the lid and cook under HIGH pressure for 90 minutes
5. Release the pressure naturally. Remove the pork roast and transfer to a baking dish
6. Bake at 400 degrees Fahrenheit
7. Transfer the cooked veggies and broth to a blender and blend to obtain a smooth texture
8. Set your pot to Saute and add the mushrooms, cook them in coconut oil for about 3-5 minutes
9. Add the blended veggies and keep Sautéing until a thick mixture is obtained
10. Shred the roasted pork and serve over the gravy. Enjoy!

Premium Pork Chili Colorado

Prepping time: 5 minutes | Cooking time: 8 hours |For 6 servings

3 pounds pork shoulder, cut into 1-inch cubes
1 teaspoon garlic powder
1 onion, chopped
1 teaspoon chipotle chili powder
1 tablespoon chili powder
1 teaspoon of sea salt

1. Add listed to Ninja Foodi
2. Lock lid and cook on SLOW COOK Mode (LOW) for 8-10 hours. Serve and enjoy!

Chapter 4: High-Quality Seafood Dishes

Hearty Swordfish Meal

Prepping time: 5 minutes | Cooking time: 150 minutes | For 4 servings

5 swordfish fillets
½ a cup of melted clarified butter
6 garlic cloves, chopped
1 tablespoon black pepper

1. Take a mixing bowl and add garlic, clarified butter, black pepper
2. Take a parchment paper and add the fillet. Cover and wrap the fish
3. Keep repeating until the fillets are wrapped up
4. Transfer wrapped fish to Ninja Foodi pot and lock lid
5. Allow them to cook for 2 and a ½ hour at high pressure. Release the pressure naturally
6. Serve and enjoy!

Gentle And Simple Fish Stew

Prepping time: 5 minutes | Cooking time: 20 minutes | For 4 servings

3 cups fish stock
1 onion, diced
1 cup broccoli, chopped
2 cups celery stalks, chopped
1 and ½ cups cauliflower, diced
1 carrot, sliced
1 pound white fish fillets, chopped

1 cup heavy cream
1 bay leaf
2 tablespoons butter
¼ teaspoon pepper
½ teaspoon salt
¼ teaspoon garlic powder

1. Set your Ninja Foodi to Saute mode and add butter, let it melt
2. Add onion and carrots, cook for 3 minutes. Stir in remaining
3. Lock lid and cook on HIGH pressure for 4 minutes. Naturally, release pressure over 10 minutes
4. Discard bay leaf . Serve and enjoy!

Cool Shrimp Zoodles

Prepping time: 5 minutes | Cooking time: 3 minutes | For 4 servings

4 cups zoodles
1 tablespoon basil, chopped
2 tablespoons Ghee
1 cup vegetable stock
2 garlic cloves, minced
2 tablespoons olive oil
½ lemon
½ teaspoon paprika

1. Set your Ninja Foodi to Saute mode and add ghee, let it heat up
2. Add olive oil as well. Add garlic and cook for 1 minute
3. Add lemon juice, shrimp and cook for 1 minute
4. Stir in rest of the and lock lid, cook on LOW pressure for 5 minutes
5. Quick release pressure and serve . Enjoy!

Heartfelt Sesame Fish

Prepping time: 8 minutes | Cooking time: 8 minutes | For 4 servings

1 and ½ pound salmon fillet
1 teaspoon sesame seeds
1 teaspoon butter, melted
½ teaspoon salt
1 tablespoon apple cider vinegar
¼ teaspoon rosemary, dried

1. Take apple cider vinegar and spray it to the salmon fillets
2. Then add dried rosemary, sesame seeds, butter and salt
3. Mix them well. Take butter sauce and brush the salmon properly
4. Place the salmon on the rack and lower the air fryer lid. Set the air fryer mode
5. Cook the fish for 8 minutes at 360 F. Serve hot and enjoy!

Awesome Sock-Eye Salmon

Prepping time: 5 minutes | Cooking time: 5 minutes | For 4 servings

4 sockeye salmon fillets
1 teaspoon Dijon mustard
¼ teaspoon garlic, minced
¼ teaspoon onion powder
¼ teaspoon lemon pepper
½ teaspoon garlic powder
¼ teaspoon salt
2 tablespoons olive oil
1 and ½ cup of water

1. Take a bowl and add mustard, lemon juice, onion powder, lemon pepper, garlic powder, salt, olive oil. Brush spice mix over salmon
2. Add water to Instant Pot. Place rack and place salmon fillets on rack
3. Lock lid and cook on LOW pressure for 7 minutes
4. Quick release pressure .Serve and enjoy!

Buttered Up Scallops

Prepping time: 10 minutes | Cooking time: 5 minutes | For 4 servings

4 garlic cloves, minced
4 tablespoons rosemary, chopped
2 pounds sea scallops
12 cup butter
Salt and pepper to taste

1. Set your Ninja Foodi to Saute mode and add butter, rosemary, and garlic
2. Saute for 1 minute. Add scallops, salt, and pepper
3. Saute for 2 minutes. Lock Crisping lid and Crisp for 3 minutes at 350 degrees F. Serve and enjoy!

NAwesome Cherry Tomato Mackerel

Prepping time: 5 minutes | Cooking time: 7 minutes | For 4 servings

4 Mackerel fillets
¼ teaspoon onion powder
¼ teaspoon lemon powder
¼ teaspoon garlic powder
½ teaspoon salt
2 cups cherry tomatoes
3 tablespoons melted butter
1 and ½ cups of water
1 tablespoon black olives

1. Grease baking dish and arrange cherry tomatoes at the bottom of the dish
2. Top with fillets sprinkle all spices. Drizzle melted butter over
3. Add water to your Ninja Foodi
4. Lower rack in Ninja Foodi and place baking dish on top of the rack
5. Lock lid and cook on LOW pressure for 7 minutes . Quick release pressure. Serve and enjoy!

Lovely Air Fried Scallops

Prepping time: 5 minutes | Cooking time: 5 minutes | For 4 servings

12 scallops
3 tablespoons olive oil
Salt and pepper to taste

1. Gently rub scallops with salt, pepper, and oil
2. Transfer to your Ninja Foodie's insert, and place the insert in your Foodi
3. Lock Air Crisping lid and cook for 4 minutes at 390 degrees F
4. Half through, make sure to give them a nice flip and keep cooking. Serve warm and enjoy!

Packets Of Lemon And Dill Cod

Prepping time: 10 minutes | Cooking time: 5-10 minutes | For 4 servings

2 tilapia cod fillets
Salt, pepper and garlic powder to taste
2 sprigs fresh dill
4 slices lemon
2 tablespoons butter

1. Layout 2 large squares of parchment paper
2. Place fillet in center of each parchment square and season with salt, pepper and garlic powder
3. On each fillet, place 1 sprig of dill, 2 lemon slices, 1 tablespoon butter
4. Place trivet at the bottom of your Ninja Foodi. Add 1 cup water into the pot
5. Close parchment paper around fillets and fold to make a nice seal
6. Place both packets in your pot . Lock lid and cook on HIGH pressure for 5 minutes
7. Quick release pressure . Serve and enjoy!

Adventurous Sweet And Sour Fish

Prepping time: 10 minutes | Cooking time: 6 minutes | For 4 servings

2 drops liquid stevia
¼ cup butter
1 pound fish chunks
1 tablespoon vinegar
Salt and pepper to taste

1. Set your Ninja Foodi to Saute mode and add butter, let it melt
2. Add fish chunks and Saute for 3 minutes. Add stevia, salt, and pepper, stir
3. Lock Crisping Lid and cook on "Air Crisp" mode for 3 minutes at 360 degrees F
4. Serve once done and enjoy!

Garlic And Lemon Prawn Delight

Prepping time: 5 minutes | Cooking time: 5 minutes | For 4 servings

2 tablespoons olive oil
1 pound prawns
2 tablespoons garlic, minced
2/3 cup fish stock
1 tablespoon butter
2 tablespoons lemon juice
1 tablespoon lemon zest
Salt and pepper to taste

1. Set your Ninja Foodi to Saute mode and add butter and oil, let it heat up
2. Stir in remaining . Lock lid and cook on LOW pressure for 5 minutes
3. Quick release pressure. Serve and enjoy!

Lovely Carb Soup

Prepping time: 5 minutes | Cooking time: 6-7 hours |For 4 servings

1 cup crab meat, cubed
1 tablespoon garlic, minced
Salt as needed
Red chili flakes as needed
3 cups vegetable broth
1 teaspoon salt

1. Coat the crab cubes in lime juice and let them sit for a while
2. Add the all (including marinated crab meat) to your Ninja Foodi and lock lid
3. Cook on SLOW COOK MODE (MEDIUM) for 3 hours
4. Let it sit for a while
5. Unlock lid and set to Saute mode, simmer the soup for 5 minutes more on LOW
6. Stir and check to season. Enjoy!

The Rich Guy Lobster And Butter

Prepping time: 15 minutes | Cooking time: 20 minutes | For 4 servings

6 Lobster Tails
4 garlic cloves,
¼ cup butter

1. Preheat the Ninja Foodi to 400 degrees F at first
2. Open the lobster tails gently by using kitchen scissors
3. Remove the lobster meat gently from the shells but keep it inside the shells
4. Take a plate and place it
5. Add some butter in a pan and allow it melt
6. Put some garlic cloves in it and heat it over medium-low heat
7. Pour the garlic butter mixture all over the lobster tail meat
8. Let the fryer to broil the lobster at 130 degrees F
9. Remove the lobster meat from Ninja Foodi and set aside
10. Use a fork to pull out the lobster meat from the shells entirely
11. Pour some garlic butter over it if needed. Serve and enjoy!

Lovely Panko Cod

Prepping time: 5 minutes | Cooking time: 15 minutes | For 6 servings

2 uncooked cod fillets, 6 ounces each
3 teaspoons kosher salt
¾ cup panko bread crumbs
2 tablespoons butter, melted
¼ cup fresh parsley, minced
1 lemon. Zested and juiced

1. Pre-heat your Ninja Foodi at 390 degrees F and place Air Crisper basket inside
2. Season cod and salt
3. Take a bowl and add bread crumbs, parsley, lemon juice, zest, butter, and mix well
4. Coat fillets with the bread crumbs mixture and place fillets in your Air Crisping basket
5. Lock Air Crisping lid and cook on Air Crisp mode for 15 minutes at 360 degrees F
6. Serve and enjoy!

Salmon Paprika

Prepping time: 5 minutes | Cooking time: 7 minutes | For 4 servings

2 wild caught salmon fillets, 1 to 1 and ½ inches thick
2 teaspoons avocado oil
2 teaspoons paprika
Salt and pepper to taste
Green herbs to garnish

1. Season salmon fillets with salt, pepper, paprika, and olive oil
2. Place Crisping basket in your Ninja Foodi, and pre-heat your Ninja Foodie at 390 degrees F
3. Place insert insider your Foodi and place the fillet in the insert, lock Air Crisping lid and cook for 7 minutes. Once done, serve the fish with herbs on top. Enjoy!

Heartfelt Air Fried Scampi

Prepping time: 5 minutes | Cooking time: 5 minutes | For 4 servings

4 tablespoons butter
1 tablespoon lemon juice
1 tablespoon garlic, minced
2 teaspoons red pepper flakes
1 tablespoon chives, chopped
1 tablespoon basil leaves, minced
2 tablespoons chicken stock
1 pound defrosted shrimp

1. Set your Foodi to Saute mode and add butter, let the butter melt and add red pepper flakes and garlic, Saute for 2 minutes
2. Transfer garlic to crisping basket, add remaining (including shrimp) to the basket
3. Return basket back to the Ninja Foodi and lock the Air Crisping lid, cook for 5 minutes at 390 degrees F. Once done, serve with a garnish of fresh basil

Ranch Warm Fillets

Prepping time: 5 minutes | Cooking time: 13 minutes | For 4 servings

¼ cup panko
½ packet ranch dressing mix powder
1 and ¼ tablespoons vegetable oil
1 egg beaten
2 tilapia fillets
A garnish of herbs and chilies

1. Pre-heat your Ninja Foodi with the Crisping Basket inside at 350 degrees F
2. Take a bowl and mix in ranch dressing and panko
3. Beat eggs in a shallow bowl and keep it on the side
4. Dip fillets in the eggs, then in the panko mix
5. Place fillets in your Ninja Foodie's insert and transfer insert to Ninja Foodi
6. Lock Air Crisping Lid and Air Crisp for 13 minutes at 350 degrees F
7. Garnish with chilies and herbs. Enjoy!

Alaskan Cod Divine

Prepping time: 10 minutes | Cooking time: 5-10 minutes | For 4 servings

1 large fillet, Alaskan Cod (Frozen)
1 cup cherry tomatoes
Salt and pepper to taste
Seasoning as you need
2 tablespoons butter
Olive oil as needed

1. Take an ovenproof dish small enough to fit inside your pot
2. Add tomatoes to the dish, cut large fish fillet into 2-3 serving pieces and lay them on top of tomatoes. Season with salt, pepper, and your seasoning
3. Top each fillet with 1 tablespoon butter and drizzle olive oil
4. Add 1 cup of water to the pot. Place trivet to the Ninja Foodi and place dish on the trivet
5. Lock lid and cook on HIGH pressure for 9 minutes. Release pressure naturally over 10 minutes
6. Serve and enjoy!

Kale And Salmon Delight

Prepping time: 10 minutes | Cooking time: 5 minutes | For 4 servings

1 lemon, juiced
2 salmon fillets
¼ cup extra virgin olive oil
1 teaspoon Dijon mustard
4 cups kale, thinly sliced, ribs
    removed
1 teaspoon salt
1 avocado, diced
1 cup pomegranate seeds
1 cup walnuts, toasted
1 cup goat parmesan cheese, shredded

1. Season salmon with salt and keep it on the side. Place a trivet in your Ninja Foodi
2. Place salmon over the trivet. Lock lid and cook on HIGH pressure for 15 minutes
3. Release pressure naturally over 10 minutes. Transfer salmon to a serving platter
4. Take a bowl and add kale, season with salt
5. Take another bowl and make the dressing by adding lemon juice, Dijon mustard, olive oil, and red wine vinegar. Season kale with dressing and add diced avocado, pomegranate seeds, walnuts and cheese. Toss and serve with the fish. Enjoy!

Ale and Cod Sandwich

Prep time: 5 minutes | Cook time: 15 minutes | Serves 4

2 eggs
8 ounces (227 g) ale
1 cup cornstarch
1 cup all-purpose flour
½ tablespoon chili powder
1 tablespoon ground cumin
1 teaspoon sea salt
1 teaspoon freshly ground black
   pepper
4 (5- to 6-ounce / 142- to 170-g) cod
   fillets, cut into 16 half-inch strips
Cooking spray
Tartar sauce, for garnish
8 slices sandwich bread

1. Insert Cook & Crisp Basket in pot. Close crisping lid. Select AIR CRISP, set temperature to 375°F (191°C), and set time to 5 minutes. Select START/STOP to begin preheating.
2. In a shallow bowl, whisk together the eggs and beer. In a medium bowl, whisk together the cornstarch, flour, chili powder, cumin, salt, and pepper.
3. Dip each strip of cod fillet in the egg mixture, then dredge in the flour mixture, coating on all sides.
4. Once unit has preheated, spray the basket with the cooking spray. Place the fish strips in the basket and coat them with cooking spray. Close crisping lid.
5. Select AIR CRISP, set temperature to 375°F (191°C), and set time to 15 minutes. Select START/STOP to begin.
6. When cooking is complete, check the fish for your desired crispiness. Remove the fish from the basket.
7. Spread tartar sauce on four slices of bread. Place four fish strips on each slice and top the sandwiches with the four remaining slices. Serve.

Garlicky Shrimp with Broccoli

Prep time: 5 minutes | Cook time: 5 minutes | Serves 4

2 tablespoons unsalted butter
1 shallot, minced
3 garlic cloves, minced
¼ cup white wine
½ cup chicken stock
Juice of ½ lemon
½ teaspoon sea salt
½ teaspoon freshly ground black
   pepper
1½ pounds (680 g) frozen shrimp,
   thawed
1 large head broccoli, cut into florets

1. Add the butter. Select SEAR/SAUTÉ and set to MED. Select START/STOP to begin.
2. Once the butter is melted, add the shallots and cook for 3 minutes. Add the garlic and cook for 1 minute.
3. Deglaze the pot by adding the wine and using a wooden spoon to scrape the bits of garlic and shallot off the bottom of the pot. Stir in the chicken stock, lemon juice, salt, pepper, and shrimp.
4. Place the broccoli florets on top of the shrimp mixture. Assemble pressure lid, making sure the pressure release valve is in the SEAL position.
5. Select PRESSURE and set to HI. Set time to 0 minutes. Select START/STOP to begin.
6. When pressure cooking is complete, quick release the pressure by moving the pressure release valve to the VENT position. Carefully remove lid when the unit has finished releasing pressure. Serve immediately.

Country Shrimp Boil

Prep time: 10 minutes | Cook time: 10 minutes | Serves 6

2 pounds (907 g) Red Bliss potatoes,
   diced
3 ears corn, cut crosswise into thirds
1 (14-ounce / 397-g) package smoked
   sausage or kielbasa, sliced into
   1-inch pieces
4 cups water
2½ tablespoons Creole seasoning
1 pound (454 g) medium (21–30
   count) shrimp, peeled and
   deveined

1. Place the potatoes, corn, sausage, water, and Creole seasoning into the pot and stir. Assemble pressure lid, making sure the pressure release valve is in the SEAL position.
2. Select PRESSURE and set to HI. Set time to 5 minutes. Select START/STOP to begin.
3. When pressure cooking is complete, quick release the pressure by turning the pressure release valve to the VENT position. Carefully remove lid when unit has finished releasing pressure.
4. Stir in the shrimp.
5. Select SEAR/SAUTÉ and set to MD:LO. Simmer for about 5 minutes, until the shrimp is cooked through.
6. When cooking is complete, serve immediately.

Lobster Lettuce Rolls

Prep time: 10 minutes | Cook time: 20 minutes | Serves 4

4 (4-ounce / 113-g) lobster tails
¼ cup mayonnaise
1 celery stalk, minced
Zest of 1 lemon
Juice of 1 lemon
¼ teaspoon celery seed
Kosher salt
Freshly ground black pepper
4 split-top hot dog buns
4 tablespoons unsalted butter, at
    room temperature
4 leaves butter lettuce

1. Insert Cook & Crisp Basket into the pot and close the crisping lid. Select AIR CRISP, set temperature to 375°F (191°C), and set time to 15 minutes. Select START/STOP to begin. Let preheat for 5 minutes.
2. Once unit has preheated, open lid and add the lobster tails to the basket. Close the lid and cook for 10 minutes.
3. In a medium bowl, mix together the mayonnaise, celery, lemon zest and juice, and celery seed, and add salt and pepper.
4. Fill a large bowl with a tray of ice cubes and enough water to cover the ice.
5. When cooking is complete, open lid. Transfer the lobster into the ice bath for 5 minutes. Close lid to keep unit warm.
6. Spread butter on the hot dog buns. Open lid and place the buns in the basket. Close crisping lid.
7. Select AIR CRISP, set temperature to 375°F (191°C), and set time to 4 minutes. Select START/STOP to begin.
8. Remove the lobster meat from the shells and roughly chop. Place in the bowl with the mayonnaise mixture and stir.
9. When cooking is complete, open lid and remove the buns. Place lettuce in each bun, then fill with the lobster salad.

Ginger and Scallion Cod Fillets

Prep time: 5 minutes | Cook time: 10 minutes | Serves 4

2 tablespoons rice vinegar
2 tablespoons soy sauce
1 tablespoon chicken stock
1 tablespoon grated fresh ginger
4 skinless cod fillets (about 1½ pounds / 680 g)
Sea salt
Freshly ground black pepper
Greens of 6 scallions, thinly sliced

1. In a small bowl, mix together the rice vinegar, soy sauce, chicken stock, and ginger.
2. Season the cod fillets on both sides with salt and pepper. Place them in the pot and cover with the vinegar mixture.
3. Select SEAR/SAUTÉ and set to MED. Bring the liquid to a low boil.
4. Once boiling, turn the heat to LO and cover with the pressure lid. Cook for 8 minutes.
5. Remove lid and add the scallion greens to the top of the fish. Cover with the pressure lid and cook for 2 minutes more. Serve.

Tuscan Cod with Red Potatoes

Prep time: 20 minutes | Cook time: 32 minutes | Serves 4

2 tablespoons canola oil, divided
1½ pounds (680 g) baby red potatoes,
    cut into ½-inch pieces
2½ teaspoons kosher salt, divided
1 teaspoon freshly ground black pepper, divided
1 cup panko bread crumbs
6 tablespoons unsalted butter, divided
2 teaspoons poultry seasoning

Juice of 1 lemon
1 medium onion, thinly sliced
1½ cups cherry tomatoes, halved
4 garlic cloves, quartered lengthwise
⅓ cup Kalamata olives, roughly chopped
4 (6-ounce / 170-g) fresh cod fillets
1 teaspoon fresh mint, finely chopped
1 lemon, cut into wedges

1. Select SEAR/SAUTÉ and set to HI. Select START/STOP to begin. Let preheat for 5 minutes.
2. Add 1 tablespoon of oil and the potatoes. Season with 1½ teaspoons of salt and ½ teaspoon of pepper. Sauté for about 15 minutes, stirring occasionally, until the potatoes are golden brown.
3. While potatoes are cooking, combine the bread crumbs, 4 tablespoons of butter, poultry seasoning, the remaining 1 teaspoon of salt and ½ teaspoon of pepper, and lemon juice in a medium bowl. Stir well.
4. Once the potatoes are browned, carefully remove them from the pot and set aside. Add the remaining 1 tablespoon of oil, then the onion. Sauté for 2 to 3 minutes, until the onions are lightly browned. Add the tomatoes, garlic, and olives and cook for about 2 minutes more, stirring occasionally. Return the potatoes to the pot, stir. Select START/STOP to pause cooking. Close crisping lid to retain heat.
5. Coat the cod on both sides with the remaining 2 tablespoons of butter. Evenly distribute the breadcrumb mixture on top of the cod, pressing the crumbs down firmly.
6. Open lid and place the Reversible Rack in the pot over the potato mixture, making sure it is the higher position. Place the cod fillets on the rack, bread-side up. Close crisping lid.
7. Select BAKE/ROAST, set temperature to 375°F (191°C), and set time to 12 minutes. Select START/STOP to begin.
8. When cooking is complete, leave the cod in the pot with the crisping lid closed for 5 minutes to rest before serving. After resting, the internal temperature of the cod should be at least 145°F (63°C) and the bread crumbs should be golden brown. Serve with potato mixture and garnish with chopped mint and lemon wedges.

Apricot Salmon with Potatoes

Prep time: 10 minutes | Cook time: 25 minutes | Serves 4

20 ounces (567 g) baby potatoes, whole
1½ cups water
4 (6-ounce / 170-g) frozen skinless salmon fillets
¼ cup apricot preserves
2 teaspoons Dijon mustard
2 tablespoons extra-virgin olive oil
½ teaspoon kosher salt
½ teaspoon freshly ground black pepper

1. Place the potatoes and water in the pot. Put Reversible Rack in pot, making sure it is in the higher position. Place salmon on the rack. Assemble pressure lid, making sure the pressure release valve is in the SEAL position.
2. Select PRESSURE and set to HI. Set time to 5 minutes. Select START/STOP to begin.
3. Mix together the apricot preserves and mustard in a small bowl.
4. When pressure cooking is complete, quick release the pressure by turning the pressure release valve to the VENT position. Carefully remove lid when unit has finished releasing pressure.
5. Carefully remove rack with salmon. Remove potatoes from pot and drain. Place the potatoes on a cutting board and, using the back of a knife, carefully press down to flatten each. Drizzle the flattened potatoes with the olive oil and season with salt and pepper.
6. Place Cook & Crisp Basket in the pot. Place the potatoes into the basket and close crisping lid.
7. Select AIR CRISP, set temperature to 390°F (199°C), and set time to 15 minutes. Select START/STOP to begin.
8. After 8 minutes, open lid, and using silicone-tipped tongs, gently flip the potatoes. Lower basket back into pot and close lid to resume cooking.
9. When cooking is complete, remove basket from pot. Return the rack with the salmon to the pot, making sure the rack is in the higher position. Gently brush the salmon with the apricot and mustard mixture.
10. Close crisping lid. Select BROIL and set time to 5 minutes. Select START/STOP to begin.
11. When cooking is complete, remove salmon and serve immediately with the potatoes.

Salmon with Rice and Brussels Sprouts

Prep time: 10 minutes | Cook time: 57 minutes | Serves 2

2 cups brown rice

2½ cups water

2 (4- to 6-ounce / 113- to 170-g) salmon fillets

4 tablespoons everything bagel seasoning, divided

1 pound (454 g) Brussels sprouts, ends trimmed, cut in half

1 tablespoon olive oil

2 tablespoons balsamic glaze

1. Place the rice and water in the cooking pot. Assemble the pressure lid, making sure the pressure release valve is in the SEAL position.
2. Select PRESSURE and set to HI. Set the time to 30 minutes. Select START/STOP to begin.
3. Meanwhile, season both sides of the salmon fillets with the everything bagel seasoning, using one tablespoon per fillet. Set aside.
4. When pressure cooking is complete, allow the pressure to release naturally for 10 minutes. After 10 minutes, quick release any remaining pressure by moving the pressure release valve to the VENT position. Carefully remove the lid when the unit has finished releasing pressure.
5. Season both sides of each salmon fillet with one tablespoon of the everything bagel seasoning.
6. In a medium bowl, combine the Brussels sprouts and olive oil. Toss to coat, and then sprinkle with one tablespoon of the everything bagel seasoning. Toss again to ensure Brussels sprouts are coated.
7. Place the Cook & Crisp Basket into the cooking pot. Close the crisping lid. Select AIR CRISP, set the temperature to 390ºF (199ºC), and set the time to 16 minutes. Select START/STOP to begin. Allow to preheat for 5 minutes, then add the sprouts to the Cook & Crisp Basket. Close the crisping lid to begin cooking.
8. After 8 minutes, open the crisping lid, lift the basket, and shake the sprouts. Lower the basket back into the pot and close the lid to resume cooking another 8 minutes or until the Brussels sprouts reach your desired crispiness.
9. Once timer is complete, transfer the sprouts to a bowl and toss with remaining tablespoon of seasoning and the balsamic glaze.
10. Close the crisping lid. Select AIR CRISP, set the temperature to 390ºF (199ºC), and set the time to 11 minutes. Select START/STOP to begin. Allow to preheat for 5 minutes, then add the salmon fillets to the Cook & Crisp basket. Close the lid to begin cooking.
11. Once timer is complete, remove fillets from basket and serve alongside sprouts and rice.

Tilapia with Rice and Avocado Salsa

Prep time: 10 minutes | Cook time: 12 minutes | Serves 4

2 cups white rice, rinsed

2 cups water

¼ cup blackening seasoning

4 (4-ounce / 113-g) tilapia fillets

2 tablespoons freshly squeezed lime juice, divided

1 bunch cilantro, minced

1 tablespoon extra-virgin olive oil

2 avocados, diced

1 large red onion, diced

2 Roma tomatoes, diced

Kosher salt

Freshly ground black pepper

1. Place the rice and water in the pot and stir. Assemble pressure lid, making sure the pressure release valve is in the SEAL position.
2. Select PRESSURE and set to HI. Set time to 2 minutes. Select START/STOP to begin.
3. Place the blackening seasoning on a plate. Dredge the tilapia fillets in the seasoning.
4. When pressure cooking is complete, allow pressure to naturally release for 10 minutes. After 10 minutes, quick release remaining pressure by turning the pressure release valve to the VENT position. Carefully remove lid when unit has finished releasing pressure.
5. Transfer the rice to a large bowl and stir in 1 tablespoon of lime juice and half the cilantro. Cover the bowl with aluminum foil and set aside.
6. Place the Reversible Rack in the pot and arrange tilapia fillets on top. Close crisping lid.
7. Select BROIL and set time to 10 minutes. Select START/STOP to begin.
8. In a medium bowl, stir together the remaining cilantro, remaining 1 tablespoon of lime juice, olive oil, avocado, onion, tomato, and season with salt and pepper.
9. When cooking is complete, open lid and lift the rack out of the pot. Serve the fish over the rice and top with avocado salsa.

White Wine Mussels with Saffron Threads

Prep time: 15 minutes | Cook time: 25 minutes | Serves 4

2 tablespoons vegetable oil

2 shallots, sliced

3 garlic cloves, minced

1 cup cherry tomatoes, halved

2 pounds (907 g) fresh mussels, washed with cold water, strained, scrubbed, and debearded, as needed

2 cups white wine (chardonnay or sauvignon blanc)

2 cups heavy cream

1½ teaspoons cayenne pepper

1½ teaspoons freshly ground black pepper

½ teaspoon saffron threads

1 loaf sourdough bread, cut into slices, for serving

1. Select SEAR/SAUTÉ and set the temperature to HI. Select START/STOP to begin and allow to preheat for 5 minutes.
2. Add oil to the pot and allow to heat for 1 minute. Add the shallots, garlic, and cherry tomatoes. Stir to ensure the ingredients are coated and sauté for 5 minutes.
3. Add the mussels, wine, heavy cream, cayenne, black pepper, and saffron threads to the pot.
4. Assemble the pressure lid, making sure the pressure release valve is in the VENT position.
5. Select STEAM and set the temperature to HI. Set the time to 20 minutes. Select START/STOP to begin.
6. When cooking is complete, carefully remove the lid.
7. Transfer the mussels and broth to bowls or eat straight from the pot. Discard any mussels that have not opened.
8. Serve with the bread and enjoy!

Pineapple Rice with Coconut-Crusted Shrimp

Prep time: 15 minutes | Cook time: 45 minutes | Serves 4

2 tablespoons canola oil

1 (20-ounce / 567-g) can diced pineapple

1 yellow onion, diced

1 cup long-grain white rice

1½ cups chicken stock

½ cup freshly squeezed lime juice

¾ cup all-purpose flour

1 tablespoon kosher salt

½ teaspoon freshly ground black pepper

2 large eggs

½ cup coconut flakes

½ cup plain panko bread crumbs

10 ounces (283 g) deveined shrimp, tails removed

Cooking spray

1. Select SEAR/SAUTÉ and set temperature to HI. Select START/STOP to begin. Let preheat for 5 minutes.
2. Add the oil and heat for 1 minute. Add the pineapple and onion. Cook, stirring frequently, for about 8 minutes, or until the onion is translucent.
3. Add the rice, chicken stock, and lime juice. Assemble pressure lid, making sure the pressure release valve is in the SEAL position.
4. Select PRESSURE and set to HI. Set time to 2 minutes. Select START/STOP to begin.
5. When pressure cooking is complete, allow press to naturally release for 10 minutes. After 10 minutes, quick release remaining pressure by turning the pressure release valve to the VENT position. Carefully remove lid when unit has finished releasing pressure.
6. Transfer the rice mixture to a bowl and cover to keep warm. Clean the cooking pot and return to the unit.
7. Create a batter station with three medium bowls. In the first bowl, mix together the flour, salt and pepper. In the second bowl, whisk the eggs. In the third bowl, combine the coconut flakes and bread crumbs. Dip each shrimp into the flour mixture. Next dip it in the egg. Finally, coat in the coconut mixture, shaking off excess as needed. Once all the shrimp are battered, spray them with cooking spray.
8. Place Cook & Crisp Basket into pot. Place the shrimp in basket and close crisping lid.
9. Select AIR CRISP, set temperature to 390°F (199°C), and set time to 10 minutes. Select START/STOP to begin.
10. After 5 minutes, open lid, then lift basket and shake the shrimp. Lower basket back into the pot and close the lid to continue cooking until the shrimp reach your desired crispiness.
11. When cooking is complete, serve the shrimp on top of the rice.

Vodka Shrimp Penne

Prep time: 5 minutes | Cook time: 11 minutes | Serves 6

2 tablespoons extra-virgin olive oil
2 tablespoons minced garlic
1 teaspoon crushed red pepper flakes
1 small red onion, diced
Kosher salt
Freshly ground black pepper
¾ cup vodka
2¾ cups vegetable stock
1 (28-ounce / 794-g) can crushed tomatoes
1 (16-ounce / 454-g) box penne pasta
1 pound (454 g) frozen shrimp, peeled and
  deveined
1 (8-ounce / 227-g) package cream cheese, cubed
4 cups shredded Mozzarella cheese

1. Select SEAR/SAUTÉ and set to MD:HI. Select START/STOP to begin. Let preheat for 5 minutes.
2. Add the olive oil, garlic, and crushed red pepper flakes. Cook until garlic is golden brown, about 1 minute. Add the onions and season with salt and pepper and cook until translucent, about 2 minutes.
3. Stir in the vodka, vegetable stock, crushed tomatoes, penne pasta, and frozen shrimp. Assemble pressure lid, making sure the pressure release valve is in the SEAL position.
4. Select PRESSURE and set temperature to HI. Set time to 6 minutes. Select START/STOP to begin.
5. When pressure cooking is complete, quick release the pressure by turning the pressure release valve to the VENT position. Carefully remove lid when unit has finished releasing pressure.
6. Stir in the cream cheese until it has melted. Layer the Mozzarella on top of the pasta. Close crisping lid.
7. Select AIR CRISP, set temperature to 400°F (204°C), and set time to 5 minutes. Select START/STOP to begin.
8. When cooking is complete, open lid and serve.

Crab and Rice Cake Casserole

Prep time: 10 minutes | Cook time: 17 minutes | Serves 8

2 tablespoons canola oil
1 large onion, chopped
2 celery stalks, chopped
1 red bell pepper, chopped
1½ cups basmati rice, rinsed
2 cups chicken stock
¼ cup mayonnaise
¼ cup Dijon mustard
3 (8-ounce / 227-g) cans lump crab meat
1 cup shredded Cheddar cheese, divided
1 (5-ounce / 142-g) sleeve butter crackers,
  crumbled

1. Select SEAR/SAUTÉ and set to HI. Select START/STOP to begin. Let preheat for 5 minutes.
2. Add the oil. Once hot, add the onion, celery, and bell pepper and stir. Cook for 5 minutes, stirring occasionally.
3. Stir in the rice and chicken stock. Assemble pressure lid, making sure the pressure release valve is in the SEAL position.
4. Select PRESSURE and set to HI. Set time to 2 minutes. Select START/STOP to begin.
5. When pressure cooking is complete, allow pressure to naturally release for 10 minutes. After 10 minutes, quick release any remaining pressure by moving the pressure release valve to the VENT position. Carefully remove lid when unit has finished releasing pressure.
6. Stir in the mayonnaise, mustard, crab, and ½ cup of Cheddar cheese. Top evenly with the crackers, then top with remaining ½ cup of cheese. Close crisping lid.
7. Select BAKE/ROAST, set temperature to 350°F (177°C), and set time to 10 minutes. Select START/STOP to begin.
8. When cooking is complete, open lid and serve immediately.

Chorizo and Shrimp Veg Potpie

Prep time: 10 minutes | Cook time: 23 minutes | Serves 6

¼ cup unsalted butter
½ large onion, diced
1 celery stalk, diced
1 carrot, peeled and diced
8 ounces (227 g) chorizo, fully cooked,
  cut into ½-inch wheels
¼ cup all-purpose flour
16 ounces (454 g) frozen tail-off shrimp,
  cleaned and deveined

¾ cup chicken stock
1 tablespoon Cajun spice mix
½ cup heavy (whipping) cream
Sea salt
Freshly ground black pepper
1 refrigerated store-bought pie crust,
  at room temperature

1. Select SEAR/SAUTÉ and set to MD:HI. Select START/STOP to begin. Let preheat for 5 minutes.
2. Add the butter. Once melted, add the onion, celery, carrot, and sausage, and cook until softened, about 3 minutes. Stir in the flour and cook 2 minutes, stirring occasionally.
3. Add the shrimp, stock, Cajun spice mix, and cream and season with salt and pepper. Stir until sauce thickens and bubbles, about 3 minutes.
4. Lay the pie crust evenly on top of the filling, folding over the edges if necessary. Make a small cut in center of pie crust so that steam can escape during baking. Close crisping lid.
5. Select BROIL and set time to 10 minutes. Select START/STOP to begin.
6. When cooking is complete, open lid and remove pot from unit. Let rest 10 to 15 minutes before serving.

Salmon, Almond, and Cranberry Rice Bowl

Prep time: 10 minutes | Cook time: 10 minutes | Serves 4

1½ cups long-grain white rice, rinsed
1½ cups water
⅓ cup dry cranberries
⅓ cup slivered almonds
Kosher salt
4 (4-ounce / 113-g) frozen salmon fillets
⅓ cup dry roasted sunflower seeds
¼ cup Dijon mustard
⅓ cup panko bread crumbs
1 tablespoon honey
1 tablespoon minced parsley

1. Place the rice, water, cranberries, and almonds in the pot. Season with salt and stir. Place Reversible Rack in pot in the higher broil position. Place a circle of aluminum foil on top of the rack, then place the salmon fillets on the foil. Assemble pressure lid, making sure the pressure release valve is in the SEAL position.
2. Select PRESSURE and set to HI. Set time to 2 minutes. Select START/STOP to begin.
3. Add the sunflower seeds, mustard, bread crumbs, honey, and parsley to a small bowl and mix well.
4. When pressure cooking is complete, allow pressure to naturally release for 10 minutes. After 10 minutes, quick release remaining pressure by moving the pressure release valve to the VENT position. Carefully remove lid when unit has finished releasing pressure.
5. Using a spoon, spread a thick, even layer of the sunflower mixture across the top of each fillet. Close crisping lid.
6. Select BROIL and set time to 8 minutes. Select START/STOP to begin. When cooking is complete, open lid and remove the rack and salmon. Use a silicone-coated spatula to fluff the rice. Serve the salmon fillets over the rice.

Bang Bang Popcorn Shrimp

Prep time: 10 minutes | Cook time: 11 minutes | Serves 4

1 cup long-grain white rice
1 cup water
16 ounces (454 g) frozen popcorn shrimp
½ cup mayonnaise
¼ cup sweet chili sauce
½ teaspoon Sriracha
2 tablespoons sliced scallions, for garnish

1. Put the rice and water in the pot and stir to combine. Assemble the Pressure Lid, making sure the pressure release valve is in the Seal position. Select Pressure and set to High. Set the time to 2 minutes, then select Start/Stop to begin.
2. When pressure cooking is complete, quick release the pressure by moving the pressure release valve to the Vent position. Carefully remove the lid when the pressure has finished releasing.
3. Place the Reversible Rack inside the pot over the rice, making sure the rack is in the higher position. Place the shrimp on the rack.
4. Close the Crisping Lid. Select Air Crisp, set the temperature to 390ºF (199ºC), and set the time to 9 minutes. Select Start/Stop to begin.
5. Meanwhile, in a medium mixing bowl, stir together the mayonnaise, sweet chili sauce, and Sriracha to create the sauce.
6. After 5 minutes of Air Crisping time, use tongs to flip the shrimp. Close the lid to resume cooking.
7. After cooking is complete, check for desired crispiness and remove the rack from the pot. Toss the shrimp in the sauce to coat evenly. Plate the rice and shrimp, garnish with the scallions, and serve.

Chapter 5: Mouthwatering Poultry Recipes

Lemon And Chicken Extravaganza

Prepping time: 5 minutes | Cooking time: 18 minutes | For 4 servings

4 bone-in, skin on chicken thighs
Salt and pepper to taste
2 tablespoons butter, divided
2 teaspoons garlic, minced
½ cup herbed chicken stock
½ cup heavy whip cream
½ a lemon, juiced

1. Season your chicken thighs generously with salt and pepper
2. Set your Foodi to sauté mode and add oil, let it heat up
3. Add thigh, Sauté both sides for 6 minutes. Remove thigh to a platter and keep it on the side
4. Add garlic, cook for 2 minutes. Whisk in chicken stock, heavy cream, lemon juice and gently stir
5. Bring the mix to a simmer and reintroduce chicken
6. Lock lid and cook for 10 minutes on HIGH pressure
7. Release pressure over 10 minutes. Serve and enjoy!

Bruschetta Chicken Meal

Prepping time: 5 minutes | Cooking time: 9 minutes | For 4 servings

2 tablespoons balsamic vinegar
1/3 cup olive oil
2 teaspoons garlic cloves, minced
1 teaspoon black pepper
½ teaspoon salt
½ cup sun-dried tomatoes, in olive oil
2 pounds chicken breasts, quartered, boneless
2 tablespoons fresh basil, chopped

1. Take a bowl and whisk in vinegar, oil, garlic, pepper, salt
2. Fold in tomatoes, basil and add breast, mix well. Transfer to fridge and let it sit for 30 minutes
3. Add everything to Ninja Foodi and lock lid, cook on High Pressure for 9 minutes
4. Quick release pressure. Serve and enjoy!

The Great Hainanese Chicken

Prepping time: 20 minutes |Cooking time: 4 hours |For 4 servings

1 ounces ginger, peeled
6 garlic cloves, crushed
6 bundles cilantro/basil leaves
1 teaspoon salt
1 tablespoon sesame oil
3 (1 and ½ pounds each) chicken
    meat, ready to cook

For Dip
2 tablespoons ginger, minced
1 teaspoon garlic, minced
1 tablespoon chicken stock
1 teaspoon sesame oil
½ teaspoon sugar
Salt to taste

1. Add chicken, garlic, ginger, leaves, and salt in your Ninja Food
2. Add enough water to fully submerge chicken, lock lid cook on SLOW COOK mode on LOW for 4 hours. Release pressure naturally
3. Take chicken out of pot and chill for 10 minutes
4. Take a bowl and add all the dipping and blend well in a food processor
5. Take chicken out of ice bath and drain, chop into serving pieces. Arrange onto a serving platter
6. Brush chicken with sesame oil. Serve with ginger dip. Enjoy!

A Genuine Hassel Back Chicken

Prepping time: 5 minutes | Cooking time: 60 minutes | For 4 servings

4 tablespoons butter
Salt and pepper to taste
2 cups fresh mozzarella cheese, thinly sliced
8 large chicken breasts
4 large Roma tomatoes, thinly sliced

1. Make few deep slits in chicken breasts, season with salt and pepper
2. Stuff mozzarella cheese slices and tomatoes in chicken slits
3. Grease Ninja Foodi pot with butter and arrange stuffed chicken breasts
4. Lock lid and BAKE/ROAST for 1 hour at 365 degrees F. Serve and enjoy!

Shredded Up Salsa Chicken

Prepping time: 5 minutes | Cooking time: 20 minutes | For 4 servings

1 pound chicken breast, skin
    and bones removed
¾ teaspoon cumin
½ teaspoon salt
Pinch of oregano
Pepper to taste
1 cup chunky salsa Keto friendly

1. Season chicken with spices and add to Ninja Foodi
2. Cover with salsa and lock lid, cook on HIGH pressure for 20 minutes
3. Quick release pressure. Add chicken to a platter and shred the chicken. Serve and enjoy!

Mexico's Favorite Chicken Soup

Prepping time: 5 minutes | Cooking time: 20 minutes | For 4 servings

2 cups chicken, shredded
4 tablespoons olive oil
½ cup cilantro, chopped
8 cups chicken broth
1/3 cup salsa
1 teaspoon onion powder
½ cup scallions, chopped
4 ounces green chilies, chopped
½ teaspoon habanero, minced
1 cup celery root, chopped
1 teaspoon cumin
1 teaspoon garlic powder
Salt and pepper to taste

1. Add all to Ninja Foodi. Stir and lock lid, cook on HIGH pressure for 10 minutes
2. Release pressure naturally over 10 minutes. Serve and enjoy!

Taiwanese Chicken Delight

Prepping time: 5 minutes | Cooking time: 10 minutes | For 4 servings

6 dried red chilis
¼ cup sesame oil
2 tablespoons ginger
¼ cup garlic, minced
¼ cup red wine vinegar
¼ cup coconut aminos
Salt as needed
1.2 teaspoon xanthan gum (for the finish)
¼ cup Thai basil, chopped

1. Set your Ninja Foodi to Saute mode and add ginger, chilis, garlic and Saute for 2 minutes
2. Add remaining . Lock lid and cook on HIGH pressure for 10 minutes
3. Quick release pressure. Serve and enjoy!

Cabbage And Chicken Meatballs

Prepping time: 10 minutes + 30 minutes | Cooking time: 4-6 minutes | For 4 servings

1 pound ground chicken
¼ cup heavy whip cream
2 teaspoons salt
½ teaspoon ground caraway seeds
1 and ½ teaspoons fresh ground black pepper, divided
1/4 teaspoon ground allspice
4-6 cups green cabbage, thickly chopped
½ cup almond milk
2 tablespoons unsalted butter

1. Transfer meat to a bowl and add cream, 1 teaspoon salt, caraway, ½ teaspoon pepper, allspice and mix it well. Let the mixture chill for 30 minutes
2. Once the mixture is ready, use your hands to scoop the mixture into meatballs
3. Add half of your balls to Ninja Foodi pot and cover with half of the cabbage
4. Add remaining balls and cover with rest of the cabbage
5. Add milk, pats of butter, season with salt and pepper
6. Lock lid and cook on HIGH pressure for 4 minutes. Quick release pressure
7. Unlock lid and serve. Enjoy!

Poached Chicken With Coconut Lime Cream Sauce

Prepping time: 5 minutes |Cooking time: 10 minutes | For 4 servings

1-ounce shallot, minced
1 ounces ginger, sliced
2 medium banana peppers,
1 cup of coconut milk
1 cup chicken stock
Juice of 1 lime, and zest
2 tablespoons fish sauce
3 pieces of 1/3 pounds each chicken breasts, meat

1. Add listed to your Ninja Foodi
2. Stir well and lock lid, cook on HIGH pressure for 10 minutes
3. Quick release pressure. Top with fresh cilantro. Serve and enjoy!

Hot And Spicy Paprika Chicken

Prepping time: 10 minutes | Cooking time: 20-25 minutes | For 4 servings

4 piece (4 ounces each) chicken
    breast, skin on
Salt and pepper to taste
½ cup sweet onion, chopped
½ cup heavy whip cream
2 teaspoons smoked paprika
½ cup sour cream
2 tablespoons fresh parsley, chopped

1. Season chicken with salt and pepper
2. Set your Foodi to Saute mode and add oil, let it heat up
3. Add chicken and sear both sides until nicely browned. Should take around 15 minutes
4. Remove chicken and transfer to a plate
5. Take a skillet and place it over medium heat, add onion and Sauté for 4 minutes
6. Stir in cream, paprika, bring the liquid to simmer. Return chicken to skillet and warm
7. Transfer the whole mixture to your Foodi and lock lid, cook on HIGH pressure for 5 minutes
8. Release pressure naturally over 10 minutes. Stir in cream, serve and enjoy!

Inspiring Turkey Cutlets

Prepping time: 10 minutes | Cooking time: 20-25 minutes | For 4 servings

1 teaspoon Greek seasoning
1 pound turkey cutlets
2 tablespoons olive oil
1 teaspoon turmeric powder
½ cup almond flour

1. Take a bowl and add Greek seasoning, turmeric powder, almond flour, and mix
2. Dredge turkey cutlets in a bowl and let them sit for 30 minutes
3. Set Ninja Foodi to Sauté mode and add oil, let it heat up. Add cutlets and Sauté for 2 minutes
4. Lock lid and cook on LOW- MEDIUM pressure for 20 minutes
5. Release pressure naturally over 10 minutes. Take it out and serve, enjoy!

Lemongrass And Tamarind Chicken

Prepping time: 10 minutes |Cooking time: 4 hours |For 4 servings

3 chicken thighs
1 ounce strips fresh turmeric
2 shallots, quartered
Handful of mustard
1 stalk lemongrass, bruised and bundled up
2 cups chicken stock
1 banana pepper
4 tablespoons olive oil
2 tablespoons tamarind paste
2 Roma tomatoes, quartered
1 radish, peeled and chopped
Fish sauce to taste
Salt and pepper to taste

1. Add listed to your Ninja Foodi
2. Stir well and lock lid, cook on HIGH pressure for 10 minutes
3. Quick release pressure. Top with fresh cilantro. Serve and enjoy!

Fluffy Whole Chicken Dish

Prepping time: 10 minutes | Cooking time: 8 hours |For 4 servings

1 cup mozzarella cheese
4 whole garlic cloves, peeled
1 whole chicken (2 pounds, cleaned and pat dried
Salt and pepper to taste
2 tablespoons fresh lemon juice

1. Stuff chicken cavity with garlic cloves and mozzarella cheese
2. Season chicken generously with salt and pepper
3. Transfer chicken to Ninja Foodi and drizzle lemon juice
4. Lock lid and set to Slow Cooker mode, let it cook on LOW for 8 hours
5. Once done, serve and enjoy!

Sensible Chettinad Chicken

Prepping time: 10 minutes | Cooking time: 15 minutes | For 4 servings

1 pound of boneless chicken
    thigh cut up into pieces
1 tablespoon of Ghee
1 bay leaf
5 curry leaves
1 inch Ginger piece
5 cloves of Garlic
¼ cup of grated coconut (fresh)
1 large onion, diced
2 medium tomatoes, diced
1 teaspoon of salt
½ a cup of water
Cilantro as needed
Whole Spices

4 pieces of Red Chili Whole Kashmiri
1 teaspoon of black peppercorns
1 teaspoon of cumin seeds
2 teaspoon of coriander seeds
5 pieces of Green coriander
1 stick of cinnamon
4 pieces of cloves
1 tablespoon of cloves
1 tablespoon of poppy seeds
1 teaspoon of fennel seeds

1. Set your Ninja Foodi to Saute mode and add whole spices and cook them until dry roasted (for about 30 seconds
2. Add garlic, ginger, grated coconut and Saute for 30 seconds more
3. Transfer the mixture to a blender and Grind until you have a paste. This is your Chettinad Spice Mix. Clean the Ninja Foodi and set your pot to Saute mode again
4. Add oil and allow it to heat it up. Add bay leaf and curry leaves, Saute for 30 seconds
5. Add diced up onions and Saute for about 30 seconds
6. Add diced up onion and Saute for 3 minutes
7. Add tomatoes, salt and ground spices and Saute for 2 minutes (including the previous blend)
8. Add chicken pieces and Saute for 3 minutes more
9. Add water and lock up the lid, cook for 5 minutes at HIGH pressure
10. Once done, do a quick release and enjoy with a garnish of cilantro. Enjoy!

Hawaiian Pinna Colada Chicken Meal

Prepping time: 10 minutes | Cooking time: 15 minutes | For 4 servings

2 pounds organic chicken thigh
1 cup fresh pineapple chunks
½ cup coconut cream
1 teaspoon cinnamon
1/8 teaspoon salt
2 tablespoons coconut aminos
½ cup green onion, chopped
Arrowroot flout

1. Add all of the to your Ninja Foodi except green onion
2. Lock up the lid and cook for 15 minutes at HIGH pressure
3. Once done, allow the pressure to release naturally. Open up the lid and stir well
4. Take a bowl and mix arrowroot flour and a tablespoon of water to make a slurry
5. Add the slurry to your pot and mix well to make a thick mixture
6. Set your pot to Saute mode and wait until the sauce is just thick enough
7. Garnish with some green onion and enjoy!

Garlic And Butter Chicken Dish

Prepping time: 10 minutes | Cooking time: 35 minutes | For 4 servings

4 pieces of chicken breasts, chopped up
¼ cup of turmeric ghee/ normal ghee
1 teaspoon of salt
10 cloves of garlic, peeled and diced up

1. Add chicken breast to the Ninja Foodi
2. Add ghee, salt, diced garlic and lock up the lid
3. Cook on HIGH pressure for 35 minutes
4. Release the pressure naturally and open the lid
5. Serve with extra ghee

Creamy Chicken Curry

Prepping time: 10 minutes | Cooking time: 10 hours |For 4 servings

10 bone-in chicken thighs, skinless
1 cup sour cream
2 tablespoons. Curry powder
1 onion, chopped
1 jar (16 ounces chunky salsa sauce

1. Add chicken thigh to your Ninja Foodi
2. Add onions, salsa, curry powder over chicken, stir and place the lid
3. Cook SLOW COOK MODE (LOW) for 10 hours. Open lid and transfer chicken to a serving platter
4. Pour sour cream into the sauce (cooking liquid) in the Ninja Foodi
5. Stir well and pour the sauce over chicken. Serve!

Lemon And Artichoke Medley

Prepping time: 10 minutes | Cooking time: 8 hours |For 6 servings

1 pound boneless and skinless chicken breast
1 pound boneless and skinless chicken thigh
14 ounces (can) artichoke hearts, packed in water and drained
1 onion, diced
2 carrots, diced
3 garlic cloves, minced
1 bay leaf
½ teaspoon pepper
3 cups turnips, peeled and cubed
6 cups chicken broth
14 cup fresh lemon juice
¼ cup parsley, chopped

1. Add the above mentioned to your Ninja Foodi except for lemon juice and parsley
2. Cook on Slow Cooker (LOW) for 8 hours. Remove the chicken and shred it up
3. Return it back to the Ninja Foodi. Season with some pepper and salt!
4. Stir in parsley and lemon juice and serve!

Awesome Sesame Ginger Chicken

Prepping time: 10 minutes | Cooking time: 10 minutes | For 4 servings

1 tablespoon rice vinegar
1 tablespoon Truvia
1 tablespoon garlic, minced
1 tablespoon fresh ginger, minced
1 tablespoon sesame oil
2 tablespoons soy sauce
1 and ½ pound boneless, skinless chicken thigh, cut into large pieces

1. Take a heatproof bowl and add soy sauce, ginger, sesame oil, garlic, Truvia and vinegar
2. Stir well to coat it. Cover bowl with foil. Add 2 cups of water to Ninja Foodie's inner pot
3. Place a trivet and place the bowl with chicken on the trivet
4. Lock lid and cook for 10 minutes on HIGH pressure. Release pressure naturally over 10 minutes
5. Remove chicken and shred it, mix it back into the bowl. Serve and enjoy!

Chicken Korma

Prepping time: 10 minutes | Cooking time: 20 minutes | For 6 servings

1 pound of chicken
For Sauce

1 ounce of cashews
1 small chopped onion
½ a cup of diced tomatoes
½ of green Serrano pepper
5 cloves of garlic
1 teaspoon of minced ginger
1 teaspoon of turmeric
1 teaspoon of Garam masala
1 teaspoon of cumin-coriander powder
½ a teaspoon of cayenne pepper
½ a cup of water

For topping

1 teaspoon of Garam masala
½ a cup of coconut milk
¼ cup of chopped cilantro

1. Add the sauce to a blender and blend them well
2. Pour the sauce to your Ninja Foodi. Place the chicken on top
3. Lock up the lid and cook on HIGH pressure for 10 minutes
4. Release the pressure naturally. Take the chicken out and cut into bite-sized portions
5. Add coconut milk, Garam masala to the pot
6. Transfer the chicken back and garnish with cilantro. Enjoy!

Turkey With Garlic Sauce

Prepping time: 10 minutes | Cooking time: 8 hours |For 6 servings

5 large onions, thinly sliced
4 garlic cloves, minced
¼ cup white wine vinegar
½ teaspoon salt
¼ teaspoon ground black pepper
¼ teaspoon cayenne pepper
4 large skinless turkey thighs

1. Gently lay the garlic and onions into the bottom of your Ninja Foodi
2. Pour in some wine with a sprinkle of salt, cayenne pepper, and black pepper.
3. Add turkey thighs and cover it up. Let it cook SLOW COOKER MODE (low) for about 8 hours.
4. Remove the turkey from the crock pot and clean up the flesh from the bones.
5. Keep the lid open and keep cooking until the liquid has completely evaporated, making sure to stir from time to time. Return the turkey to the pot.
6. Nestle the turkey into the mix. Serve hot. Enjoy!

Awesome Ligurian Chicken

Prepping time: 10 minutes | Cooking time: 15 minutes | For 4 servings

2 garlic cloves, chopped
3 sprigs fresh rosemary
2 sprigs fresh sage
½ bunch parsley
3 lemon, juiced
4 tablespoons extra virgin olive oil
1 teaspoon salt
¼ teaspoon pepper
1 and ½ cup of water
1 whole chicken, cut into parts
3 and ½ ounces black gourmet salt-cured olives
1 fresh lemon

1. Take a bowl and add chopped up garlic, parsley, sage, and rosemary
2. Pour lemon juice, olive oil to a bowl and season with salt and pepper
3. Remove the chicken skin and from the chicken pieces and carefully transfer them to a dish
4. Pour the marinade on top of the chicken pieces and allow them to chill for 2-4 hours
5. Set your Ninja Foodi to Saute mode and add olive oil, allow it to heat up
6. Add chicken and browned on all sides
7. Measure out the marinade and add to the pot (it should cover the chicken, add a bit of water if needed). Lock up the lid and cook on HIGH pressure for 10 minutes
8. Release the pressure naturally. The chicken out and transfer to a platter
9. Cover with a foil and allow them to cool. Set your pot in Saute mode and reduce the liquid to ¼
10. Add the chicken pieces again to the pot and allow them to warm
11. Sprinkle a bit of olive, lemon slices, and rosemary. Enjoy!

Creative French Chicken

Prepping time: 10 minutes | Cooking time: 15 minutes | For 4 servings

For Marinade

2 teaspoon of Herbes De Provence
2 tablespoon of olive oil
1 tablespoon of prepped Dijon mustard
1 tablespoon of cider vinegar
½ a teaspoon of salt
1 teaspoon of pepper
1 tablespoon of minced garlic
1 pound of boneless and skinless chicken thigh

For Cooking

2 tablespoon of butter
8 cloves of garlic, chopped
¼ cup of water
¼ cup of cream

1. 1. Take a bowl and add all of the marinade and whisk well
2. Add chicken thigh and the chicken to marinate for 30 minutes at room temperature
3. Set your Ninja Foodi to Saute mode and add butter, allow the butter to heat up
4. Add chopped garlic and sauté for 2-3 minutes
5. Add chicken and Saute for 3-5 minutes until slightly browned
6. Add the marinade from the chicken bowl alongside a ¼ cup of water
7. Lock up the lid and cook on HIGH pressure for 5 minutes. Release the pressure naturally over 10 minutes. Remove the chicken and transfer to a platter
8. Add ¼ cup of cream to the pot and stir. Once the sauce thickens, transfer the chicken thigh to the pot and serve!

Daring Salted Baked Chicken

Prepping time: 10 minutes | Cooking time: 30 minutes | For 6 servings

2 teaspoons ginger, minced
1 and ¼ teaspoons salt
¼ teaspoons five spice
  powder
Dash of white pepper
5-6 chicken legs

1. Season the chicken legs by placing them in a large mixing bowl
2. Pour 2 teaspoon of ginger, 1 and a ¼ teaspoon of kosher salt, ¼ teaspoon of five spice powder and mix
3. Transfer them to a parchment paper
4. Wrap up tightly and place them to a shallow dish
5. Place a steamer rack in your Ninja Foodi and add 1 cup of water
6. Place the chicken dish onto the rack
7. Lock up the lid and cook on HIGH pressure for 18-26 minutes
8. Release the pressure naturally
9. Open the lid and unwrap the paper
10. Pour the juice into a small bowl
11. Transfer the chicken on a wire rack and broil for a while
12. Serve immediately with the cooking liquid used as a dipping sauce

Worthy Ghee-Licious Chicken

Prepping time: 10 minutes | Cooking time: 8 minutes | For 6 servings

2-3 pounds boneless chicken thigh
1 tablespoon ghee
1 and a ½ large onion, chopped
3 and ½ teaspoons salt
2 teaspoons garlic powder
2 teaspoons ginger powder
2 heaping teaspoons turmeric
1 and ½ teaspoon cayenne powder
1 and ½ cup stewed tomatoes
1 cup stewed tomatoes
2 cans of coconut milk
2 heaping teaspoons Garam masala
½ cup almond, sliced
½ cup cilantro

1. Set your Ninja Foodi to Saute mode and add ghee, allow it to melt
2. Add 2 teaspoon of salt alongside onion and cook well
3. Add ginger, garlic, turmeric, paprika, cayenne pepper and mix well
4. Add your canned tomatoes alongside coconut milk and mix
5. Add chicken and give it a nice stir
6. Lock up the lid and cook on HIGH pressure for about 8 minutes
7. Once done, pour coconut cream, tomato paste, and Garam Masala
8. Garnish with some cilantro and serve with a sprinkle of sliced up almonds. Enjoy!

Hearty Duck Breast Meal

Prepping time: 120 minutes | Cooking time: 30 minutes | For 4 servings

2 duck breast halves, boneless and skin on
1 teaspoon salt
2 teaspoons fresh garlic, minced
½ teaspoon black pepper
1/3 teaspoon thyme
1/3 teaspoon peppercorn
1 tablespoon olive oil
1 tablespoon apricot, peeled and cored
2 teaspoons date paste

1. Clean the duck breast and rub the spices all over. Cover and allow it to chill for 2 hours
2. Rinse the spices off and place the breast in a zip bag, seal it up making sure to remove as much air as possible. (look on the internet for immersion sealing method for best results
3. Add 5 cups of water to your Ninja Foodi
4. Set your Ninja Foodi to Saute mode and allow the water to heat up for about 20 minutes
5. Place the bag in the water bath and keep it for 35-40 minutes
6. Remove the bag from water and pat the breasts dry
7. Sear the skin side of the duck breast in a nonstick frying pan with about 1 tablespoon of oil over medium-high heat. Turn the breast over and cook for 20 seconds more
8. Prepare the apricot sauce by mixing apricot and date paste in a small pot and bringing the mix to a boil, followed by a simmer for 5 minutes at low heat
9. Slice the duck breast and serve with apricot sauce. Serve the duck breast with the sauce. Enjoy!

Fancy Chicken Chile Verde

Prepping time: 120 minutes | Cooking time: 25 minutes | For 4 servings

1/3 cup water
3 pounds chicken breasts, skinless
¾ pound quartered tomatillos
¾ pound poblano peppers, seeds and stems discarded
½ pound Anaheim pepper, seeds and stems discarded
4-5 jalapeno pepper stems removed and halved
1 white onion, quartered
4-6 medium garlic clove, peeled
1 tablespoon ground cumin
½ tablespoon paprika
1 tablespoon salt
1 tablespoon pepper
1 tablespoon ground cinnamon
1 tablespoon red boat fish sauce

1. Add Anaheim, tomatillos, pepper, poblano pepper, jalapeno pepper, onion, cumin, garlic, paprika, salt and chicken to your Ninja Foodi. Add water to cover them
2. Lock up the lid and cook on HIGH pressure for 25 minutes
3. Release the pressure naturally over 10 minutes
4. Add the red boat fish sauce to a blender and puree the sauce
5. Take the chicken out from your Instant Pot and shred it using a fork, return it back to the pot
6. Add puree and stir. Serve over lettuce wraps and enjoy!

Roasted Whole Chicken

Prep time: 10 minutes | Cook time: 40 minutes | Serves 4

1 (4½- to 5-pound / 2.0- to 2.3-kg) whole chicken
1 head garlic
2 fresh whole sprigs rosemary
2 fresh whole sprigs parsley
1 lemon, halved
¼ cup hot water
¼ cup white wine
Juice of 2 lemons

¼ cup unsalted butter, melted
3 tablespoons extra-virgin olive oil
5 garlic cloves, minced
2 teaspoons minced fresh parsley
2 teaspoons minced fresh rosemary
½ teaspoon sea salt
¼ teaspoon freshly ground black pepper

1. Discard the neck from inside the chicken cavity and remove any excess fat and leftover feathers. Rinse the chicken inside and out under running cold water. Stuff the garlic head into the chicken cavity along with the rosemary and parsley sprigs and lemon halves. Tie the legs together with cooking twine.
2. Add the water, wine, and lemon juice. Place the chicken into the Cook & Crisp Basket and insert the basket in the pot. Assemble pressure lid, making sure the pressure release valve is in the SEAL position.
3. Select PRESSURE and set to HI. Set time to 15 minutes. Select START/STOP to begin.
4. When pressure cooking is complete, quick release the pressure by moving the pressure release valve to the VENT position. Carefully remove lid when the unit has finished releasing pressure.
5. In a small bowl, combine the butter, olive oil, minced garlic, minced parsley, minced rosemary, salt, and pepper. Brush the mixture over the chicken. Close crisping lid.
6. Select AIR CRISP, set temperature to 400°F (204°C), and set time to 20 minutes. Select START/STOP to begin.
7. Cooking is complete when the internal temperature of the chicken reaches 165°F (74°C) on a meat thermometer inserted into the thickest part of the meat (it should not touch the bone). Carefully remove the chicken from the basket using 2 large serving forks.
8. Let the chicken rest for 10 minutes before carving and serving.

Chinese Flavor Spicy Chicken with Cashew

Prep time:10 minutes | Cook time: 13 minutes | Serves 4

1 pound (454 g) chicken breast, cut into
    ½-inch pieces
4 tablespoons stir-fry sauce, divided
3 tablespoons canola oil
12 arbol chiles
1 teaspoon Sichuan peppercorns
2 teaspoons grated fresh ginger
2 garlic cloves, minced
¾ cup cashews
6 scallions, cut into 1-inch pieces
2 teaspoons dark soy sauce
½ teaspoon sesame oil

1. Place the chicken in a zip-top bag and add 2 tablespoons of stir-fry sauce. Let marinate for 4 hours, or overnight.
2. Select SEAR/SAUTÉ and set to HI. Select START/STOP to begin. Let preheat for 5 minutes.
3. Add the oil, chiles, peppercorns, ginger, and garlic and cook for 1 minute.
4. Add half the chicken and cook for 2 minutes, stirring occasionally. Transfer the chicken to a plate and set aside. Add the remaining chicken and cook for 2 minutes, stirring occasionally. Return the first batch of chicken to the pot and add the cashews. Cook for 2 minutes, stirring occasionally.
5. Add the scallions, soy sauce, sesame oil, and remaining 2 tablespoons of stir-fry sauce to pot and cook for 1 minute, stirring frequently.
6. When cooking is complete, serve immediately over steamed rice, if desired.

Stir-Fried Chicken and Broccoli Rice Bowl

Prep time: 5 minutes | Cook time: 20 minutes | Serves 4

1 cup long-grain white rice
1 cup chicken stock
2 tablespoons canola oil
3 boneless, skinless chicken breasts, cut
    into 1-inch cubes
1 medium head broccoli, cut into 1-inch
    florets
2 teaspoons kosher salt
½ teaspoon freshly ground black pepper
1 tablespoon ground ginger
¼ cup teriyaki sauce
Sesame seeds, for garnish

1. Place the rice and chicken stock into the pot. Assemble pressure lid, making sure the pressure release valve is in the SEAL position.
2. Select PRESSURE and set to HI. Set time to 2 minutes. Select START/STOP to begin.
3. When pressure cooking is complete, allow pressure to naturally release for 10 minutes. After 10 minutes, quick release remaining pressure by turning the pressure release valve to the VENT position. Carefully remove lid when unit has finished releasing pressure.
4. Transfer the rice to a bowl and cover to keep warm. Clean the cooking pot and return to unit.
5. Select SEAR/SAUTÉ and set to HI. Select START/STOP to begin. Let preheat for 5 minutes.
6. Add the oil and heat for 1 minute. Add the chicken and cook, stirring frequently, for about 6 minutes.
7. Stir in the broccoli, salt, pepper, and ginger. Cook for 5 minutes, stirring frequently. Stir in the teriyaki sauce and cook, stirring frequently, until the chicken has reached internal temperature of 165°F (74°C) on a food thermometer.
8. Serve the chicken and broccoli mixture over the rice. Garnish with sesame seeds if desired.

Chicken and Bean Burrito Rice Bowl

Prep time: 5 minutes | Cook time: 10 minutes | Serves 4

1 pound (454 g) boneless, skinless chicken breasts, cut into
    1-inch chunks
1 tablespoon chili powder
1½ teaspoons cumin
1 teaspoon sea salt
1 teaspoon freshly ground black pepper
½ teaspoon paprika
¼ teaspoon garlic powder
¼ teaspoon onion powder
¼ teaspoon cayenne pepper
¼ teaspoon dried oregano
1 cup chicken stock
¼ cup water
1¼ cups of your favorite salsa
1 (15-ounce / 425-g) can corn kernels, drained
1 (15-ounce / 425-g) can black beans, rinsed and drained
1 cup rice
¾ cup shredded Cheddar cheese

1. Add the chicken, chili powder, cumin, salt, black pepper, paprika, garlic powder, onion powder, cayenne pepper, oregano, chicken stock, water, salsa, corn, and beans and stir well.
2. Add the rice to the top of the ingredients in the pot. Assemble pressure lid, making sure the pressure release valve is in the SEAL position.
3. Select PRESSURE and set to HI. Set time to 10 minutes. Select START/STOP to begin.
4. When pressure cooking is complete, quick release the pressure by moving the pressure release valve to the VENT position. Carefully remove lid when the unit has finished releasing pressure.
5. Add the cheese and stir. Serve immediately.

Chicken Rice Pilaf

Prep time: 5 minutes | Cook time: 14 minutes | Serves 4

1 (6-ounce / 170-g) box rice pilaf
1¾ cups water
1 tablespoon unsalted butter
4 boneless, skin-on chicken thighs
1 tablespoon extra-virgin olive oil
1 teaspoon kosher salt
1 teaspoon garlic powder

1. Place the rice pilaf, water, and butter in the pot and stir.
2. Place Reversible Rack in pot, making sure it is in the higher position. Place the chicken thighs on the rack. Assemble pressure lid, making sure the pressure release valve is in the SEAL position.
3. Select PRESSURE and set to HI. Set time to 4 minutes. Select START/STOP to begin.
4. Stir together the olive oil, salt, and garlic powder in a small bowl.
5. When pressure cooking is complete, quick release the pressure by moving the pressure release valve to the VENT position. Carefully remove lid when unit has finished releasing pressure.
6. Brush the chicken with the olive oil mixture. Close crisping lid.
7. Select BROIL and set time to 10 minutes. Select START/STOP to begin.
8. When cooking is complete, serve the chicken with the rice.

Jerk Chicken with Sweet Mash

Prep time: 10 minutes | Cook time: 20 minutes | Serves 6

4 boneless, skin-on chicken thighs
½ cup spicy jerk marinade
3 large sweet potatoes, peeled and cut into 1-inch cubes
½ cup unsweetened full-fat coconut milk

Kosher salt
Freshly ground black pepper
2 bananas, peeled and quartered
2 tablespoons agave nectar

1. Place the chicken thighs and jerk marinade in a container, rubbing the marinade all over the chicken. Cover the container with plastic wrap and marinate 15 minutes.
2. Place the sweet potatoes, coconut milk, salt, and pepper in the pot. Place Reversible Rack in pot, making sure it is in the higher position. Place the chicken skin-side up on the rack, leaving space between the pieces. Assemble pressure lid, making sure the pressure release valve is in the SEAL position.
3. Select PRESSURE and set to HI. Set time to 4 minutes. Select START/STOP to begin.
4. When pressure cooking is complete, quick release the pressure by turning the pressure release valve to the VENT position. Carefully remove lid when unit has finished releasing pressure.
5. Place the bananas in the spaces between chicken thighs. Close crisping lid.
6. Select BROIL and set time to 15 minutes. Select START/STOP to begin.
7. After 10 minutes, remove the bananas and set aside. Turn over the chicken thighs. Close lid and continue cooking.
8. When cooking is complete, remove rack and chicken and let rest 5 to 10 minutes. Add the roasted bananas and agave nectar and mash them along with the sweet potatoes. Once rested, serve the chicken and sweet potato and banana mash.

Parmesan and Mozzarella Chicken Cutlets

Prep time: 5 minutes | Cook time: 20 minutes | Serves 4

1 cup all-purpose flour
1 teaspoon sea salt
2 eggs, beaten
2 tablespoons water
1 cup seasoned bread crumbs
½ cup grated Parmesan cheese
4 (6-ounce / 170-g) chicken cutlets
2 tablespoons extra-virgin olive oil
¼ cup marinara sauce
1 cup shredded Mozzarella cheese

1. Place the flour and salt in a shallow bowl and stir. In another shallow bowl, add the eggs and water, whisking to combine. Place the bread crumbs and Parmesan cheese in a third shallow bowl.
2. Dredge each piece of chicken in the flour. Tap off any excess, then coat the chicken in the egg wash. Transfer the chicken to the breadcrumb mixture and evenly coat. Repeat until all the chicken is coated.
3. Place Reversible Rack in pot, making sure it is in the higher position. Place the chicken on the rack and brush lightly with the oil. Close crisping lid.
4. Select AIR CRISP, set temperature to 325ºF (163ºC), and set time to 15 minutes. Select START/STOP to begin.
5. After 15 minutes, open lid and spread the marinara sauce on top of the chicken. Top with the Mozzarella. Close crisping lid.
6. Select BROIL and set time to 5 minutes. Select START/STOP to begin.
7. When the cheese is fully melted, cooking is complete. Serve.

Bacon and Chicken Penne

Prep time: 5 minutes | Cook time: 10 minutes | Serves 4

3 strips bacon, chopped
½ pound (227 g) boneless, skinless chicken breast, cut into ½-pieces
1 teaspoon dried basil
1 teaspoon dried oregano
¼ teaspoon sea salt
1 tablespoon unsalted butter
3 garlic cloves, minced
1 cup chicken stock
1½ cups water
8 ounces (227 g) dry penne pasta
½ cup half-and-half
½ cup grated Parmesan cheese, plus more for serving

1. Select SEAR/SAUTÉ and set to HI. Select START/STOP to begin. Let preheat for 5 minutes.
2. Add the bacon and cook, stirring frequently, for about 5 minutes or until crispy. Using a slotted spoon, transfer the bacon to a paper towel-lined plate to drain.
3. Season the chicken with the basil, oregano, and salt, coating all the pieces.
4. Add the butter, chicken, and garlic and sauté for 2 minutes, until the chicken begins to brown and the garlic is fragrant.
5. Add the chicken stock, water, and penne pasta. Assemble pressure lid, making sure the pressure release valve is in the SEAL position.
6. Select PRESSURE and set to HI. Set time to 3 minutes. Select START/STOP to begin.
7. When pressure cooking is complete, allow pressure to naturally release for 2 minutes. After 2 minutes, quick release remaining pressure by moving the pressure release valve to the VENT position. Carefully remove lid when unit has finished releasing pressure.
8. Add the half-and-half, cheese, and bacon, and stir constantly to thicken the sauce and melt the cheese. Serve immediately, with additional Parmesan cheese to garnish.

Chicken Spaghetti Carbonara

Prep time: 5 minutes | Cook time: 15 minutes | Serves 4

4 strips bacon, chopped

1 medium onion, diced

1½ pounds (680 g) chicken breast, cut into ¾ inch-cubes

6 garlic cloves, minced

2 cups chicken stock

8 ounces (227 g) dry spaghetti, with noodles broken in half

2 cups freshly grated Parmesan cheese, plus more for serving

2 eggs

Sea salt

Freshly ground black pepper

1. Select SEAR/SAUTÉ and set to HI. Select START/STOP to begin. Let preheat for 5 minutes.
2. Add the bacon and cook, stirring frequently, for about 6 minutes, or until crispy. Using a slotted spoon, transfer the bacon to a paper towel-lined plate to drain. Leave any bacon fat in the pot.
3. Add the onion, chicken, and garlic and sauté for 2 minutes, until the onions start to become translucent and the garlic is fragrant.
4. Add the chicken stock and spaghetti noodles. Assemble pressure lid, making sure the pressure release valve is in the SEAL position.
5. Select PRESSURE and set to HI. Set time to 6 minutes. Select START/STOP to begin.
6. When pressure cooking is complete, allow pressure to naturally release for 5 minutes. After 5 minutes, quick release remaining pressure by moving the pressure release valve to the VENT position. Carefully remove lid when unit has finished releasing pressure.
7. Add the cheese and stir to fully combine. Close the crisping lid, leaving the unit off, to keep the heat inside and allow the cheese to melt.
8. Whisk the eggs until full beaten.
9. Open lid, select SEAR/SAUTÉ, and set to LO. Select START/STOP to begin. Add the eggs and stir gently to incorporate, taking care to ensure the eggs are not scrambling while you work toward your desired sauce consistency. If your pot gets too warm, turn unit off.
10. Add the bacon back to the pot and season with salt and pepper. Stir to combine. Serve, adding more cheese as desired.

Baked Ranch Chicken and Bacon

Prep time: 10 minutes | Cook time: 30 minutes | Serves 6

1 pound (454 g) chicken breast, cut in 1-inch cubes

2 tablespoons extra-virgin olive oil

3 tablespoons ranch seasoning mix, divided

4 strips bacon, chopped

1 small onion, chopped

2 garlic cloves, minced

1 cup long-grain white rice

2 cups chicken broth

½ cup half-and-half

2 cups shredded Cheddar cheese, divided

2 tablespoons chopped fresh parsley

1. Select SEAR/SAUTÉ and set to HI. Select START/STOP to begin. Let preheat for 5 minutes.
2. In a large bowl, toss the chicken with the olive oil and 2 tablespoons of ranch seasoning mix.
3. Add the bacon to the pot and cook, stirring frequently, for about 6 minutes, or until crispy. Using a slotted spoon, transfer the bacon to a paper towel-lined plate to drain.
4. Add the onion and cook for about 5 minutes. Add the garlic and cook for 1 minute more. Add the chicken and stir, cooking until chicken is cooked through, about 3 minutes.
5. Add the rice, chicken broth, and remaining ranch mix. Assemble pressure lid, making sure the pressure release valve is in the SEAL position.
6. Select PRESSURE and set to HI. Set time to 7 minutes. Select START/STOP to begin.
7. When complete, quick release the pressure by turning the valve to the VENT position. Carefully remove lid when unit has finished releasing pressure.
8. Stir in half-and-half and 1 cup of Cheddar cheese. Top with the remaining 1 cup of cheese. Close crisping lid.
9. Select BROIL and set time to 8 minutes. Select START/STOP to begin. When cooking is complete, serve garnished with fresh parsley.

Tuscan Chicken and Spinach Penne

Prep time: 10 minutes | Cook time: 6 minutes | Serves 8

2 pounds (907 g) chicken stock
1 (7-ounce / 198-g) jar oil-packed sun-dried tomatoes, drained
2 teaspoons Italian seasoning
3 garlic cloves, minced
1 pound (454 g) chicken breast, cubed
1 (16-ounce / 454-g) box penne pasta
4 cups spinach
1 (8-ounce / 227-g) package cream cheese, cubed
1 cup shredded Parmesan cheese
Kosher salt
Freshly ground black pepper

1. Place the chicken stock, sun-dried tomatoes, Italian seasoning, garlic, chicken breast, and pasta and stir. Assemble pressure lid, making sure the pressure release valve is in the SEAL position.
2. Select PRESSURE and set to HI. Set time to 6 minutes. Select START/STOP to begin.
3. When pressure cooking is complete, quick release the pressure by turning the pressure release valve to the VENT position. Carefully remove lid when unit has finished releasing pressure.
4. Add the spinach and stir, allowing it to wilt with the residual heat. Add the cream cheese, Parmesan cheese, salt and pepper and stir until melted. Serve.

Slow Cooked Garlic Chicken Thighs

Prep time: 5 minutes | Cook time: 4 hours | Serves 6

6 (4- to 6-ounce / 113- to 170-g) bone-in, skin-on, chicken thighs
10 garlic cloves, peeled
6 cups chicken broth
1 cup dry white wine
2 teaspoons dried oregano
2 teaspoons kosher salt
1 teaspoon freshly ground black pepper
¼ cup capers, drained
1 tablespoon chopped fresh parsley

1. Place the chicken, garlic cloves, chicken broth, wine, oregano, salt, and pepper in the cooking pot.
2. Assemble pressure lid, making sure the pressure release valve is in the VENT position. Select SLOW COOK and set to HI. Set time to 4 hours. Select START/STOP to begin.
3. When cooking is complete, carefully remove the lid. Stir in the capers.
4. Serve garnished with fresh parsley.

Buttermilk-Breaded Crispy Chicken

Prep time: 15 minutes | Cook time: 30 minutes | Serves 4

1½ pounds (680 g) boneless, skinless chicken breasts
1 to 2 cups buttermilk
2 large eggs
¾ cup all-purpose flour
¾ cup potato starch
½ teaspoon granulated garlic, divided
1 teaspoon salt, divided
2 teaspoons freshly ground black pepper, divided
1 cup bread crumbs
½ cup panko bread crumbs
Olive oil or cooking spray

1. In a large bowl, combine the chicken breasts and buttermilk, turning the chicken to coat. Cover the bowl with plastic wrap and refrigerate the chicken to soak at least 4 hours or overnight.
2. In a medium shallow bowl, whisk the eggs. In a second shallow bowl, stir together the flour, potato starch, ¼ teaspoon of granulated garlic, ½ teaspoon of salt, and 1 teaspoon of pepper. In a third shallow bowl, stir together the bread crumbs, panko, remaining ¼ teaspoon of granulated garlic, remaining ½ teaspoon of salt, and remaining 1 teaspoon of pepper.
3. Working one piece at a time, remove the chicken from the buttermilk, letting the excess drip into the bowl. Dredge the chicken in the flour mixture, coating well on both sides. Then dip the chicken in the eggs, coating both sides. Finally, dip the chicken in the bread crumb mixture, coating both sides and pressing the crumbs onto the chicken. Spritz both sides of the coated chicken pieces with olive oil.
4. Place the Cook & Crisp Basket into the unit.
5. Select AIR CRISP, set the temperature to 400°F (204°C), and set the time to 30 minutes. Select START/STOP to begin and allow to preheat for 5 minutes.
6. Spritz both sides of the coated chicken pieces with olive oil. Working in batches as needed, place the chicken breasts in the Cook & Crisp Basket, ensuring the chicken pieces do not touch each other.
7. After 12 minutes, turn the chicken with a spatula so you don't tear the breading. Close the crisping lid and continue to cook, checking the chicken for an internal temperature of 165°F (74°C).
8. When cooking is complete, transfer the chicken to a wire rack to cool.

Broccoli and Chicken Casserole

Prep time: 10 minutes | Cook time: 30 minutes | Serves 6

4 (8-ounce / 227-g) boneless, skinless chicken breasts
2 cups chicken stock
1 cup whole milk
1 (10½-ounce / 298-g) cans condensed Cheddar cheese soup
1 teaspoon paprika
2 cups shredded Cheddar cheese
Kosher salt
Freshly ground black pepper
2 cups crushed buttered crackers

1. Place the chicken and stock in the pot. Assemble pressure lid, making sure the pressure release valve is in the SEAL position.
2. Select PRESSURE and set to HI. Set timer to 20 minutes. Select START/STOP to begin.
3. When pressure cooking is complete, quick release the pressure by turning the pressure release valve to the VENT position. Carefully remove lid when unit has finished releasing pressure.
4. Using silicone-tipped utensils, shred the chicken inside the pot.
5. Add the milk, condensed soup, paprika, and cheese. Stir to combine with the chicken. Season with salt and pepper. Top with the crushed crackers. Close crisping lid.
6. Select AIR CRISP, set temperature to 360ºF (182ºC), and set time to 10 minutes. Select START/STOP to begin.
7. When cooking is complete, open lid and let cool before serving.

Marinara Chicken and Mozzarella Stick Casserole

Prep time: 5 minutes | Cook time: 35 minutes | Serves 6

2 (11-ounce / 312-g) boxes frozen breaded Mozzarella sticks
4 (6-ounce / 170-g) frozen boneless, skinless chicken breasts
½ cup water
1 (23-ounce / 652-g) jar marinara sauce

1. Remove the Mozzarella sticks from freezer and let sit at room temperature for 15 to 20 minutes to assure easy chopping.
2. Place the chicken and water in the pot. Assemble pressure lid, making sure the pressure release valve is in the SEAL position.
3. Select PRESSURE and set to HI. Set time to 20 minutes. Select START/STOP to begin.
4. Chop up the Mozzarella sticks.
5. When pressure cooking is complete, quick release the pressure by moving the pressure release valve to the VENT position. Carefully remove lid when unit has finished releasing pressure.
6. Using a silicone-tipped utensil, shred the chicken inside the pot. Stir in the marinara sauce. Evenly sprinkle the top of chicken with the pieces of Mozzarella sticks. Close crisping lid.
7. Select BAKE/ROAST, set temperature to 390ºF (199ºC), and set time to 15 minutes. Select START/STOP to begin.
8. After 10 minutes, open lid and check the Mozzarella sticks for desired crispiness and doneness. If necessary, cook for up to 5 minutes more.
9. When cooking is complete, open lid and serve.

Chapter 6: Healthy Vegan/Vegetarian Ninja Foodi Recipes

Comfortable Mushroom Soup

Prepping time: 10 minutes | Cooking time: 10 minutes | For 6 servings

1 small onion, diced
8 ounces white button
   mushrooms, chopped
8 ounces portabella mushrooms
2 garlic cloves, minced
¼ cup dry white wine vinegar
2 and ½ cup mushroom stock
2 teaspoons salt
1 teaspoon fresh thyme
¼ teaspoon black pepper

Cashew Cream

1/3 cup of raw cashew
½ a cup of mushroom stock

1. Add onion, mushroom to the pot and set your Ninja Foodi to Saute mode
2. Cook for 8 minutes and stir from time to time
3. Add garlic and Saute for 2 minutes more. Add wine and Saute until evaporated
4. Add thyme, pepper, salt, Mushroom stock, and stir
5. Lock up the lid and cook on HIGH pressure for 5 minutes
6. Perform quick release. Transfer cashew and water to the blender and blend well
7. Remove lid and transfer mix to the blender. Blend until smooth. Server and enjoy!

Chives And Radishes Platter

Prepping time: 10 minutes | Cooking time: 7 minutes | For 4 servings

2 cups radishes, quartered
½ cup chicken stock
Salt and pepper to taste
2 tablespoons melted ghee
1 tablespoon chives, chopped
1 tablespoon lemon zest, grated

1. Add radishes, stock, salt, pepper, zest to your Ninja Foodi and stir
2. Lock lid and cook on HIGH pressure for 7 minutes
3. Quick release pressure. Add melted ghee, toss well. Sprinkle chives and enjoy!

Garlic And Swiss Chard Garlic

Prepping time: 10 minutes |Cooking time: 4 minutes | For 4 servings

2 tablespoons ghee
3 tablespoons lemon juice
½ cup chicken stock
4 bacon slices, chopped
1 bunch Swiss chard, chopped
½ teaspoon garlic paste
Salt and pepper to taste

1. Set your Ninja Foodi to Saute mode and add bacon, stir well and cook for a few minutes
2. Add ghee, lemon juice, garlic paste, and stir. Add Swiss chard, salt, pepper, and stock
3. Lock lid and cook on HIGH pressure for 3 minutes. Quick release pressure and serve. Enjoy!

Healthy Rosemary And Celery Dish

Prepping time: 10 minutes | Cooking time: 5 minutes | For 4 servings

1 pound celery, cubed
1 cup of water
2 garlic cloves, minced
Salt and pepper
¼ teaspoon dry rosemary
1 tablespoon olive oil

1. Add water to your Ninja Foodi and place steamer basket
2. Add celery cubs to basket and lock lid, cook on HIGH pressure for 4 minutes
3. Quick release pressure. Take a bowl and add mix in oil, garlic, and rosemary. Whisk well
4. Add steamed celery to the bowl and toss well, spread on a lined baking sheet
5. Broil for 3 minutes using the Air Crisping lid at 250 degrees F. Serve and enjoy!

Awesome Veggie Hash

Prepping time: 10 minutes | Cooking time: 15 minutes | For 4 servings

1 cups cauliflower, chopped
1 teaspoon mustard
½ cup dark leaf kale, chopped
1 tablespoon lemon juice
½ cup spinach, chopped
½ teaspoon salt
2 garlic cloves
½ teaspoon pepper
6 whole eggs
3 teaspoons coconut oil

1. Set your Ninja Foodi to Saute mode and add coconut oil, add garlic, cook until fragrant
2. Add chopped cauliflower and cook for 5 minutes
3. Stir in all except eggs, cook for 2 minutes
4. Stir in eggs, lock lid and cook for 2 minutes on HIGH pressure. Quick release pressure.Enjoy!

Thyme And Carrot Dish With Dill

Prepping time: 5 minutes | Cooking time: 5 minutes | For 4 servings

½ cup of water
1 pound baby carrots
3 tablespoons stevia
1 tablespoon thyme, chopped
1 tablespoon dill, chopped
Salt and pepper to taste
2 tablespoons ghee

1. Add trivet to your Ninja Foodi, add carrots and add water
2. Lock lid and cook on HIGH pressure for 3 minutes. Quick release pressure
3. Drain and transfer to a bowl. Set your Ninja Foodi to Saute mode and add ghee, let it melt
4. Add stevia, thyme dill, and carrots. Stir well for a few minutes. Serve and enjoy!

Creative Coconut Cabbage

Prepping time: 10 minutes | Cooking time: 7 minutes | For 4 servings

2 tablespoons lemon juice
1/3 medium carrot, sliced
½ ounces, yellow onion, sliced
1/2 cup cabbage, shredded
1 teaspoon turmeric powder
1 ounce dry coconut
½ tablespoon mustard powder
½ teaspoon mild curry powder
1 large garlic cloves, diced
1 and ½ teaspoons salt
1/3 cup water
3 tablespoons olive oil
3 large whole eggs
3 large egg yolks

1. Set your Ninja Foodi to Saute mode and add oil, stir in onions, salt and cook for 4 minutes
2. Stir in spices, garlic and Saute for 30 seconds
3. Stir in rest of the , lock lid and cook on HIGH pressure for 3 minutes
4. Naturally, release pressure over 10 minutes. Serve and enjoy!

Complete Cauliflower Zoodles

Prepping time: 10 minutes | Cooking time: 8 minutes | For 6 servings

2 tablespoons butter
2 cloves garlic
7-8 cauliflower florets
1 cup vegetable broth
2 teaspoons salt
2 cups spinach, coarsely chopped
2 green onions, chopped
1 pound of zoodles (Spiralized Zucchini)

Garnish

Chopped sun-dried tomatoes
Balsamic vinegar
Gorgonzola cheese

1. Set your Ninja Foodi to Saute mode and add butter, allow the butter to melt
2. Add garlic cloves and Saute for 2 minutes
3. Add cauliflower, broth, salt and lock up the lid and cook on HIGH pressure for 6 minutes
4. Prepare the zoodles. Perform a naturally release over 10 minutes
5. Use an immersion blender to blend the mixture in the pot to a puree
6. Pour the sauce over the zoodles
7. Serve with a garnish of cheese, sun-dried tomatoes and a drizzle of balsamic vinegar. Enjoy!

Simple Mushroom Hats And Eggs

Prepping time: 10 minutes | Cooking time: 9 minutes | For 1 serving)

4 ounces mushroom hats
1 teaspoon butter, melted
4 quail eggs
½ teaspoon ground black pepper
¼ teaspoon salt

1. Spread the mushroom hats with the butter inside. Then beat the eggs into mushroom hats
2. Sprinkle with salt and ground black pepper. Transfer the mushroom hats on the rack
3. Lower the air fryer lid. Cook the meat for 7 minutes at 365 F
4. Check the mushroom, if it is not cooked fully then cook them for 2 minutes more
5. Serve and enjoy!

Ginger And Butternut Bisque Yum

Prepping time: 10 minutes | Cooking time: 8 minutes | For 6 servings

1 cup of diced yellow onion
4 minced cloves of garlic
2 teaspoon of peeled and chopped ginger
1 cup of chopped carrot
1 green apple chopped
1 peeled and chopped butternut squash
1 teaspoon salt
2 cups of water
¼ cup of finely chopped parsley
Black pepper

1. Prepare the accordingly and keep them on the side
2. Set your Ninja Foodie to Saute mode and add onions, cook for minutes
3. Add just a splash of water . Add garlic, carrot, ginger, apple, squash, and salt
4. Give it a nice stir. Add water and lock up the lid
5. Cook on HIGH pressure for 5 minutes. Naturally, release the pressure
6. Allow it to cool for 15 minutes
7. Blend the soup in batches, or you may use an immersion blender as well to blend in the pot until it is creamy. Add parsley and season with some black pepper. Serve and enjoy!

Hearty Cheesy Cauliflower

Prepping time: 10 minutes | Cooking time: 35 minutes | For 6 servings

1 tablespoon Keto-Friendly mustard
1 head cauliflower
1 teaspoon avocado mayonnaise
½ cup parmesan cheese, grated
¼ cup butter, cut into small pieces

1. Set your Ninja Foodi to Saute mode and add butter, let it melt
2. Add cauliflower and Saute for 3 minutes
3. Add rest of the and lock lid, cook on HIGH pressure for 30 minutes
4. Release pressure naturally over 10 minutes. Serve and enjoy!

Mesmerizing Spinach Quiche

Prepping time: 10 minutes | Cooking time: 33 minutes | For 4 servings_

1 tablespoon butter, melted
1 pack (10 ounces frozen spinach, thawed
5 organic eggs, beaten
Salt and pepper to taste
3 cups Monterey Jack Cheese, shredded

1. Set your Ninja Foodi to Saute mode and let it heat up, add butter and let the butter melt
2. Add spinach and Saute for 3 minutes, transfer the Sautéed spinach to a bowl
3. Add eggs, cheese, salt, and pepper to a bowl and mix it well
4. Transfer the mixture to greased quiche molds and transfer the mold to your Foodi
5. Close the lid and choose the "Bake/Roast" mode and let it cook for 30 minutes at 360 degrees F. Once done, open lid and transfer the dish out
6. Cut into wedges and serve. Enjoy!

Running Away Broccoli Casserole

Prepping time: 10 minutes | Cooking time: 7 minutes | For 4 servings

1 tablespoon extra-virgin olive oil
1 pound broccoli, cut into florets
1 pound cauliflower, cut into florets
¼ cup almond flour
2 cups of coconut milk
½ teaspoon ground nutmeg
Pinch of pepper
1 and ½ cup shredded Gouda cheese, divided

1. Pre-heat your Ninja Foodi by setting it to Saute mode
2. Add olive oil and let it heat up, add broccoli and cauliflower
3. Take a medium bowl stir in almond flour, coconut milk, nutmeg, pepper, 1 cup cheese and add the mixture to your Ninja Foodi. Top with ½ cup cheese and lock lid, cook on HIGH pressure for 5 minutes. Release pressure naturally over 10 minutes . Serve and enjoy!

Spaghetti Squash Fancy Noodles

Prepping time: 10 minutes | Cooking time: 7 minutes | For 6 servings

2 pound of spaghetti squash
1 cup of water

1. Take a paring knife and cut the spaghetti squash in half
2. Take a largely sized spoon and scoop out the center seeds and discard the gunk
3. Place the Ninja Foodi steamer insert inside the inner pot of your Ninja Foodi. Add 1 cup of water
4. Add the half-cut squashes to the steamer insert, making sure that the cut part if facing up
5. Lock up the lid and cook on HIGH pressure for 7 minutes
6. Once done, perform a quick release. Take the squash out and fork out the strings
7. Serve with sauce or your favorite topping!

Dill And Garlic Fiesta Platter

Prepping time: 10 minutes | Cooking time: 10-15 minutes | For 6 servings

3 cups carrots, chopped
1 tablespoon melted butter
½ teaspoon garlic salt
1 tablespoon fresh dill, minced
1 cup of water

1. Add listed to Ninja Foodi. Stir and lock lid, cook on HIGH pressure for 10 minutes
2. Release pressure naturally over 10 minutes. Quick release pressure
3. Serve with topping of dill, enjoy

Quick Red Cabbage

Prepping time: 10 minutes | Cooking time: 10 minutes | For 6 servings

6 cups red cabbage, chopped
1 tablespoon apple cider vinegar
½ cup Keto-Friendly applesauce
1 cup of water
3 garlic cloves, minced
1 small onion, chopped
1 tablespoon olive oil
Salt and pepper to taste

1. Add olive oil to Ninja Foodi
2. Set it to Saute mode and let it heat up, add onion and garlic and Saute for 2 minutes
3. Add remaining and stir. Lock lid and cook on HIGH pressure for 10 minutes
4. Quick release pressure. Stir well and serve. Enjoy!

Simple Rice Cauliflower

Prepping time: 10 minutes | Cooking time: 15 minutes | For 4 servings

1 large cauliflower head
2 tablespoons olive oil
¼ teaspoon salt
½ teaspoon dried parsley
½ teaspoon cumin
¼ teaspoon turmeric
¼ teaspoon paprika
Fresh cilantro
Lime wedges

1. Wash the cauliflower well and trim the leaves
2. Place a steamer rack on top of the pot and transfer the florets to the rack
3. Add 1 cup of water into the Ninja Foodi.Lock up the lid and cook on HIGH pressure for 1 minute
4. Once done, do a quick release.Transfer the flower to a serving platter
5. Set your pot to Saute mode and add oil, allow the oil to heat up
6. Add flowers back to the pot and cook, making sure to break them using a potato masher
7. Add spices and season with a bit of salt. Give a nice stir and squeeze a bit of lime
8. Serve and enjoy!

Very Spicy Cauliflower Steak

Prepping time: 10 minutes | Cooking time: 4 minutes | For 6 servings

1 large head cauliflower
2 tablespoon extra-virgin olive oil
2 teaspoon paprika
2 teaspoon ground cumin
¾ teaspoon kosher salt
1 cup fresh cilantro, chopped
1 lemon, quartered

1. Place the steamer rack into your Ninja Foodi. Add 1 and a ½ cups of water
2. Remove the leaves from the cauliflower and trim the core to ensure that it is able to sit flat
3. Carefully place it on the steam rack. Take a small bowl and add olive oil, cumin, paprika, salt
4. Drizzle the mixture over the cauliflower
5. Lock up the lid and cook on HIGH pressure for 4 minutes
6. Quick release the pressure. Lift the cauliflower to a cutting board and slice into 1-inch steaks
7. Divide the mixture among serving plates and sprinkle with cilantro. Serve and enjoy!

Authentic Indian Palak Paneer

Prepping time: 10 minutes | Cooking time: 5 minutes | For 4 servings

2 teaspoons olive oil
5 garlic cloves, chopped
1 tablespoon fresh ginger, chopped
1 large yellow onion, chopped
½ jalapeno chile, chopped
1 pound fresh spinach
2 tomatoes, chopped
2 teaspoons ground cumin
½ teaspoon cayenne
2 teaspoons Garam masala
1 teaspoon ground turmeric
1 teaspoon salt
½ cup of water
1 and ½ cup paneer cubes
½ cup heavy whip cream

1. Pre-heat your Ninja Foodi using Saute mode on HIGH heat, once the pot is hot, add oil and let it shimmer. Add garlic, ginger and chile, Saute for 2-3 minutes
2. Add onion, spinach, tomatoes, cumin, cayenne, garam masala, turmeric, salt, and water
3. Lock lid and cook on HIGH pressure for 2 minutes. Release pressure naturally over 10 minutes
4. Use an immersion blender to puree the mixture to your desired consistency
5. Gently stir in paneer and top with a drizzle of cream. Enjoy!

All-Time Mixed Vegetable Curry

Prepping time: 10 minutes | Cooking time: 3 minutes | For 6 servings

3 cups leeks, sliced
6 cups rainbow chard, stems and leaves, chopped
1 cup celery, chopped
2 tablespoons garlic, minced
1 teaspoon dried oregano
1 teaspoon salt
2 teaspoons fresh ground black pepper
3 cups chicken broth
2 cups yellow summer squash, sliced into 1/ inch slices
¼ cup fresh parsley, chopped
¾ cup heavy whip cream
4-6 tablespoons parmesan cheese, grated

1. Add leeks, chard, celery, 1 tablespoon garlic, oregano, salt, pepper and broth to your Ninja Foodi
2. Lock lid and cook on HIGH pressure for 3 minutes. Quick release pressure
3. Open the lid and add more broth, set your pot to Saute mode and adjust heat to HIGH
4. Add yellow squash, parsley and remaining 1 tablespoon garlic
5. Let it cook for 2-3 minutes until the squash is soft. Stir in cream and sprinkle parmesan
6. Serve and enjoy!

Chapter 7: Soups and Stews

Pumpkin Soup

Prep time: 10 minutes | Cook time: 23 minutes | Serves 8

¼ cup unsalted butter
½ small onion, diced
1 celery stalk, diced
1 carrot, diced
2 garlic cloves, minced
1 (15-ounce / 425-g) can pumpkin purée
1½ teaspoons poultry spice blend
3 cups chicken stock
1 (8-ounce / 227-g) package cream cheese
1 cup heavy (whipping) cream
¼ cup maple syrup
Sea salt
Freshly ground black pepper

1. Select SEAR/SAUTÉ and set to HI. Select START/STOP to begin. Let preheat for 5 minutes.
2. Add the butter. Once melted, add the onions, celery, carrot, and garlic. Cook, stirring occasionally, for 3 minutes
3. Add the pumpkin, poultry spice, and chicken stock. Assemble pressure lid, making sure the pressure release valve is in the SEAL position.
4. Select PRESSURE and set to HI. Set time to 15 minutes. Select START/STOP to begin.
5. When pressure cooking is complete, quick release the pressure by turning the pressure release valve to the VENT position. Carefully remove lid when the unit has finished releasing pressure.
6. Whisk in the cream cheese, heavy cream, and maple syrup. Season with salt and pepper. Using an immersion blender, purée the soup until smooth.

Beef and Potato Goulash

Prep time: 15 minutes | Cook time: 55 minutes | Serves 6

½ cup all-purpose flour
1 tablespoon kosher salt
½ teaspoon freshly ground black
    pepper
2 pounds (907 g) beef stew meat
2 tablespoons canola oil
1 medium red bell pepper, seeded and
    chopped
4 garlic cloves, minced
1 large yellow onion, diced
2 tablespoons smoked paprika
1½ pounds (680 g) small Yukon Gold
    potatoes, halved
2 cups beef broth
2 tablespoons tomato paste
¼ cup sour cream
Fresh parsley, for garnish

1. Select SEAR/SAUTÉ and set to HI. Select START/STOP to begin. Let preheat for 5 minutes.
2. Mix together the flour, salt, and pepper in a small bowl. Dip the pieces of beef into the flour mixture, shaking off any extra flour.
3. Add the oil and let heat for 1 minute. Place the beef in the pot and brown it on all sides, about 10 minutes.
4. Add the bell pepper, garlic, onion, and smoked paprika. Sauté for about 8 minutes or until the onion is translucent.
5. Add the potatoes, beef broth, and tomato paste and stir. Assemble pressure lid, making sure the pressure release valve is in the SEAL position.
6. Select PRESSURE and set to LO. Set time to 30 minutes. Select START/STOP to begin.
7. When pressure cooking is complete, quick release the pressure by moving the pressure release valve to the VENT position. Carefully remove lid when unit has finished releasing pressure.
8. Add the sour cream and mix thoroughly. Garnish with parsley, if desired, and serve immediately.

Rice and Mushroom Soup

Prep time: 10 minutes | Cook time: 30 minutes | Serves 6

5 medium carrots, chopped
5 celery stalks, chopped
1 onion, chopped
3 garlic cloves, minced
1 cup wild rice
8 ounces (227 g) fresh mushrooms, sliced
6 cups vegetable broth
1 teaspoon kosher salt
1 teaspoon poultry seasoning
½ teaspoon dried thyme

1. Place all the ingredients in the pot. Assemble pressure lid, making sure the pressure release valve is in the SEAL position.
2. Select PRESSURE and set to HI. Set time to 30 minutes. Select START/STOP to begin.
3. When pressure cooking is complete, quick release the pressure by turning the pressure release valve to the VENT position. Carefully remove lid when unit has finished releasing pressure.
4. Serve.

Bacon and Cheddar Potato Soup

Prep time: 15 minutes | Cook time: 30 minutes | Serves 6

5 slices bacon, chopped
1 onion, chopped
3 garlic cloves, minced
4 pounds (1.8 kg) Russet potatoes, peeled and chopped
4 cups chicken broth
1 cup whole milk
½ teaspoon sea salt
½ teaspoon freshly ground black pepper
1½ cups shredded Cheddar cheese
Sour cream, for serving (optional)
Chopped fresh chives, for serving (optional)

1. Select SEAR/SAUTÉ and set to HI. Select START/STOP to begin. Let preheat for 5 minutes.
2. Add the bacon, onion, and garlic. Cook, stirring occasionally, for 5 minutes. Set aside some of the bacon for garnish.
3. Add the potatoes and chicken broth. Assemble pressure lid, making sure the pressure release valve is in the SEAL position.
4. Select PRESSURE and set to HI. Set time to 10 minutes, then select START/STOP to begin.
5. When pressure cooking is complete, quick release the pressure by moving the pressure release valve to the VENT position. Carefully remove lid when unit has finished releasing pressure.
6. Add the milk and mash the ingredients until the soup reaches your desired consistency. Season with the salt and black pepper. Sprinkle the cheese evenly over the top of the soup. Close crisping lid.
7. Select BROIL and set time to 5 minutes. Select START/STOP to begin.
8. When cooking is complete, top with the reserved crispy bacon and serve with sour cream and chives (if using).

Italian Sausage Soup

Prep time: 10 minutes | Cook time: 18 minutes | Serves 8

1 tablespoon extra-virgin olive oil
1½ pounds (680 g) hot Italian sausage, ground
1 pound (454 g) sweet Italian sausage, ground
1 large yellow onion, diced
2 tablespoons minced garlic
4 large Russet potatoes, cut in ½-inch thick quarters
5 cups chicken stock
2 tablespoons Italian seasoning
2 teaspoons crushed red pepper flakes
Salt
Freshly ground black pepper
6 cups kale, chopped
½ cup heavy (whipping) cream

1. Select SEAR/SAUTÉ. Set temperature to MD:HI. Select START/STOP to begin. Let preheat for 5 minutes.
2. Add the olive oil and hot and sweet Italian sausage. Cook, breaking up the sausage with a spatula, until the meat is cooked all the way through, about 5 minutes.
3. Add the onion, garlic, potatoes, chicken stock, Italian seasoning, and crushed red pepper flakes. Season with salt and pepper. Stir to combine. Assemble pressure lid, making sure the pressure release valve is in the SEAL position.
4. Select PRESSURE and set to HI. Set time to 10 minutes. Select START/STOP to begin.
5. When pressure cooking is complete, quick release the pressure by turning the pressure release valve to the VENT position. Carefully remove lid when the unit has finished releasing pressure.
6. Stir in the kale and heavy cream. Serve.

Butternut Squash and Orzo Soup

Prep time: 10 minutes | Cook time: 28 minutes | Serves 8

4 slices uncooked bacon,
    cut into ½-inch pieces
12 ounces (340 g) butternut squash,
    peeled and cubed
1 green apple, cut into small cubes
Kosher salt
Freshly ground black pepper
1 tablespoon minced fresh oregano
2 quarts (1.8 kg) chicken stock
1 cup orzo

1. Select SEAR/SAUTÉ and set temperature to HI. Select START/STOP to begin. Let preheat for 5 minutes.
2. Place the bacon in the pot and cook, stirring frequently, about 5 minutes, or until fat is rendered and the bacon starts to brown. Using a slotted spoon, transfer the bacon to a paper towel-lined plate to drain, leaving the rendered bacon fat in the pot.
3. Add the butternut squash, apple, salt, and pepper and sauté until partially soft, about 5 minutes. Stir in the oregano.
4. Add the bacon back into the pot along with the chicken stock. Bring to a boil for about 10 minutes, then add the orzo. Cook for about 8 minutes, until the orzo is tender. Serve.

Pork, Bean, and Hominy Stew

Prep time: 15 minutes | Cook time: 30 minutes | Serves 8

2 pounds (907 g) boneless pork shoulder,
    cut into 1-inch pieces
¼ cup all-purpose flour
¼ cup unsalted butter
½ small onion, diced
1 carrot, diced
1 celery stalk, diced
2 garlic cloves, minced
1 tablespoon tomato paste
1 tablespoon cumin
1 tablespoon smoked paprika
4 cups chicken stock
1 (10-ounce / 283-g) can diced
    tomatoes with chiles
1 (15-ounce / 425-g) can black beans,
    rinsed and drained
1 (15-ounce / 425-g) can hominy,
    rinsed and drained
Sea salt
Freshly ground black pepper

1. In a large bowl, coat the pork pieces with the flour.
2. Select SEAR/SAUTÉ and set to HI. Select START/STOP to begin. Let preheat for 5 minutes.
3. Add the butter. Once melted, add the pork and sear for 5 minutes, turning the pieces so they begin to brown on all sides.
4. Add the onion, carrot, celery, garlic, tomato paste, cumin, and paprika and cook, stirring occasionally, for 3 minutes.
5. Add the chicken stock and tomatoes. Assemble pressure lid, making sure the pressure release valve is in the SEAL position.
6. Select PRESSURE and set to HI. Set time to 15 minutes. Select START/STOP to begin.
7. When pressure cooking is complete, quick release the pressure by turning the pressure release valve to the VENT position. Carefully remove lid when the unit has finished releasing pressure.
8. Select SEAR/SAUTÉ and set to HI. Select START/STOP to begin.
9. Whisk in the beans and hominy. Season with salt and pepper and cook for 2 minutes. Serve.

Haddock and Biscuit Chowder

Prep time: 15 minutes | Cook time: 30 minutes | Serves 8

5 strips bacon, sliced
1 white onion, chopped
3 celery stalks, chopped
4 cups chicken stock
2 Russet potatoes, rinsed and cut in 1-inch pieces
4 (6-ounce / 170-g) frozen haddock fillets
Kosher salt
½ cup clam juice
⅓ cup all-purpose flour
2 (14-ounce / 397-g) cans evaporated milk
1 (14-ounce / 397-g) tube refrigerated biscuit dough

1. Select SEAR/SAUTÉ and set to HI. Select START/STOP to begin. Let preheat for 5 minutes.
2. Add the bacon and cook, stirring frequently, for 5 minutes. Add the onion and celery and cook for an additional 5 minutes, stirring occasionally.
3. Add the chicken stock, potatoes, and haddock filets. Season with salt. Assemble pressure lid, making sure the pressure release valve is in the SEAL position.
4. Select PRESSURE and set to HI. Set time to 5 minutes. Select START/STOP to begin.
5. Whisk together the clam juice and flour in a small bowl, ensuring there are no flour clumps in the mixture.
6. When pressure cooking is complete, quick release the pressure by moving the pressure release valve to the VENT position. Carefully remove lid when unit has finished releasing pressure.
7. Select SEAR/SAUTÉ and set to MED. Select START/STOP to begin. Add the clam juice mixture, stirring well to combine. Add the evaporated milk and continue to stir frequently for 3 to 5 minutes, until chowder has thickened to your desired texture.
8. Place the Reversible Rack in the pot in the higher position. Place the biscuits on the rack; it may be necessary to tear the last biscuit or two into smaller pieces in order to fit them all on the rack. Close crisping lid.
9. Select BAKE/ROAST, set temperature to 350°F (177°C), and set time to 12 minutes. Select START/STOP to begin.
10. After 10 minutes, check the biscuits for doneness. If desired, cook for up to an additional 2 minutes.
11. When cooking is complete, open lid and remove rack from pot. Serve the chowder and top each portion with biscuits.

Coconut Shrimp and Pea Bisque

Prep time: 10 minutes | Cook time: 15 minutes | Serves 4

¼ cup red curry paste
2 tablespoons water
1 tablespoon extra-virgin olive oil
1 bunch scallions, sliced
1 pound (454 g) medium (21-30 count) shrimp, peeled and deveined
1 cup frozen peas
1 red bell pepper, diced
1 (14-ounce / 397-g) can full-fat coconut milk
Kosher salt

1. In a small bowl, whisk together the red curry paste and water. Set aside.
2. Select SEAR/SAUTÉ and set to MED. Select START/STOP to begin. Let preheat for 3 minutes.
3. Add the oil and scallions. Cook for 2 minutes.
4. Add the shrimp, peas, and bell pepper. Stir well to combine. Stir in the red curry paste. Cook for 5 minutes, until the peas are tender.
5. Stir in coconut milk and cook for an additional 5 minutes until shrimp is cooked through and the bisque is thoroughly heated.
6. Season with salt and serve immediately.

Shrimp and White Fish Stew

Prep time: 10 minutes | Cook time: 46 minutes | Serves 6

2 tablespoons extra-virgin olive oil
1 yellow onion, diced
1 fennel bulb, tops removed and bulb diced
3 garlic cloves, minced
1 cup dry white wine
2 (14½-ounce / 411-g) cans fire-roasted tomatoes
2 cups chicken stock
1 pound (454 g) medium (21-30 count) shrimp, peeled and deveined
1 pound (454 g) raw white fish (cod or haddock), cubed
Salt
Freshly ground black pepper
Fresh basil, torn, for garnish

1. Select SEAR/SAUTÉ and set to MED. Select START/STOP to begin. Let preheat for 3 minutes.
2. Add the olive oil, onions, fennel, and garlic. Cook for about 3 minutes, until translucent.
3. Add the white wine and deglaze, scraping any stuck bits from the bottom of the pot using a silicone spatula. Add the roasted tomatoes and chicken stock. Simmer for 25 to 30 minutes. Add the shrimp and white fish.
4. Select SEAR/SAUTÉ and set to MD:LO. Select START/STOP to begin.
5. Simmer for 10 minutes, stirring frequently, until the shrimp and fish are cooked through. Season with salt and pepper.
6. Ladle into bowl and serve topped with torn basil.

Chicken and Black Bean Enchilada Soup

Prep time: 5 minutes | Cook time: 30 minutes | Serves 8

1 tablespoon extra-virgin olive oil
1 small red onion, diced
2 (10-ounce / 283-g) cans fire-roasted tomatoes with chiles
1 (15-ounce / 425-g) can corn
1 (15-ounce / 425-g) can black beans, rinsed and drained
1 (10-ounce / 283-g) can red enchilada sauce
1 (10-ounce / 283-g) can tomato paste
3 tablespoons taco seasoning
2 tablespoons freshly squeezed lime juice
2 (8-ounce / 227-g) boneless, skinless chicken breasts
Salt
Freshly ground black pepper

1. Select SEAR/SAUTÉ and set temperature to MD:HI. Select START/STOP to begin. Let preheat for 5 minutes.
2. Place the olive oil and onion in the pot. Cook until the onions are translucent, about 2 minutes.
3. Add the tomatoes, corn, beans, enchilada sauce, tomato paste, taco seasoning, lime juice, and chicken. Season with salt and pepper and stir. Assemble pressure lid, making sure the pressure release valve is in the SEAL position.
4. Select PRESSURE and set to HI. Set time to 9 minutes. Select START/STOP to begin.
5. When pressure cooking is complete, allow pressure to naturally release for 10 minutes. After 10 minutes, quick release remaining pressure by moving the pressure release valve to the VENT position. Carefully remove lid when unit has finished releasing pressure.
6. Transfer the chicken breasts to a cutting board. Using two forks, shred the chicken. Return the chicken back to the pot and stir. Serve in a bowl with toppings of choice, such as shredded cheese, crushed tortilla chips, sliced avocado, sour cream, cilantro, and lime wedges, if desired.

Chicken and Egg Noodle Soup

Prep time: 10 minutes | Cook time: 19 minutes | Serves 8

2 tablespoons unsalted butter
1 large onion, chopped
2 carrots, chopped
2 celery stalks, chopped
2 pounds (907 g) boneless chicken breast
4 cups chicken broth
4 cups water
1 tablespoon chopped fresh parsley
1 teaspoon dried thyme
1 teaspoon dried oregano
½ teaspoon sea salt
½ teaspoon freshly ground black pepper
5 ounces (142 g) egg noodles

1. Select SEAR/SAUTÉ and set to HI. Select START/STOP to begin. Let preheat for 5 minutes.
2. Add the butter. Once melted, add the onion, carrots, and celery. Cook, stirring occasionally, for 5 minutes.
3. Add the chicken, chicken broth, water, parsley, thyme, oregano, salt, and pepper. Assemble pressure lid, making sure the pressure release valve is in the SEAL position.
4. Select PRESSURE and set to HI. Set time to 8 minutes. Select START/STOP to begin.
5. When pressure cooking is complete, quick release the pressure by moving the pressure release valve to the VENT position. Carefully remove lid when unit has finished releasing pressure.
6. Remove the chicken from the soup and shred it with two forks. Set aside.
7. Add the egg noodles. Select SEAR/SAUTÉ and set to MED. Select START/STOP to begin.
8. Cook for 6 minutes, uncovered, or until the noodles are tender. Stir the shredded chicken back into the pot. Serve.

Chicken and Mixed Vegetable Potpie Soup

Prep time: 15 minutes | Cook time: 1 hour | Serves 6

4 (8-ounce / 227-g) chicken breasts
2 cups chicken stock
2 tablespoons unsalted butter
1 yellow onion, diced
16 ounces (454 g) frozen mixed
    vegetables
1 cup heavy (whipping) cream
1 (10½-ounce / 298-g) can condensed
    cream of chicken soup
2 tablespoons cornstarch
2 tablespoons water
Salt
Freshly ground black pepper
1 (16.3-ounce / 462-g) tube
    refrigerated biscuit dough

1. Place the chicken and stock in the pot. Assemble pressure lid, making sure the pressure release valve is in the SEAL position.
2. Select PRESSURE and set to HI. Set time to 15 minutes. Select START/STOP to begin.
3. Once pressure cooking is complete, quick release the pressure by turning the pressure release valve to the VENT position. Carefully remove lid when the unit has finished releasing pressure.
4. Using a silicone-tipped utensil, shred the chicken.
5. Select SEAR/SAUTÉ and set to MED. Add the butter, onion, mixed vegetables, cream, and condensed soup and stir. Select START/STOP to begin. Simmer for 10 minutes.
6. In a small bowl, whisk together the cornstarch and water. Slowly whisk the cornstarch mixture into the soup. Set temperature to LO and simmer for 10 minutes more. Season with salt and pepper.
7. Carefully arrange the biscuits on top of the simmering soup. Close crisping lid.
8. Select BAKE/ROAST, set temperature to 325°F (163°C), and set time to 15 minutes. Select START/STOP to begin.
9. When cooking is complete, remove the biscuits. To serve, place a biscuit in a bowl and ladle soup over it.

Chicken and Corn Tortilla Soup

Prep time: 10 minutes | Cook time: 20 minutes | Serves 8

1 tablespoon extra-virgin olive oil
1 onion, chopped
1 pound (454 g) boneless, skinless chicken
    breasts
6 cups chicken broth
1 (12-ounce / 340-g) jar salsa
4 ounces (113 g) tomato paste
1 tablespoon chili powder
2 teaspoons cumin
½ teaspoon sea salt
½ teaspoon freshly ground black pepper
1 pinch of cayenne pepper
1 (15-ounce / 425-g) can black beans,
    rinsed and drained
2 cups frozen corn
Tortilla strips, for garnish

1. Select SEAR/SAUTÉ and set to temperature to HI. Select START/STOP to begin. Let preheat for 5 minutes.
2. Place the olive oil and onions into the pot and cook, stirring occasionally, for 5 minutes.
3. Add the chicken breast, chicken broth, salsa, tomato paste, chili powder, cumin, salt, pepper, and cayenne pepper. Assemble pressure lid, making sure the pressure release valve is in the SEAL position.
4. Select PRESSURE and set to HI. Set time to 10 minutes. Select START/STOP to begin.
5. When pressure cooking is complete, allow pressure to naturally release for 10 minutes. After 10 minutes, quick release remaining pressure by moving the pressure release valve to the VENT position. Carefully remove lid when unit has finished releasing pressure.
6. Transfer the chicken breasts to a cutting board and shred with two forks. Set aside.
7. Add the black beans and corn. Select SEAR/SAUTÉ and set to MD. Select START/STOP to begin. Cook until heated through, about 5 minutes.
8. Add shredded chicken back to the pot. Garnish with tortilla strips, serve, and enjoy!

Tomatillo Chicken Thigh Stew

Prep time: 15 minutes | Cook time: 46 minutes | Serves 4

3 medium onions, quartered
3 garlic cloves, whole
2 poblano peppers, seeded and quartered
½ pound (227 g) tomatillos
2 small jalapeño peppers, seeded and quartered (optional)
2 tablespoons canola oil, divided
Kosher salt

Freshly ground black pepper
2½ pounds (1.1 kg) boneless, skinless chicken thighs (6 to 8 pieces)
1 cup chicken stock
1 teaspoon cumin
1 tablespoon oregano
1 tablespoon all-purpose flour
1 cup water

1. Place Cook & Crisp Basket in pot and close crisping lid. Select AIR CRISP and set to HIGH. Set time to 25 minutes. Select START/STOP to begin. Let preheat for 5 minutes.
2. Place the onions, garlic, poblano peppers, tomatillos, jalapeños, 1 tablespoon of canola oil, salt, and pepper in a medium-sized bowl and mix until vegetables are evenly coated.
3. Once unit has preheated, open lid and place the vegetables in the basket. Close lid and cook for 20 minutes.
4. After 10 minutes, open lid, then lift basket and shake the vegetables or toss them with silicone-tipped tongs. Lower basket back into pot and close lid to continue cooking.
5. When cooking is complete, remove basket and vegetables and set aside.
6. Select SEAR/SAUTÉ and set to HI. Select START/STOP to begin. Let preheat for 5 minutes.
7. Season the chicken thighs with salt and pepper.
8. After 5 minutes, add the remaining 1 tablespoon of oil and chicken. Sear the chicken, about 3 minutes on each side.
9. Add the chicken stock, cumin, and oregano. Scrape the pot with a rubber or wooden spoon to release any pieces that are sticking to the bottom. Assemble pressure lid, making sure the pressure release valve is in the SEAL position.
10. Select PRESSURE and set to HI. Set time to 10 minutes. Select START/STOP to begin.
11. Remove the vegetables from the basket and roughly chop.
12. In a small bowl, add the flour and water and stir.
13. When pressure cooking is complete, quick release the pressure by turning the pressure release valve to the VENT position. Carefully remove lid when unit has finished releasing pressure.
14. Remove the chicken and shred it using two forks.
15. Select SEAR/SAUTÉ and set to MED. Select START/STOP to begin. Return the chicken and vegetables and stir with a rubber or wooden spoon, being sure to scrape the bottom of the pot. Slowly stir in the flour mixture. Bring to a simmer and cook for 10 minutes, or until the broth becomes clear and has thickened.
16. When cooking is complete, serve as is or garnish with sour cream, lime, cilantro, and a flour tortilla for dipping.

Jamaican Jerk Chicken and Cabbage Stew

Prep time: 15 minutes | Cook time: 28 minutes | Serves 6

2 tablespoons canola oil
6 boneless, skinless chicken thighs, cut in 2-inch pieces
2 tablespoons Jamaican jerk spice
1 white onion, peeled and chopped
2 red bell peppers, chopped
½ head green cabbage, core removed and cut into 2-inch pieces
1½ cups wild rice blend, rinsed
4 cups chicken stock
½ cup prepared Jamaican jerk sauce
Kosher salt

1. Select SEAR/SAUTÉ and set to HI. Select START/STOP to begin. Let preheat for 5 minutes.
2. Add the oil, chicken, and jerk spice and stir. Cook for 5 minutes, stirring occasionally.
3. Add the onions, bell pepper, and cabbage and stir. Cook for 5 minutes, stirring occasionally.
4. Add the wild rice and stock, stirring well to combine. Assemble pressure lid, making sure the pressure release valve is in the SEAL position.
5. Select PRESSURE and set to HI. Set time to 18 minutes. Select START/STOP to begin.
6. When pressure cooking is complete, allow pressure to naturally release for 10 minutes. After 10 minutes, quick release any remaining pressure by moving the pressure release valve to the VENT position. Carefully remove lid when unit has finished releasing pressure.
7. Add the jerk sauce to pot, stirring well to combine. Let the stew sit for 5 minutes, allowing it to thicken. Season with salt and serve.

Chapter 8: Holiday And Weekend Ninja Recipes

Simple Weeknight Vanilla Yogurt

Prepping time: 10 minutes + 9 hours|Cooking time: 3 hours |For 4 servings

½ cup full-fat milk
¼ cup yogurt started
1 cup heavy cream
½ tablespoon vanilla extract
2 teaspoons stevia

1. Add milk to your Ninja Foodi and stir in heavy cream, vanilla extract, stevia
2. Stir well, let the yogurt sit for a while. Lock lid and cook on SLOW COOKER mode for 3 hours
3. Take a small bowl and add 1 cup milk with the yogurt starter, bring this mixture to the pot
4. Lock lid and wrap Foodi in two small towels. Let it sit for 9 hours (to allow it to culture)
5. Refrigerate and serve. Enjoy!

The Great Family Lemon Mousse

Prepping time: 10 minutes |Cooking time: 12 minutes | For 4 servings

1-2 ounces cream cheese, soft
½ cup heavy cream
1/8 cup fresh lemon juice
½ teaspoon lemon liquid stevia
2 pinch salt

1. Take a bowl and mix in cream cheese, heavy cream, lemon juice, salt, and stevia
2. Pour mixture into a ramekin and transfer to Ninja Foodi
3. Lock lid and choose the Bake/Roast mode and bake for 12 minutes at 350 degrees F
4. Check using a toothpick if it comes out clean. Serve and enjoy!

Tangy Berry Slices

Prepping time: 20 minutes | Cooking time: 15 minutes | For 4 servings

1 cup cottage cheese
½ teaspoon stevia
¼ cup ground pecans
½ cup strawberries
¼ cup whipped cream
¼ cup butter

1. Set your Ninja Food to Saute mode and add butter, add pecans and toss until coated
2. Divide mixture into 3 ramekins and press them down
3. Blend cheese and stevia, puree until smooth. Place cheese mixture on top of the pecan crust
4. Cover with fresh strawberry slices, top with whipped cream. Chill and enjoy!

Over The Weekend Apple And Sprouts

Prepping time: 10 minutes | Cooking time: 10 minutes | For 4 servings

1 green apple, julienned
1 and ½ teaspoon olive oil
4 cups alfalfa sprouts
Salt and pepper to taste
¼ cup of coconut milk

1. Set your Ninja Foodi to Saute mode and add oil, let it heat up
2. Add apple, sprouts, and stir. Lock lid and cook on HIGH pressure for 5 minutes
3. Add salt, pepper, coconut milk and stir well. Serve3 and enjoy!

Generous Gluten Free Pancakes

Prepping time: 10 minutes | Cooking time: 16 minutes | For 4 servings

1/3 cup almond flour
½ cup of water
½ teaspoon chili powder
1 Serrano pepper, minced
4 tablespoons coconut oil
3 tablespoons coconut cream
¼ teaspoon turmeric powder
1 handful cilantro, chopped
6 large eggs
1 teaspoon salt
¼ teaspoon pepper
½ inch ginger, grated
½ red onion, chopped

1. Take a bowl and add coconut milk, almond flour, spices, and blend well
2. Stir in ginger, Serrano, cilantro, red onion and mix
3. Grease interior of Ninja Foodi with coconut oil, pour batter in pot and Lock lid, cook on LOW pressure for 30 minutes. Release pressure naturally over 10 minutes
4. Remove pancake to a platter and serve. Enjoy!

Fancy Holiday Lemon Custard

Prepping time: 10 minutes |Cooking time: 20 minutes | For 4 servings

5 egg yolks
¼ cup fresh squeezed lemon juice
1 tablespoon lemon zest
1 teaspoon pure vanilla extract
1/3 teaspoon liquid stevia
2 cups heavy cream
1 cup whipped coconut cream

1. Take a medium sized bowl and whisk in yolks, lemon juice, zest, vanilla, and liquid stevia
2. Whisk in heavy cream, divide the mixture between 4 ramekins
3. Place the included rack in your Ninja Foodi and place ramekins in the rack
4. Add just enough water to reach halfway to the sides of the ramekins
5. Lock lid and cook on HIGH pressure for 20 minutes. Release pressure naturally over 10 minutes
6. Remove ramekins and let them cool down
7. Chill in fridge, top with whipped coconut cream and enjoy!

Gentle Peanut Butter Cheesecake

Prepping time: 10 minutes |Cooking time: 20 minutes | For 4 servings

1/8 cup smooth peanut butter
2 whole eggs
½ teaspoon stevia
½ teaspoon vanilla extract
½ cup sour cream
2 tablespoons smooth peanut butter
    (additional)
Pinch of stevia
2 cups cream cheese

1. Use a blender and mix in cheese, peanut butter, eggs, stevia and vanilla extract
2. Pour mixture in springform pan, cover with aluminum foil
3. Add 2 cups water to your Ninja Foodi, place pan on a trivet
4. Lock lid and cook on HIGH pressure for 20 minutes. Release pressure naturally over 10 minutes
5. Let it cool down. Add your desired toppings and spread on top. Enjoy!

Decisive Crème Brulee

Prepping time: 10 minutes |Cooking time: 20 minutes | For 4 servings

1 cup heavy cream
½ tablespoon vanilla extract
3 egg yolks
1 pinch salt
¼ cup stevia

1. Take a bowl and mix in egg yolks, vanilla extract, salt, and heavy cream
2. Mix well and beat the mixture until combined well
3. Divide mixture between 4 greased ramekins and evenly transfer the ramekins to your Ninja Foodi. Lock lid and select the "Bake/Roast" mode, bake for 35 minutes at 365 degrees F
4. Remove ramekin from Ninja Foodi and wrap with plastic wrap. Refrigerate to chill for 3 hours
5. Serve and enjoy!

The Cool Pot-De-Crème

Prepping time: 10 minutes |Cooking time: 20 minutes | For 4 servings

6 egg yolks
2 cups heavy whip cream
1/3 cup cocoa powder
1 tablespoon pure vanilla extract
½ teaspoon liquid stevia
Whipped coconut cream for garnish
Shaved dark chocolate for garnish

1. Take a medium sized bowl and whisk in yolks, heavy cream, cocoa powder, vanilla and stevia
2. Pour mixture in 1 and ½ quart baking dish, transfer to Nina Foodi insert
3. Add water to reach about half of the ramekin
4. Lock lid and cook on HIGH pressure for 12 minutes, quick release pressure
5. Remove baking dish from the insert and let it cool
6. Chill in fridge and serve with a garnish of coconut cream, shaved chocolate shavings. Enjoy!

Humming Key Lime Curd

Prepping time: 10 minutes |Cooking time: 10 minutes | For 4 servings

3 ounces unsalted butter
1 cup liquid stevia
2 large eggs
2 large egg yolks
2/3 cup fresh key lime juice
1-2 teaspoons key lime zest

1. Take food How Toor and add butter and stevia for 2 minutes
2. Slowly add the eggs and yolks to the processor and process To for 1 minute
3. Add Key Lime Juice to the blender and mix well. The mix should look curdled
4. Pour the mix into 3 one cup sized Mason Jars and lock up the lid
5. Place 1 and a ½ cups of water to your Ninja Foodi. Add the steamer basket/trivet
6. Place jars on the basket. Lock up the lid and cook for 10 minutes at HIGH pressure
7. Once done, allow the pressure to release naturally. Remove the jars and open the lids
8. Add Key Lime Zest to the curd and stir well. Place the lid and slightly tighten it
9. Cool for 20 minutes or chill in your fridge overnight. Enjoy!

Runny Eggs In A Cup

Prepping time: 5 minutes | Cooking time: 5 minutes | For 4 servings

4 whole eggs
1 cup mixed veggies, diced
½ cup cheddar cheese, shredded
¼ cup half and half
Salt and pepper to taste
½ cup shredded cheese

1. Take a bowl and add eggs, cheese, veggies, half and a half, pepper, salt and chop up cilantro
2. Mix well and divide the mix amongst four ½ a pint wide mouth mason jars (or similar containers. Slightly put the lid on top
3. Add 2 cups of water to your pot and place a steamer rack on top
4. Place the egg jars on your steamer. Lock up the lid and cook for 5 minutes at HIGH pressure
5. Quick release the pressure. Remove the jars and top them up with ½ a cup of cheese
6. Serve immediately or broil a bit to allow the cheese to melt

Simple Party Week Poached Pears

Prepping time: 10 minutes |Cooking time: 10 minutes | For 6 servings

6 firm pears, peeled
1 bottle of dry red wine
1 bay leaf
4 garlic cloves, minced
1 stick cinnamon
1 fresh ginger, minced
1 and 1/3 cup stevia
Mixed Italian herbs as needed

1. Peel the pears leaving the stems attached. Pour wine into your Ninja Foodi
2. Add bay leaf, cinnamon, cloves, ginger, stevia, and stir
3. Add pears to the pot and lock up the lid and cook on HIGH pressure for 9 minutes
4. Perform a quick release. Take the pears out using tong and keep them on the side
5. Set the pot to Saute mode and allow the mixture to reduce to half
6. Drizzle the mixture over the pears and enjoy!

A Wedding Worthy Coconut Cake

Prepping time: 10 minutes |Cooking time: 10 minutes | For 4 servings

Dry

1 cup almond flour
½ cup unsweetened shredded coconut
1/3 cup Truvia
1 teaspoon of apple pie spice
1 teaspoon of baking powder

Wet

¼ cup melted butter
2 lightly whisked eggs
½ cup heavy whipping cream

1. Add all dry in a bowl and add the wet one at a time, making sure to gently stir after each addition. Empty batter into a pan and cover with foil
2. Add water 1-2 cups of water to Ninja Foodi, place steamer rack
3. Place pan in a steamer rack and lock lid. Cook on HIGH pressure for 40 minutes
4. Naturally, release pressure over 10 minutes. Quick release pressure
5. Remove pan and let it cool for 15-20 minutes. Flip it over onto a platter and garnish as needed. Serve and enjoy!

Uniform Dark Chocolate Cake

Prepping time: 10 minutes | Cooking time: 3 hours 10 minutes | For 4 servings

1 cup + 2 tablespoons almond flour
1 and ½ teaspoons baking powder
½ cup of cocoa powder
½ cup granular swerve
3 tablespoons unflavored whey powder/egg white protein powder
¼ teaspoon salt
2/3 cup almond milk, unsweetened
3 large whole eggs
¾ teaspoon vanilla extract
6 tablespoons melted butter
1/3 cup chocolate chips, sugar-free

1. Prepare a six quart Ninja Foodi and grease with oil
2. Add whey protein powder, almond flour, sweetener, baking powder, salt, cocoa powder
3. Fold in butter, eggs, vanilla extract, milk and mix well. Stir in chips and pour batter into the pot
4. Lock lid and SLOW COOK (HIGH) for 3 hours until a toothpick comes out clean from the center
5. Remove heat and let it cool for 20 minutes, slice and serve. Enjoy!

Party Night Lamb Gyros

Prepping time: 10 minutes | Cooking time: 25 minutes | For 8 servings

8 garlic cloves
1 and ½ teaspoon salt
2 teaspoons dried oregano
1 and ½ cups of water
2 pounds lamb meat, ground
2 teaspoons rosemary
½ teaspoon pepper
1 small onion, chopped
2 teaspoons ground marjoram

1. Add onions, garlic, marjoram, rosemary, salt and pepper to a food processor
2. Process until combined well, add ground lamb meat and process again
3. Press meat mixture gently into a loaf pan. Transfer the pan to your Ninja Foodi pot
4. Lock lid and select "Bake/Roast" mode. Bake for 25 minutes at 375 degrees F
5. Transfer to serving the dish and enjoy!

Chapter 9: 5 Ingredients Or Less Ninja Foodi Recipes

The Coolest New York Strip Steak

Prepping time: 10 minutes | Cooking time: 9 minutes | For 4 servings

24 ounces NY strip steak
½ teaspoon ground black pepper
1 teaspoon salt

1. Add steaks on a metal trivet and place trivet on your Ninja Foodi
2. Season with salt and pepper
3. Add 1 cup water to the pot (below steaks. Lock lid and cook on HIGH pressure for 1 minute
4. Quick release pressure.
5. Place Air Crisp lid and Air Crisp for 8 minutes for a medium-steak. Remove from pot and enjoy!

French Onion Pork Chops

Prepping time: 5 minutes | Cooking time: 20 minutes | For 4 servings

4 pork chops
10 ounces French Onion Soup
½ cup sour cream
10 ounces chicken broth

1. Add pork chops to your Ninja Foodi. Add broth. Lock lid and cook on HIGH pressure for 12 minutes. Release pressure naturally over 10 minutes.
2. Whisk sour cream and French Onion Soup and pour mixture over pork.
3. Set your Ninja Foodi to Saute mode and cook for 6-8 minutes more. Serve and enjoy!

Hearty Apple Infused Water

Prepping time: 10 minutes |Cooking time: 4 minutes | For 4 servings

1 whole apple, chopped
5 sticks of cinnamon

1. Place the above-mentioned to a mesh steamer basket
2. Place the basket in your pot. Add water to barely cover the content.
3. Lock up the lid and cook on HIGH pressure for 5 minutes
4. Once the cooking is done, quick release the pressure
5. Remove the steamer basket and discard the cooked produce
6. Allow the flavored water to cool and chill. Serve!

Simple And Easy Chicken Breast

Prepping time: 5 minutes | Cooking time: 10 minutes | For 4 servings

4 chicken breasts, skinless
1 and ¼ cup of water

1. Add water to Ninja Foodi . Add frozen chicken and lock lid. Cook on HIGH pressure for 10 minutes. Quick release pressure. Open the lid and use just as you want it.

Italian Dark Kale Crisps

Prepping time: 5 minutes | Cooking time: 10 minutes | For 4 servings

2 cups kale, Italian dark-leaf
1 teaspoon yeast
2 tablespoons coconut oil
½ teaspoon chili flakes
¼ teaspoon salt

1. Take a bowl and tear the kale roughly and place it into the bowl
2. Sprinkle the kale with coconut oil, yeast, chili flakes and salt
3. Mix up the kale well till it becomes consistent
4. Insert the air fryer basket and in the Ninja Foodi and then transfer the kale
5. Air fryer the meal for 10 minutes. Serve and enjoy!

Quick Ginger And Sesame Chicken

Prepping time: 5 minutes | Cooking time: 10 minutes | For 4 servings

1 and ½ pounds chicken thighs, no skin
2 tablespoons coconut aminos
1 tablespoon agave
1 tablespoon ginger, minced
1 tablespoon garlic-sesame oil
1 tablespoon rice vinegar
Red onion, sliced for salad
Carrots julienned for salad
Cucumbers julienned for salad

1. Slice thigh into large chunks and add rest of the to a heat-safe dish
2. Place foil over the bowl. Add 2 cups water to Ninja Foodi
3. Place steamer rack in Ninja Foodi and place the bowl over the rack
4. Lock lid and cook on HIGH pressure for 10 minutes. Naturally, release pressure over 10 minutes
5. Shred meat and serve with a tossing of the salad. Enjoy!

Butter Melted Broccoli Florets

Prepping time: 10 minutes | Cooking time: 8 minutes | For 4 servings

4 tablespoons butter
Salt and pepper to taste
2 pounds broccoli florets
1 cup whip cream

1. Arrange basket in the bottom of your Ninja Foodi and add water
2. Place florets on top of the basket. Lock lid and cook on HIGH pressure for 5 minutes
3. Quick release pressure and transfer florets to the pot itself
4. Season with salt, pepper and add butter
5. Lock crisping lid and Air Crisp on 360 degrees F 3 minutes
6. Transfer to a serving plate. Serve and enjoy!

The Epic Fried Eggs

Prepping time: 5 minutes | Cooking time: 10 minutes | For 2 servings

4 eggs
¼ teaspoon ground black pepper
1 teaspoon butter, melted
¾ teaspoon salt

1. Take a small egg pan and brush it with butter. Beat the eggs in the pan
2. Sprinkle with the ground black pepper and salt. Transfer the egg pan in the pot
3. Lower the air fryer lid. Cook the meat for 10 minutes at 350 F. Serve immediately and enjoy!

Gentle Keto Butter Fish

Prepping time: 10 minutes | Cooking time: 30 minutes | For 6 servings

1 pound salmon fillets
2 tablespoons ginger/garlic paste
3 green chilies, chopped
Salt and pepper to taste
¾ cup butter

1. Season salmon fillets with ginger, garlic paste, salt, pepper
2. Place salmon fillets to Ninja Foodi and top with green chilies and butter
3. Lock lid and BAKE/ROAST for 30 minutes at 360 degrees F
4. Bake for 30 minutes and enjoy!

Sensational Carrot Puree

Prepping time: 10 minutes |Cooking time: 4 minutes | For 4 servings

1 and a ½ pound carrots, chopped
1 tablespoon of butter at room temperature
1 tablespoon of agave nectar
¼ teaspoon of sea salt
1 cup of water

1. Clean and peel your carrots properly. Roughly chop up them into small pieces
2. Add 1 cup of water to your Pot
3. Place the carrots in a steamer basket and place the basket in the Ninja Foodi
4. Lock up the lid and cook on HIGH pressure for 4 minutes. Perform a quick release
5. Transfer the carrots to a deep bowl and use an immersion blender to blend the carrots
6. Add butter, nectar, salt, and puree. Taste the puree and season more if needed. Enjoy!

Simple Broccoli Florets

Prepping time: 10 minutes | Cooking time: 6 minutes | For 4 servings

4 tablespoons butter, melted
Salt and pepper to taste
2 pounds broccoli florets
1 cup whipping cream

1. Place a steamer basket in your Ninja Foodi (bottom part) and add water
2. Place florets on top of the basket and lock lid
3. Cook on HIGH pressure for 5 minutes. Quick release pressure
4. Transfer florets from the steamer basket to the pot. Add salt, pepper, butter, and stir
5. Lock crisping lid and cook on Air Crisp mode for 360 degrees F. Serve and enjoy!

Awesome Magical 5 Ingredient Shrimp

Prepping time: 10 minutes | Cooking time: 15 minutes | For 4 servings

---

2 tablespoons butter
½ teaspoon smoked paprika
1 pound shrimps, peeled and deveined
Lemongrass stalks
1 red chili pepper, seeded and chopped

1. Take a bowl and mix all of the well, except lemongrass and marinate for 1 hour
2. Transfer to Ninja Foodi and lock lid, BAKE/ROAST for 15 minutes at 345 degrees F
3. Once done, serve and enjoy!

Romantic Mustard Pork

Prepping time: 10 minutes | Cooking time: 30 minutes | For 4 servings

---

2 tablespoons butter
2 tablespoons Dijon mustard (Keto-Friendly)
4 pork chops
Salt and pepper to taste
1 tablespoon fresh rosemary, coarsely chopped

1. Take a bowl and add pork chops, cover with Dijon mustard and carefully sprinkle rosemary, salt, and pepper. Let it marinate for 2 hours
2. Add butter and marinated pork chops to your Ninja Foodi pot
3. Lock lid and cook on Low-Medium Pressure for 30 minutes
4. Release pressure naturally over 10 minutes. Take the dish out, serve and enjoy!

Creative And Easy Lamb Roast

Prepping time: 10 minutes | Cooking time: 60 minutes | For 6 servings

---

2 pounds lamb roast
1 cup onion soup
1 cup beef broth
Salt and pepper to taste

1. Transfer lamb roast to your Ninja Foodi pot. Add onion soup, beef broth, salt, and pepper
2. Lock lid and cook on Medium-HIGH pressure for 55 minutes
3. Release pressure naturally over 10 minutes. Transfer to serving bowl, serve and enjoy!

Crispy Tofu And Mushrooms

Prepping time: 10 minutes | Cooking time: 10 minutes | For 2 servings

---

8 tablespoons parmesan cheese, shredded
2 cups fresh mushrooms, chopped
2 blocks tofu, pressed and cubed
Salt and pepper to taste
8 tablespoons butter

1. Take a bowl and mix in tofu, salt, and pepper
2. Set your Ninja Foodi to Saute mode and add seasoned tofu, Saute for 5 minutes
3. Add mushroom, cheese and Saute for 3 minutes. Lock crisping lid and Air Crisp for 3 minutes at 350 degrees F. Transfer to serving plate and enjoy!

A Hearty Sausage Meal

Prepping time: 10 minutes | Cooking time: 20 minutes | For 6 servings

4 whole eggs
4 sausages, cooked and sliced
2 tablespoons butter
½ cup mozzarella cheese, grated
½ cup cream

1. Take a bowl and mix everything
2. Add egg mix to your Ninja Foodi, top with cheese and sausage slices
3. Lock pressure lid and select "BAKE/ROAST" mode and cook for 20 minutes at 345 degrees F
4. Take it out once done, serve and enjoy!

Deserving Mushroom Saute

Prepping time: 10 minutes | Cooking time: 15 minutes | For 8 servings

1 pound white mushrooms, stems trimmed
2 tablespoons unsalted butter
½ teaspoon salt
¼ cup of water

1. Quarter medium mushrooms and cut any large mushrooms into eight
2. Put mushrooms, butter, and salt in your Foodi's inner pot
3. Add water and lock pressure lid, making sure to seal the valve
4. Cook on HIGH pressure for 5 minutes, quick release pressure once did
5. Once done, set your pot to Saute mode on HIGH mode and bring the mix to a boil over 5 minutes until all the water evaporates
6. Once the butter/water has evaporated, stir for 1 minute until slightly browned. Enjoy!

Slightly Zesty Lamb Chops

Prepping time: 5 minutes |Cooking time: 40 minutes | For 4 servings

4 tablespoons butter
3 tablespoons lemon juice
4 lamb chops, with bone
2 tablespoons almond flour
1 cup picante sauce

1. Coat chops with almond flour, keep them on the side
2. Set your Ninja Foodi to Saute mode and add butter, chops
3. Saute for 2 minutes, add picante sauce and lemon juice
4. Lock lid and cook on HIGH pressure for 40 minutes. Release naturally and serve, enjoy!

Bacon And Scrambled Egg

Prepping time: 10 minutes | Cooking time: 5-10 minutes | For 2 servings

4 strips bacon
2 whole eggs
1 tablespoon milk
Salt and pepper to taste

1. Add bacon inside your Ninja Foodi. Lock Crisping Lid and set it to Air Crisp mode
2. Cook for 3 minutes at 390 degrees F. Flip and cook for 2 minutes more
3. Remove bacon and keep it on the side. Take a bowl and whisk in eggs and milk
4. Season with salt and pepper. Set your Ninja Foodi to Saute mode
5. Add eggs, cook until firm. Serve and enjoy!

Delicious Creamy Crepes

Prepping time: 5 minutes |Cooking time: 30 minutes | For 4 servings

1 and ½ teaspoon Splenda
3 organic eggs
3 tablespoons coconut flour
½ cup heavy cream
3 tablespoons coconut oil, melted and divided

1. Take a bowl and mix in 1 and ½ tablespoons coconut oil, Splenda, eggs, salt and mix well
2. Beat well until mixed. Add coconut flour and keep beating. Stir in heavy cream, beat well
3. Set your Ninja Foodi to Saute mode and add ¼ of the mixture
4. Saute for 2 minutes on each side. Repeat until all are used up. Enjoy!

Egg Stuffed Avocado Dish

Prepping time: 10 minutes | Cooking time: 5 minutes | For 6 servings

½ tablespoon fresh lemon juice
1 medium ripe avocado, peeled, pitted and chopped
6 organic eggs, boiled, peeled and cut in half lengthwise
Salt to taste
½ cup fresh watercress, trimmed

1. Place steamer basket at the bottom of your Ninja Foodie. Add water
2. Add watercress on the basket and lock lid
3. Cook on HIGH pressure for 3 minutes, quick release the pressure and drain the watercress
4. Remove egg yolks and transfer them to a bowl
5. Add watercress, avocado, lemon juice, salt into the bowl and mash with a fork
6. Place egg whites in a serving bowl and fill them with the watercress and avocado dish
7. Serve and enjoy!

Lovely Asparagus Bites

Prepping time: 5 minutes |Cooking time: 10 minutes | For 4 servings

1 cup asparagus
½ cup coconut, desiccated
½ cup feta cheese

1. Add coconut in a shallow dish, coat asparagus with coconut
2. Transfer to Ninja Foodi and top with feta cheese
3. Lock Crisping lid and Air Crisp for 10 minutes at 360 degrees F. Serve and enjoy!

Easy to Make Mustard Pork Chops

Prepping time: 5 minutes |Cooking time: 30 minutes | For 4 servings

2 tablespoons butter
2 tablespoons Dijon mustard
4 pork chops
Salt and pepper to taste
1 tablespoon fresh rosemary

1. Marinate pork chops with Dijon mustard, rosemary, salt, and pepper for 2 hours
2. Put butter and marinated pork chops in Ninja Foodi. Lock lid and cook on LOW pressure for 30 minutes. Release naturally and enjoy!

Generous Lemon Mousse

Prepping time: 5 minutes + chill time |Cooking time: 12 minutes | For 4 servings

1-ounce cream cheese, soft
½ cup heavy cream
1/8 cup fresh lemon juice
½ teaspoon lemon liquid stevia
2 pinch salt

1. Mix in cream cheese, heavy cream, lemon juice, salt and stevia in a bowl
2. Pour mix into ramekins and transfer ramekins to Ninja Foodi
3. Lock lid and cook on BAKE/ROAST mode for 12 minutes at 350 degrees F
4. Pour mixture into serving glass and chill for 3 hours, serve and enjoy!

Terrific Baked Spinach Quiche

Prepping time: 10 minutes | Cooking time: 5-10 minutes | For 2 servings

1 tablespoons butter, melted
1 pack frozen spinach, thawed
5 organic eggs, beaten
Salt and pepper to taste
3 cups monetary jack cheese, shredded

1. Set your pot to Saute mode and add butter, spinach
2. Saute for 3 minutes, transfer dish out of the bowl
3. Add eggs, Monterey Jack cheese, salt, pepper to a bowl and transfer to the greased mold
4. Place molds inside Ninja Foodi and lock lid, cook on BAKE/ROAST mode for 30 minutes at 360 degrees F. Remove from Ninja Foodi and cut into wedges. Serve and enjoy!

Juicy Keto Lamb Roast

Prepping time: 5 minutes |Cooking time: 55 minutes | For 4 servings

2 pounds lamb roast
1 cup onion soup
1 cup beef broth
Salt and pepper

1. Add lamb roast to Ninja Foodi, add onion soup, beef broth, salt, and pepper
2. Lock lid and cook on HIGH pressure for 55 minutes
3. Release pressure naturally over 10 minutes. Serve and enjoy!

Chapter 10: 20 Minutes Ninja Foodi Recipes

Quick And Easy Buttery Pancake

Prepping time: 5 minutes | Cooking time: 10 minutes | For 4 servings

2 cups cream cheese
2 cups almond flour
6 large whole eggs
1/4 teaspoon salt
2 tablespoons butter
¼ teaspoon ground ginger
½ teaspoon cinnamon powder

1. Take a large bowl and add cream cheese, eggs, 1 tablespoon butter. Blend on high until creamy. Slow add flour and keep beating. Add salt, ginger, cinnamon. Keep beating until fully mixed. Set your Ninja Foodi to Saute mode and grease stainless steel insert. Add butter and heat it up. Add ½ cup batter and cook for 2-3 minutes, flip and cook the other side
2. Repeat with the remaining batter, Enjoy!

Decisive Asian Brussels

Prepping time: 5 minutes | Cooking time: 4 minutes | For 4 servings

1 pound Brussels, halved
3 tablespoons chicken stock
Salt and pepper to taste
1 teaspoon toasted sesame seeds
1 tablespoon green onions, chopped
1 and ½ tablespoons stevia
1 tablespoon coconut aminos
2 tablespoons olive oil
1 tablespoon Keto sriracha sauce

1. Take a bowl and mix in oil, coconut aminos, Sriracha, stevia, salt, pepper and whisk well
2. Put Brussels to Ninja Foodi and add sriracha mix, stock, green onions, sesame, stir
3. Lock lid and cook on HIGH pressure for 4 minutes. Serve and enjoy!

Busy Man's Bacon Jalapeno

Prepping time: 6 minutes | Cooking time: 3 minutes | For 3 servings

6 jalapeno peppers
6 bacon strips, chopped and cooked
¼ teaspoon ground cumin
1 teaspoon garlic, minced
1-ounces ground beef, cooked
6 tablespoons cream cheese
½ teaspoon salt

1. Trim the ends of the peppers and remove the seeds
2. Add cream cheese, ground cumin and salt then mix them
3. Then add ground beef and stir well. Add bacon
4. Put the mixture into the peppers. Transfer on the rack. Lower the air fryer lid
5. Cook the jalapenos for 3 minutes at 365 F. Serve immediately and enjoy!

Lovely Bok Choy Soup

Prepping time: 5 minutes | Cooking time: 13 minutes | For 4 servings

4 chicken thighs
4 cups beef bone broth
1 pound Bok choy
Salt and pepper to taste
¼ teaspoon dried dill weed
1 teaspoon bay leaf

1. Add chicken thigh to Ninja Foodi, add 1 cup broth. Lock lid and cook on HIGH pressure for 8 minutes. Release pressure naturally over 10 minutes. Add remaining and lock lid again. Cook on HIGH pressure for 5 minutes more
2. Quick release pressure. Serve and enjoy!

Mushroom Hats Stuffed With Cheese

Prepping time: 10 minutes | Cooking time: 6 minutes | For 3 servings

10 ounces mushroom hats
2 ounces parmesan, grated
½ teaspoon oregano, dried
1-ounce fresh parsley, chopped
1-ounce cheddar cheese, grated
2 tablespoons cream cheese
½ teaspoon chili flakes

1. Mix together the chopped parsoley, cream cheese, chili flakes, grated cheese, and dried oregano. Fill up the mushroom hats with the cheese mixture
2. Place the mushroom hats in the rack. Lower the air fryer lid
3. Cook the meat for 6 minutes at 400 F. Then check the mushroom cooked or not if you want you can cook for 2-3 minutes more. Serve hot and enjoy!

A King's Favorite Egg Salad

Prepping time: 5 minutes | Cooking time: 15 minutes | For 2 servings

3 eggs
1 teaspoon olive oil
½ white onion, sliced
1 avocado, chopped
3 tablespoons heavy cream
½ teaspoon paprika
½ teaspoon salt

1. Take a trivet and place the eggs into it. Lower the air fryer lid
2. Cook the eggs for 15 minutes at 270 F
3. In between, combine heavy cream, salt, chopped avocado, onion and paprika
4. Once cooked, let the chill in the icy water and then peel them
5. Cut the eggs into the quarters and add in the avocado mixture
6. Then stir the salad. Serve and enjoy!

Come-Back Cauliflower And Parm

Prepping time: 5 minutes | Cooking time: 4 minutes | For 4 servings

1 cauliflower head
½ cup vegetable stock
2 garlic cloves, minced
Salt and pepper to taste
1/3 cup grated parmesan
1 tablespoons parsley, chopped
3 tablespoons olive oil

1. Take a bowl and add oil, garlic, salt, pepper cauliflower, and toss. Transfer to Ninja Foodi
2. Add stock and lock lid, cook on HIGH pressure for 4 minutes
3. Add parsley, parmesan and toss. Serve and enjoy!

The Chorizo Flavored Casserole

Prepping time: 5 minutes | Cooking time: 10 minutes | For 3 servings

3 eggs, whisked
2 ounces chorizo, chopped
3 ounces cauliflower hash brown, cooked
1-ounces mozzarella, sliced
¾ cup almond milk
½ teaspoon butter
1/3 teaspoon chili flakes

1. Start with melting butter then whisk it with chorizo, chili flakes, eggs, and almond milk
2. Add hash brown and stir well. Take a cake pan and put the egg mixture into it
3. Then place in the Ninja Foodi. Close the Air Crisping lid and crisp on Air Crisp mode for 2 minutes at 365 F. Serve and enjoy!

Sensible Chinese Salad

Prepping time: 5 minutes | Cooking time: 5 minutes | For 4 servings

2 tablespoons sesame oil
1 yellow onion, chopped
1 teaspoon garlic, minced
1 pound cabbage, shredded
¼ cup rice wine vinegar
¼ teaspoon Szechuan pepper
½ teaspoon salt
1 tablespoon coconut aminos

1. Set your Ninja Foodi to Saute mode and add oil, let it heat up
2. Add onion and cook until tender. Add rest of and stir
3. Lock lid and cook on HIGH pressure for 3 minutes. Quick release pressure
4. Transfer cabbage mix to the salad bowl and serve. Enjoy!

Mushroom And Bok Choy Health Bite

Prepping time: 7 minutes | Cooking time: 7 minutes | For 3 servings

10 ounces bok choy, chopped
1 tablespoon coconut oil
5 ounces white mushrooms, chopped
1 teaspoon salt

1. Mix together the mushrooms and bok choy. Add all the and mix them well
2. Sprinkle with coconut oil and salt. Make a shake to the and place them into Ninja Foodi. Lower the air fryer lid. Cook the side dish for 7 minutes at 400 F
3. Stir generously. Serve hot and enjoy!

Cool Cabbage Soup

Prepping time: 5 minutes | Cooking time: 5 minutes | For 4 servings

½ pound Capoccolo, chopped
Salt and pepper to taste
½ teaspoon cayenne pepper
1 onion, chopped
1 celery stalk, chopped
1 parsnip, chopped
1 pound cabbage, cut into wedges
2 cups broth
1 cup tomatoes, pureed
1 cup of water
1 bay leaf

1. Add listed to Ninja Foodi. Lock lid and cook on HIGH pressure for 3 minutes
2. Quick release pressure once did. Ladle soup to serving bowls and serve, enjoy!

Sensible Steamed Keto Salad

Prepping time: 5 minutes | Cooking time: 5 minutes | For 4 servings

1 cup of water
8 tomatoes, sliced
2 tablespoons extra virgin olive oil
½ cup Halloumi cheese, crumbled
2 garlic cloves, smashed
2 tablespoons fresh basil, snipped

1. Add 1 cup water to Ninja Foodi. Place steamer rack to the Foodi
2. Place tomatoes on rack and lock lid, cook on HIGH pressure for 3 minutes
3. Quick release pressure. Remove lid toss tomato with remaining . Serve and enjoy!

Okra And Bacon Delight

Prepping time: 5 minutes | Cooking time: 4 minutes | For 4 servings

2 tablespoons olive oil
1 red onion, chopped
½ pound okra
1 teaspoon ginger-garlic paste
4 slices pancetta, chopped
1 t teaspoon celery seeds
½ teaspoon caraway seeds
½ teaspoon cayenne pepper
½ teaspoon turmeric powder
1 cup of water
1 cup tomato puree

1. Set your Ninja Foodi to Saute mode, add olive oil and let it heat up
2. Add onion and Saute until tender. Add okra, ginger garlic paste, Saute for 1 minute
3. Stir in remaining . Lock lid and cook on HIGH pressure for 3 minutes
4. Quick release pressure and serve. Enjoy!

Awesome Luncheon Green Beans

Prepping time: 10 minutes | Cooking time: 5 minutes | For 4 servings

1 pound fresh green beans
2 tablespoons butter
1 garlic clove, minced
Salt and pepper to taste
1 and ½ cups of water

1. Add listed to Ninja Foodi. Lock lid and cook on High Pressure for 5 minutes
2. Quick release pressure. Serve and enjoy!

Powerful Keto Tuscan Soup

Prepping time: 5 minutes | Cooking time: 5 minutes | For 4 servings

2 tablespoons butter, melted
½ cup leeks, sliced
2 garlic cloves, minced
4 cups broccoli rabe, broken into pieces
2 cups of water
2 cups broth, homemade
1 zucchini, shredded
1 carrot, trimmed and grated
Salt to taste
¼ teaspoon ground pepper

1. Set your Ninja Foodi to Saute mode and let it heat up
2. Add butter and let it melt, add leeks and cook for 2 minutes
3. Add minced garlic, cook for 40 seconds. Add remaining
4. Lock lid and cook on LOW pressure for 3 minutes. Quick release. Serve and enjoy!

Turnip Greens And Sausage

Prepping time: 10 minutes | Cooking time: 5 minutes | For 4 servings

2 teaspoons sesame oil
2 pork sausage, casing removed, sliced
2 garlic cloves, minced
1 medium leek, chopped
1 cup of turkey bone stock
1 pound turnip greens
Salt and pepper to taste
1 bay leaf
1 tablespoon black sesame seeds

1. Set your Ninja Foodi to Saute mode and add sesame oil, let it heat up
2. Add sausage and cook until browned
3. Add garlic, leeks and cook for 2 minutes. Add greens, stock, salt, pepper and bay leaf
4. Lock lid and cook for 3 minutes on LOW pressure. Quick release pressure
5. Serve with a garnish of black sesame seeds. Enjoy!

Easy And Cheesy Asparagus

Prepping time: 10 minutes | Cooking time: 3 minutes | For 4 servings

1 and ½ pounds fresh asparagus
2 tablespoons olive oil
4 garlic cloves, minced
Salt and pepper to taste
½ cup Colby cheese, shredded

1. Add 1 cup water to Ninja Foodi. Add steamer basket to Ninja Foodi
2. Place asparagus and drizzle asparagus with olive oil
3. Scatter garlic over asparagus. Season with salt and pepper
4. Lock lid and cook on HIGH pressure for 1 minute. Quick release pressure
5. Serve with cheese scattered on top. Enjoy!

Crisped Up Sweet Fish

Prepping time: 10 minutes | Cooking time: 6 minutes | For 4 servings

2 drops liquid stevia
¼ cup butter
1 pound fish chunks
1 tablespoon vinegar
Salt and pepper to taste

1. Set your Ninja Foodi to Saute mode, add butter and fish chunks
2. Saute for 3 minutes and add stevia, salt, and pepper
3. Lock crisping lid and Air Crisp for 3 minutes at 360 degrees F
4. Transfer to serving bowl and serve. Enjoy!

Flimsy Buffalo Fish

Prepping time: 5 minutes | Cooking time: 11 minutes | For 4 servings

6 tablespoons butter
¾ cup Franks red hot sauce
6 fish fillets
Salt and pepper to taste
2 teaspoons garlic powder

1. Set your Ninja Foodi to Saute mode and add butter, fish fillets
2. Saute for 3 minutes and add salt, pepper and garlic powder
3. BAKE/ROAST for 8 minutes at 340 degrees F. Transfer to serving plate and enjoy!

Tomato And Zucchini Rosemary

Prepping time: 10 minutes |Cooking time: 3 minutes | For 4 servings

2 tablespoons olive oil
2 garlic cloves, chopped
1 pound zucchini, sliced
½ cup tomato puree
½ cup of water
1 teaspoon dried thyme
½ teaspoon dried oregano
½ teaspoon dried rosemary

1. Set your Ninja Foodi to Saute mode and add olive oil, let it heat up
2. Add garlic and cook until aromatic. Add rest of the and stir
3. Lock lid and cook on LOW pressure for 3 minutes. Quick release pressure and serve. Enjoy!

Herbed Up 13 Minutes Cod

Prepping time: 5 minutes | Cooking time: 8 minutes | For 4 servings

4 garlic cloves, minced
2 teaspoons coconut aminos
¼ cup butter
6 whole eggs
2 small onions, chopped
3 cod fish fillets, skinless and cut into rectangular pieces
2 green chilies, chopped
Salt and pepper to taste

1. Add listed to a shallow dish except for cod and beat well
2. Dip each fillet in the mix and keep it on the side. Transfer fillets to basket and lock lid
3. Air Crisp for 8 minutes at 330 degrees F. Serve and enjoy!

New Broccoli Pops

Prepping time: 6 minutes | Cooking time: 12 minutes | For 4 servings

1/3 cup parmesan cheese, grated
2 cups cheddar cheese, grated
Salt and pepper to taste
3 eggs, beaten
3 cups broccoli florets
1 tablespoon olive oil

1. Add broccoli into a food processor and pulse until finely crumbled
2. Transfer broccoli to a large-sized bowl and add remaining to the bowl, mix well
3. Make small balls using the mixture and let them chill for 30 minutes
4. Place balls in your Ninja Foodi pot and Air Crisping lid. Let it cook for 12 minutes at 365 degrees F on the "Air Crisp" mode. Once done, remove and enjoy!

Great Salmon Stew

Prepping time: 5 minutes | Cooking time: 8 minutes | For 4 servings

1 cup homemade fish broth
Salt and pepper to taste
1 medium onion, chopped
1 pound salmon fillet, cubed
1 tablespoon butter

1. Season salmon fillets with salt and pepper
2. Set your Ninja Foodi to Saute mode and add butter and onions
3. Saute for 3 minutes, add salmon and fish broth
4. Lock lid and cook on HIGH pressure for 8 minutes
5. Release pressure naturally over 10 minutes. Transfer to serving plate, serve and enjoy!

Creative Srilankan Coconut Dish

Prepping time: 10 minutes | Cooking time: 10 minutes | For 4 servings

1 tablespoon coconut oil
1 medium brown onion, halved and sliced
1 and ½ teaspoon salt
2 large garlic cloves, diced
½ a long red chili, sliced
1 tablespoon yellow mustard seeds
1 tablespoon turmeric powder
1 medium cabbage, quartered, shredded and sliced
1 medium carrot, peeled and sliced
2 tablespoons lime juice
½ cup desiccated unsweetened coconut
1 tablespoon olive oil
1/3 cup water

1. Set your Ninja Foodi to Saute mode and add coconut oil, once the oil is hot and add onion and half of the salt. Saute for 3-4 minutes
2. Add garlic, chili, and spices and Saute for 30 seconds
3. Add cabbage, lime juice, carrots, coconut, and olive oil and stir well. Add water and stir
4. Lock up the lid and cook on HIGH pressure for 5 minutes
5. Release the pressure naturally over 5 minutes followed by a quick release
6. Serve as a side with chicken/fish. Enjoy!

Chapter 11: Awesome Snacks And Appetizers

Inspiring Cauliflower Hash Browns

Prepping time: 10 minutes | Cooking time: 30 minutes | For 6 servings

6 whole eggs
4 cups cauliflower rice
¼ cup milk
1 onion, chopped
3 tablespoons butter
1 and ½ cups cooked ham, chopped
½ cup shredded cheese

1. Set your Ninja Foodi to sauté mode and add butter, let the butter heat up
2. Add onions and cook for 5 minutes until tender. Add iced cauliflower to pot and stir
3. Lock the Air Crisping lid and Air Crisp for 15 minutes, making sure to give them a turn about halfway through
4. Take a small bowl and mix in eggs and milk, pour mixture over browned cauliflower
5. Sprinkle ham over top. Press Air Crispy again and crisp for 10 minutes more
6. Sprinkle cheddar cheese on top and lock lid, let the crisp for 1 minute more until the cheese melts. Serve and enjoy!

Everybody's Favorite Cauliflower Patties

Prepping time: 5 minutes |Cooking time: 20 minutes | For 4 servings

3 whole eggs
1 chili pepper, chopped
½ teaspoon garlic powder
Salt and pepper to taste
2 cups cauliflower, chopped
¾ cups olive oil
¼ cup cheddar cheese
¼ cup whole mozzarella cheese

1. Cut cauliflower into small florets, remove leaves and cut out a core
2. Add 1 cup water to Ninja Food, transfer florets to steamer basket and place it on a trivet in your Ninja Foodi. Lock lid and cook on HIGH pressure for 5 minutes
3. Mash steamed cauliflower and dry them, add shredded cheese, eggs, chili, salt and pepper
4. Mix well and shape into flat patties
5. Heat up oil in your Ninja Foodi and set to Saute mode, shallow fry patties until crisp on both sides. Serve and enjoy!

Kale And Almonds Mix

Prepping time: 10 minutes |Cooking time: 4 minutes | For 4 servings

1 cup of water
1 big kale bunch, chopped
1 tablespoon balsamic vinegar
1/3 cup toasted almonds
3 garlic cloves, minced
1 small yellow onion, chopped
2 tablespoons olive oil

1. Set your Ninja Foodi on Saute mode and add oil, let it heat up
2. Stir in onion and cook for 3 minutes. Add garlic, water, kale, and stir
3. Lock lid and cook on HIGH pressure for 4 minutes. Quick release pressure
4. Add salt, pepper, vinegar, almonds and toss well. Serve and enjoy!

Simple Treat Of Garlic

Prepping time: 10 minutes |Cooking time: 5 minutes | For 4 servings

1 tablespoon extra-virgin olive oil
2 garlic cloves, minced
2 large-sized Belgian endive, halved lengthwise
½ cup apple cider vinegar
½ cup broth
Salt and pepper to taste
1 teaspoon cayenne pepper

1. Set your Ninja Foodi to Saute mode and add oil, let the oil heat up
2. Add garlic and cook for 30 seconds unto browned
3. Add endive, vinegar, broth, salt, pepper, and cayenne
4. Lock lid and cook on LOW pressure for 2 minutes. Quick release pressure and serve. Enjoy!

Buttered Up Garlic And Fennel

Prepping time: 10 minutes |Cooking time: 5 minutes | For 4 servings

½ stick butter
2 garlic cloves, sliced
½ teaspoon salt
1 and ½ pounds fennel bulbs, cut into wedges
¼ teaspoon ground black pepper
½ teaspoon cayenne
¼ teaspoon dried dill weed
1/3 cup dry white wine
2/3 cup stock

1. Set your Ninja Foodi to Saute mode and add butter, let it heat up
2. Add garlic and cook for 30 seconds. Add rest of the
3. Lock lid and cook on LOW pressure for 3 minutes. Remove lid and serve. Enjoy!

Obvious Paprika And Cabbage

Prepping time: 10 minutes |Cooking time: 4 minutes | For 4 servings

1 and ½ pounds green cabbage, shredded
Salt and pepper to taste
3 tablespoon ghee
1 cup vegetable stock
¼ teaspoon sweet paprika

1. Set your Ninja Foodi to Saute mode and add ghee, let it melt
2. Add cabbage, salt, pepper, and stock, stir well
3. Lock lid and cook on HIGH pressure for 7 minutes. Quick release pressure
4. Add paprika and toss well. Divide between plates and serve. Enjoy!

Authentic Western Omelet

Prepping time: 5 minutes | Cooking time: 34 minutes | For 2 servings

3 eggs, whisked
3 ounces chorizo, chopped
1-ounces Feta cheese, crumbled
5 tablespoons almond milk
¾ teaspoon chili flakes
¼ teaspoon salt
1 green pepper, chopped

1. Add all the and mix them well. Stir it gently. Take an omelet pan and pour the mixture into it. Preheat your Ninja Foodi at "Roast/Bake" mode at 320 F.
2. Cook for 4 minutes. After that, transfer the pan with an omelet in Ninja Foodi
3. Cook for 30 minutes more at the same mode. Serve hot and enjoy!

Bowl Full Of Broccoli Salad

Prepping time: 10 minutes |Cooking time: 5 minutes | For 4 servings

1 pound broccoli, cut into florets
2 tablespoons balsamic vinegar
2 garlic cloves, minced
1 teaspoon mustard seeds
1 teaspoon cumin seeds
Salt and pepper to taste
1 cup cottage cheese, crumbled

1. Add 1 cup water to your Ninja Foodi. Place steamer basket
2. Place broccoli in basket and lock lid, cook on HIGH pressure for 5 minutes
3. Quick release pressure and remove lid. Toss broccoli with other and serve. Enjoy!

Rise And Shine Breakfast Casserole

Prepping time: 10 minutes | Cooking time: 10 minutes | For 6 servings

4 whole eggs
1 tablespoons milk
1 cup ham, cooked and chopped
½ cup cheddar cheese, shredded
¼ teaspoon salt
¼ teaspoon ground black pepper

1. Take a baking pan (small enough to fit into your Ninja Foodi) bowl, and grease it well with butter. Take a medium bowl and whisk in eggs, milk, salt, pepper and add ham, cheese, and stir. Pour mixture into baking pan and lower the pan into your Ninja Foodi
2. Set your Ninja Foodi Air Crisp mode and Air Crisp for 325 degrees F for 7 minutes
3. Remove pan from eggs and enjoy!

Cauliflower And Egg Dish

Prepping time: 10 minutes |Cooking time: 4 minutes | For 4 servings

21 ounces cauliflower, separated into
    florets
1 cup red onion, chopped
1 cup celery, chopped
½ cup of water
Salt and pepper to taste
2 tablespoons balsamic vinegar
1 teaspoon stevia
4 boiled eggs, chopped
1 cup Keto Friendly mayonnaise

1. Add water to Ninja Foodi
2. Add steamer basket and add cauliflower, lock lid and cook on High Pressure for 5 minutes
3. Quick release pressure. Transfer cauliflower to bowl and add eggs, celery, onion and toss
4. Take another bowl and mix in mayo, salt, pepper, vinegar, stevia and whisk well
5. Add a salad, toss well. Divide into salad bowls and serve. Enjoy!

Just A Simple Egg Frittata

Prepping time: 10 minutes |Cooking time: 15 minutes | For 4 servings

5 whole eggs
¾ teaspoon mixed herbs
1 cup spinach
¼ cup shredded cheddar cheese
½ cup mushrooms
Salt and pepper to taste
¾ cup half and half
2 tablespoons butter

1. Dice mushrooms, chop spinach finely
2. Set your Ninja Foodi to Saute mode and add spinach, mushrooms
3. Whisk eggs, milk, cream cheese, herbs, and Sautéed vegetables in a bowl and mix well
4. Take a 6-inch baking pan and grease it well
5. Pour mixture and transfer to your Ninja Foodie (on a trivet)
6. Cook on HIGH pressure for 2 minutes. Quick release pressure. Serve and enjoy!

Ultimate Cheese Dredged Cauliflower Snack

Prepping time: 10 minutes | Cooking time: 30 minutes | For 4 servings

1 tablespoon mustard
1 head cauliflower
1 teaspoon avocado mayonnaise
½ cup parmesan cheese, grated
¼ cup butter, cut into small pieces

1. Set your Ninja Foodi to Saute mode and add butter and cauliflower
2. Saute for 3 minutes. Add remaining and stir
3. Lock lid and cook on HIGH pressure for 30 minutes. Release pressure naturally over 10 minutes
4. Serve and enjoy!

The Great Mediterranean Spinach

Prepping time: 10 minutes | Cooking time: 15 minutes | For 4 servings

4 tablespoons butter
2 pounds spinach, chopped and boiled
Salt and pepper to taste
2/3 cup Kalamata olives, halved and pitted
1 and ½ cups feta cheese, grated
4 teaspoons fresh lemon zest, grated

1. Take a bowl and mix in spinach, butter, salt, pepper and mix well
2. Transfer to Ninja Foodi the seasoned spinach
3. Lock Air Crisper and Air Crisp for 15 minutes at 350 degrees F. Serve and enjoy!

Quick Turkey Cutlets

Prepping time: 10 minutes | Cooking time: 22 minutes | For 4 servings

1 teaspoon Greek seasoning
1 pound turkey cutlets
2 tablespoons olive oil
1 teaspoon turmeric powder
½ cup almond flour

1. Add Greek seasoning, turmeric powder, almond flour to a bowl
2. Dredge turkey cutlets in it and keep it on the side for 30 minutes
3. Set your Foodi to Saute mode and add oil and cutlets, Saute for 2 minutes
4. Lock lid and cook on LOW-MEDIUM pressure for 20 minutes
5. Quick release pressure. Serve and enjoy!

Veggies Dredged In Cheese

Prepping time: 10 minutes | Cooking time: 30 minutes | For 4 servings

2 onions, sliced
2 tomatoes, sliced
2 zucchinis, sliced
2 teaspoons olive oil
2 cups cheddar cheese, grated
2 teaspoons mixed dried herbs
Salt and pepper to taste

Arrange all the listed to your Ninja Foodi. Top with olive oil, herbs, cheddar, salt and pepper. Lock lid and Air Crisp for 30 minutes at 350 degrees F. Serve and enjoy!

Egg Dredged Casserole

Prepping time: 10 minutes | Cooking time: 5 minutes | For 6 servings

4 whole eggs
1 tablespoons milk
1 tomato, diced
½ cup spinach
¼ teaspoon salt
¼ teaspoon ground black pepper

1. Take a baking pan (small enough to fit Ninja Foodi) and grease it with butter
2. Take a medium bowl and whisk in eggs, milk, salt, pepper, add veggies to the bowl and stir
3. Pour egg mixture into the baking pan and lower the pan into the Ninja Foodi
4. Close Air Crisping lid and Air Crisp for 325 degrees for 7 minutes
5. Remove the pan from eggs and enjoy hot!

Excellent Bacon And Cheddar Frittata

Prepping time: 10 minutes | Cooking time: 10 minutes | For 6 servings

6 whole eggs
2 tablespoons milk
½ cup bacon, cooked and chopped
1 cup broccoli, cooked
½ cup shredded cheddar cheese
¼ teaspoon salt
¼ teaspoon ground black pepper

1. Take a baking pan (small enough to fit into your Ninja Foodi) bowl, and grease it well with butter. Take a medium sized bowl and add eggs, milk, salt, pepper, bacon, broccoli, and cheese. Stir well. Pour mixture into your prepared baking pan and lower pan into your Foodi, close Air Crisping lid. Air Crisp for 7 minutes at 375 degrees F. Remove pan and enjoy!

Pork Packed Jalapeno

Prepping time: 10 minutes | Cooking time: 10 minutes | For 6 servings

2 pounds pork sausage, ground
2 cups parmesan cheese, shredded
2 pounds large sized jalapeno peppers sliced lengthwise and seeded
2 (8 ounces packages, cream cheese, softened
2 (8 ounces bottles, ranch dressing

1. Take a bowl and add pork sausage, cream cheese, ranch dressing and mix well
2. Slice jalapeno in half, remove seeds and clean them
3. Stuff sliced jalapeno pieces with pork mixture
4. Place peppers in crisping basket and transfer basket to your Ninja Foodi
5. Lock Air Crisping lid and cook on Air Crisp mode for 10 minutes at 350 degrees F
6. Cook in batches if needed, serve and enjoy!

Juicy Garlic Chicken Livers

Prepping time: 10 minutes | Cooking time: 8 hours |For 6 servings

1 pound chicken livers
8 garlic cloves, minced
8 ounces cremini mushrooms, quartered
4 slices uncooked bacon, chopped
1 onion, chopped
1 cup bone broth
1 teaspoon dried thyme
1 teaspoon dried rosemary
1 teaspoon salt
1 teaspoon freshly ground black pepper
¼ cup fresh parsley, chopped

1. Add livers, bacon, garlic, mushrooms, onion, thyme, broth, rosemary to Ninja Foodi
2. Season with salt and pepper. Place lid and cook on SLOW COOK Mode (LOW) for 8 hours
3. Remove lid and stir in parsley. Serve and enjoy!

The Original Zucchini Gratin

Prepping time: 10 minutes | Cooking time: 15 minutes | For 4 servings

2 zucchinis
1 tablespoon fresh parsley, chopped
2 tablespoons bread crumbs
4 tablespoons parmesan cheese, grated
1 tablespoon vegetable oil
Salt and pepper to taste

1. Pre-heat your Ninja Foodi to 300 degrees F for 3 minutes
2. Slice zucchini lengthwise to get about 8 equal sizes pieces
3. Arrange pieces in your Crisping Basket (skin side down)
4. Top each with parsley, bread crumbs, cheese, oil, salt, and pepper
5. Return basket Ninja Foodi basket and cook for 15 minutes at 360 degrees F
6. Once done, serve with sauce. Enjoy!

Quick Bite Zucchini Fries

Prepping time: 10 minutes | Cooking time: 10 minutes | For 4 servings

1-2 pounds of zucchini, sliced into 2 and ½ inch sticks
Salt to taste
1 cup cream cheese
2 tablespoons olive oil

1. Add zucchini in a colander and season with salt, add cream cheese and mix
2. Add oil into your Ninja Foodie's pot and add Zucchini
3. Lock Air Crisping Lid and set the temperature to 365 degrees F and timer to 10 minutes
4. Let it cook for 10 minutes and take the dish out once done, enjoy!

Pickled Up Green Chili

Prepping time: 5 minutes | Cooking time: 11 minutes | For 4 servings

1 pound green chilies
1 and ½ cups apple cider vinegar
1 teaspoon pickling salt
1 and ½ teaspoon sugar
¼ teaspoon garlic powder

1. Add the listed to your pot. Lock up the lid and cook on HIGH pressure for 11 minutes. Release the pressure naturally
2. Spoon the mixture into jars and cover the slices with cooking liquid, making sure to completely submerge the chilies. Serve!

Vegetable Tamales

Prep time: 15 minutes | Cook time: 23 minutes | Makes 2 dozen tamales

For the Squash and Pepper Filling:
3 tablespoons vegetable oil
2 medium yellow summer squash, finely diced
1 red bell pepper, seeded, r ibbed, and finely diced
1 jalapeño, seeded and finely diced
4 garlic cloves, minced
1 medium yellow onion, finely diced
1 teaspoon chili powder
1 teaspoon ground cumin

1 (15-ounce / 425-g) can tomato sauce
1 cup vegetable broth
2 teaspoons kosher salt

For the Tamales:
24 dried corn husks
4½ cups instant yellow corn masa flour (see Note, this page)
3¾ teaspoons kosher salt
3 teaspoons baking powder
¾ cup vegetable shortening, at room temperature

Make the Filling

1. Set the Foodi to Sear/Saute on High. Add the oil to the inner pot and heat for 4 minutes. Add the squash and cook until softened, about 6 minutes, stirring once halfway through. Stir in the bell pepper, jalapeño, and garlic and continue to cook until softened, about 4 minutes, stirring often. Add the onion, chili powder, and cumin and cook until softened and aromatic, about 4 minutes more, stirring once.

2. Add the tomato sauce, vegetable broth, and salt. Lock on the Pressure Lid, making sure the valve is set to Seal, and set to Pressure on High for 1 minute. When the timer reaches 0, quick-release the pressure and carefully remove the lid. Transfer the squash and bell pepper mixture to a medium bowl and set aside to cool to room temperature. Wash and dry the Foodi's inner pot.

Make the Tamales

3. Arrange the corn husks vertically in the crisping basket (see this page), folding the edges in, and place the basket in the Foodi's inner pot. Add 3 cups water and lock on the Pressure Lid, making sure the valve is set to Seal, then set the Foodi to Pressure on High for 0 minutes. When the timer reaches 0, quick-release the pressure and carefully remove the lid. Remove the crisping basket and set aside. Leave the water in the pot.

4. Place the masa in a medium bowl and whisk in the salt and baking powder. Add the vegetable shortening and pinch it into the flour mixture (as you would if making pie dough), rubbing the shortening into the flour until there aren't any fat bits larger than a pea. Add the water from the inner pot and use a spoon to stir the mixture until it forms a batter of sorts.

5. Place a corn husk on your work surface, ribbed side down, and unfold the husk so it lies flat. Gently spread about 3 tablespoons of the masa dough on the husk in an even layer all the way to the edges of the husk. Add about 2 tablespoons of the filling to the middle of the masa and spread it, leaving a ¼-inch border around the edges. Fold in the sides of the tamale, followed by the bottom. Set the tamale into the crisping basket (it's easiest to place the crisping basket on its side; see photograph on right), seam side down, like a little package. Repeat with the remaining husks, dough, and filling.

6. Place 2 cups water in the Foodi's inner pot. Arrange the tamales in the crisping basket so that the folded ends are at the bottom of the basket and the open tops are pointing upward. Place the basket in the Foodi, then lock on the Pressure Lid, making sure the valve is set to Seal, and set to Pressure on High for 10 minutes. When the timer reaches 0, quick-release the pressure and carefully remove the lid. Allow the tamales to cool slightly before serving or store them, when completely cooled, in an airtight container.

Artichokes with Melted Butter

Prep time: 5 minutes | Cook time: 12 minutes | Serves 6

3 globe artichokes, stems and top leaves trimmed, if desired
2 teaspoons kosher salt
1 lemon, halved
4 tablespoons butter, melted

1. Add ½ cup water, the artichokes, and the salt to the Foodi's inner pot. Squeeze the lemon halves over the artichokes and then add them to the pot as well. Lock on the Pressure Lid, making sure the valve is set to Seal, and set to Pressure on High for 12 minutes. When the timer reaches 0, quick-release the pressure and carefully open the lid.
2. Serve the artichokes with melted butter.

Chicken Wings

Prep time: 5 minutes | Cook time: 40 minutes | Serves 2

1½ cups hot sauce
6 whole chicken wings, split into drumettes and flats
½ teaspoon kosher salt
Celery sticks, for garnish (optional)
Carrot sticks, for garnish (optional)
Blue cheese dressing, for garnish (optional)
Ranch dressing, for garnish (optional)

1. Place ½ cup of the hot sauce and 1 cup water in the Foodi's inner pot and stir to combine. Place the wings in the crisping basket and set the basket into the inner pot. Lock on the Pressure Lid, making sure the valve is set to Seal, and set to Pressure on High for 2 minutes. When the timer reaches 0, quick-release the pressure and carefully remove the lid.
2. Sprinkle the wings with the salt. Drop the Crisping Lid and set the Foodi to Air Crisp at 390°F (199°C) for 40 minutes, or until crisp and blistered.
3. Lift the lid and remove the basket with the wings. Add the remaining 1 cup hot sauce to the pot, and toss the wings with the sauce in the pot. Transfer the wings to a platter and serve with your favorite accoutrements.

Hot Blackberry Chicken Wing Sauce

Prep time: 5 minutes | Cook time: 8 minutes | Makes 1 cup

4 tablespoons unsalted butter
6 ounces (170 g) fresh blackberries
2 serrano chiles, roughly chopped (for less heat, remove the seeds and membranes)
1 teaspoon freshly ground black pepper

1. Place the butter, blackberries, chiles, pepper, and ½ cup water into the Foodi's inner pot. Lock on the Pressure Lid, making sure the valve is set to Seal, and set to Pressure on High for 2 minutes. When the timer reaches 0, quick-release the pressure and carefully remove the lid.
2. Use a silicone potato masher to mash the blackberries until they are uniformly pulverized. Set the Foodi to Sear/Sauté on High and cook the mixture until thickened, about 6 minutes.
3. Strain the sauce through a fine-mesh sieve and into a bowl, pressing on the mixture to extract as much juice as possible. Discard the seeds and remaining bits of pepper in the sieve. Immediately toss the sauce with unsauced chicken wings or transfer to an airtight container and refrigerate for up to 1 week before warming, stirring, and adding to wings.

Homemade Hummus

Prep time: 10 minutes | Cook time: 30 minutes | Makes 6 cup

1 pound (454 g) dried chickpeas
4 teaspoons cumin seeds
Zest of 1 lemon and juice of 2 lemons
¾ cup tahini
1 cup extra-virgin olive oil
1 tablespoon toasted sesame oil
2 garlic cloves, minced
2 teaspoons kosher salt
Pita, for serving (optional)
Bread, for serving (optional)
Vegetable sticks, for serving (optional)

1. Place the chickpeas into the Foodi's inner pot. Add 5 cups water, half the cumin seeds, and the lemon zest to the pot. Lock on the Pressure Lid, making sure the valve is set to Seal, and set to Pressure on High for 30 minutes. When the timer reaches 0, turn off the Foodi and let the pressure naturally release for 15 minutes, then quick-release any remaining pressure and carefully remove the lid.
2. Drain the chickpeas (reserve the cooking liquid) using the crisping basket as a colander. Add the cooked chickpeas to the Foodi's inner pot.
3. While the chickpeas are still hot, add the remaining cumin seeds, tahini, olive oil, sesame oil, garlic, lemon juice, and salt. Use a silicone potato masher or silicone spatula to smash and stir everything together. (Alternatively, you can transfer everything to a food processor or blender and process until smooth.) Use the reserved cooking liquid as needed to thin the mash to your desired thickness—I usually end up adding about 1 cup of cooking liquid. Transfer the hummus to an airtight container and refrigerate until cool. Serve with pita, bread, or vegetable sticks.

Breaded Jalapeño Poppers

Prep time: 5 minutes | Cook time: 10 minutes | Makes 24 poppers

1½ cups breadcrumbs
3 large eggs
1 (8-ounce / 227-g) package cream cheese, transferred to a zippered plastic bag to warm to room temperature
1 (26-ounce / 737-g) can whole pickled jalapeños, drained, stemmed, halved lengthwise, and seeds and ribs removed
Cooking spray

1. Place the breadcrumbs in a medium bowl. Add the eggs to another small bowl and lightly whisk.
2. Snip off one of the bottom corners of the cream cheese–filled bag and use it like a pastry bag to fill the jalapeños to their rims with cream cheese.
3. Line a freezer-safe container with plastic wrap. Spray the plastic wrap with cooking spray.
4. Dip the filled jalapeños in the egg, then roll them in the breadcrumbs, then repeat with the egg and breadcrumbs so the jalapeños get a double coating.
5. Place the stuffed jalapeños in the prepared container without overlapping (though the sides can touch). If you run out of space in the container, spray the jalapeños with cooking spray, cover with plastic wrap, spray the wrap, and add another layer. Cover the container with plastic wrap and freeze for at least 4 hours or up to 1 week.
6. Insert the crisping basket into the Foodi's inner pot and spray with cooking spray. Add 9 poppers to the basket and spray the tops of the poppers. Drop the Crisping Lid and set the Foodi to Air Crisp at 390°F (199°C) for 10 minutes, or until the poppers are browned and bubbling. Lift the lid and remove the basket from the Foodi pot. Repeat for the remaining poppers. Cool for 5 minutes before eating.

Mexican Cheese Chicken Taquitos

Prep time: 5 minutes | Cook time: 15 minutes | Makes 6 taquitos

1½ cups shredded cooked chicken
1½ cups shredded Mexican-style cheese
¼ cup your favorite salsa
6 (8-inch) flour tortillas
Cooking spray
Sour cream, for garnish (optional)
Salsa, for garnish (optional)
Nacho cheese, for garnish (optional)

1. Combine the chicken, cheese, and salsa in a medium bowl, mashing until it holds together.
2. Shape ¼ cup of the chicken mixture into a log and place in the center of a tortilla, then tightly roll it up, securing it with a toothpick. Repeat with the remaining filling and tortillas.
3. Place the crisping basket in the Foodi's inner pot, spray it with cooking spray, and place 3 taquitos in the basket. Add the small rack to the basket, spray the rack (and the top of the taquitos) with cooking spray, and add the other 3 taquitos. Spray the tops of the second taquito layer.
4. Drop the Crisping Lid and set to Air Crisp at 390°F (199°C) for 15 minutes, or until the taquitos are golden and crisp, rotating the positioning of the taquitos every 5 minutes. Lift the lid and carefully remove the taquitos from the Foodi. Allow them to cool slightly before serving with salsa, sour cream, or nacho cheese for dipping.

Gruyère Cheese Fondue

Prep time: 5 minutes | Cook time: 5 minutes | Serves 4

1 garlic clove, crushed
1½ cups dry white wine
1 tablespoon cornstarch
1 pound (454 g) Gruyère cheese, cubed
Toasted cubes of bread, for serving (optional)
Steamed and cooled broccoli florets, for serving (optional)
Roasted baby potatoes, for serving (optional)
Grapes, for serving (optional)
Strawberries, for serving (optional)

1. Rub the garlic all over the inside of the Foodi's inner pot and then discard.
2. Mix ½ cup of the wine with the cornstarch. Add the remaining wine to the Foodi's inner pot and set the Foodi to Sear/Saute on High. When the wine begins to simmer, after about 5 minutes, whisk in the cornstarch mixture and return the mixture to a simmer.
3. Slowly add small handfuls of the cheese, allowing it to melt and incorporate before adding the next handful, whisking constantly to prevent the cheese from clumping.
4. When all the cheese is added, allow the fondue to come to a boil, stirring often to prevent it from scorching, then transfer to a fondue pot. (If you want to serve it directly out of the Foodi, set it to Keep Warm so the cheese doesn't cool too much between dips.) Serve with your favorite fondue accoutrements.

Spicy Harissa

Prep time: 10 minutes | Cook time: 6 minutes | Makes 1 cup

2 ounces dried red chiles
4 garlic cloves, minced
1 tablespoon coriander seeds
2 teaspoons ground cumin
¼ cup peanut oil or vegetable oil
1 tablespoon tomato paste
1 teaspoon kosher salt
1 tablespoon fresh lemon juice

1. Use kitchen shears to snip off the stem ends from the chiles and carefully shake out the seeds, using a paring knife to slice away any bits of tough veining inside the chiles. Use the kitchen shears to cut the chiles into tiny pieces over the Foodi's inner pot. Add the garlic, coriander, cumin, oil, and ¾ cup water. Whisk in the tomato paste until it is dissolved.
2. Lock on the Pressure Lid, making sure the valve is set to Seal, and set to Pressure on High for 1 minute. When the timer reaches 0, turn off the Foodi and quick-release the pressure. Carefully remove the lid—be careful not to get steam in your eyes!
3. Set the Foodi to Sear/Saute on High and cook until thickened, about 5 minutes. Turn off the Foodi and stir in the salt and lemon juice. Transfer the harissa to a storage container and allow to cool to room temperature before covering and refrigerating. (The harissa can be refrigerated for up to 1 week.)

Patatas Bravas

Prep time: 10 minutes | Cook time: 31 minutes | Serves 4

2 tablespoons unsalted butter
2 teaspoons sweet paprika
1 teaspoon hot smoked paprika
1½ cups canned tomato sauce
1 tablespoon minced fresh oregano
1 tablespoon sugar
1 tablespoon hot sauce of choice
½ teaspoon onion powder
¼ teaspoon garlic powder
1 teaspoon kosher salt
1½ pounds (680 g) baby yellow potatoes
2 tablespoons peanut oil or vegetable oil

1. Add the butter and both paprikas to the Foodi's inner pot and set the Foodi to Sear/Saute on High. Stir until the butter is bubbling, about 3 minutes.
2. Add the tomato sauce, oregano, sugar, hot sauce, onion powder, garlic powder, and ½ teaspoon of the salt. Stir and cook until the mixture returns to a simmer, about 3 minutes. Pour the sauce from the pot into a heat-safe mixing bowl and set aside.
3. Add the potatoes to the inner pot along with the oil and the remaining ½ teaspoon salt. Stir to coat the potatoes with the oil and then transfer them to the Crisping Basket. Set the basket into the inner pot, drop the Crisping Lid, and set the Foodi to Air Crisp at 390°F (199°C) for 25 minutes, or until the potatoes are crisp and browned. Serve hot with the sauce.

Ultimate Layered Nachos

Prep time: 5 minutes | Cook time: 18 minutes | Serves 4

Cooking spray
8 (6-inch) corn tortillas, cut into sixths (like a pie)
Kosher salt
8 ounces (227 g) Mexican-style cheese, shredded
Refried Black Beans, for garnish (optional)
Sliced pickled jalapeños, for garnish (optional)
Diced red onion, for garnish (optional)
Pitted and sliced black olives, for garnish (optional)
Guacamole, for garnish (optional)
Sour cream, for garnish (optional)
Cilantro, for garnish (optional)
Salsa, for garnish (optional)

Spray the crisping basket with cooking spray, add the tortillas to the basket, and place in the Foodi's inner pot. Spray the tortillas liberally with cooking spray. Drop the Crisping Lid and set to Air Crisp at 390°F (199°C) for 15 minutes, or until the tortillas are brown and crispy.

Lift the lid and season the chips with salt. Remove the crisping basket and spray the bottom and sides of the Foodi's inner pot with cooking spray. Add a handful of cheese to the pot, then a handful of the chips, another handful of cheese, another handful of chips, and so on, making the last layer cheese.

Drop the Crisping Lid and set the Foodi to Bake/Roast at 375°F (190°C) for 3 minutes, or until cheese is melted throughout.

Lift the lid and carefully remove the inner pot from the Foodi. Flip the chips out and onto a platter. Add your choice of toppings and serve with plenty of salsa and your fave nacho accoutrements.

Pão de Queijo

Prep time: 10 minutes | Cook time: 20 minutes | Makes 8 large rolls

1¼ cups whole milk
6 tablespoons vegetable oil
2 teaspoons kosher salt
4 cups tapioca flour
2 large eggs
1½ cups finely grated Pecorino cheese
1 cup packaged shredded Mozzarella (not fresh)
Cooking spray

1. Place the milk, ½ cup water, the oil, and salt in the Foodi's inner pot. Set the Foodi to Sear/Saute on High and cook until the liquid is boiling, about 5 minutes.
2. Place the tapioca flour in a large bowl. Using a silicone spatula, slowly beat the hot milk mixture into the tapioca flour until it is super sticky, like lumpy glue. Don't be scared. Add 2 of the eggs to the batter, one at a time, followed by the cheeses, beating until the batter is well combined.
3. Spray the Foodi's inner pot with cooking spray. Drop the Crisping Lid and set the Foodi to Bake/Roast at 375°F (190°C) for 5 minutes to preheat.
4. Lift the lid. Spray a ¼-cup measuring cup with cooking spray, and use it to place 4 scoops of batter into the inner pot, spacing them far enough apart so they don't touch. Drop the Crisping Lid and set the Foodi to Bake/Roast at 375°F (190°C) for 10 minutes, or until the rolls are browned. Lift the lid and transfer the rolls to a plate. Continue baking in batches until all the dough is used up. The extra rolls can be rewarmed using the Air Crisp function at 390°F (199°C) for 5 to 10 minutes.

Golden Brown Potato Chips

Prep time: 5 minutes | Cook time: 14 minutes | Serves 2

1 large russet potato, peeled
Cooking spray
Kosher salt, to taste

1. Fill a medium bowl with water and use a vegetable peeler to shave thin slices off the potato, adding them to the water as you peel (so they don't discolor). Let the slices soak at least 20 minutes and up to 1 hour, then drain the potato slices and pat them dry.
2. Spray the crisping basket with cooking spray, add the potatoes to the basket, and place the basket in the Foodi's inner pot. Spray the potatoes liberally with cooking spray, tossing them around to ensure the spray gets on every slice.
3. Drop the Crisping Lid and set to Air Crisp at 390°F (199°C) for 14 to 18 minutes (14 minutes for golden brown chips and 18 minutes for darker, earthier chips), until golden brown. Lift the lid and toss the chips often while cooking. Lift the lid when finished and season the chips with salt while hot. Serve warm or at room temperature.

Crispy Fries

Prep time: 5 minutes | Cook time: 40 minutes | Serves 2

3 large russet potatoes
2 teaspoons kosher salt, plus more as needed
Cooking spray

1. Place the potatoes in the Foodi's crisping basket and set the basket into the Foodi's inner pot. Fill the pot with water to reach the maximum fill line. Then remove the potatoes, one at a time, to peel them before returning them to the water. Once the potatoes are peeled, put one on a cutting board and cut it into ½-inch fries (thicker than McDonald's, about the size of Wendy's). Return the cut potato to the water and repeat with the remaining 2 potatoes (keeping the potatoes in water prevents them from turning brown).
2. Reserve ½ cup of the water from the inner pot and drain the potatoes. Return the reserved ½ cup water to the potatoes in the Foodi's inner pot and add the salt. Lock on the Pressure Lid, making sure the valve is set to Seal, and set to Pressure on High for 0 minutes. When the timer reaches 0, quick-release the pressure and carefully remove the lid. Transfer the potatoes to a kitchen towel–lined baking sheet and blot them dry with another kitchen towel.
3. Spray the potatoes heavily with cooking spray, tossing gently to evenly coat them. Add them to the crisping basket, insert the basket into the Foodi inner pot, drop the Crisping Lid, and set the Foodi to Air Crisp at 275°F (135°C) for 10 minutes, or until the fries are limp and pale.
4. Lift the lid and spray the fries with more oil. Drop the Crisping Lid again and set the Foodi to Air Crisp at 400°F (205°C) for 30 minutes, or until the fries are browned and crisp. Lift the lid and sprinkle with more salt if you like, then serve hot.

Dried Watermelon Jerky

Prep time: 5 minutes | Cook time: 12 hours | Makes ½ cup

1 cup seedless watermelon (1-inch) cubes

1. Arrange the watermelon cubes in a single layer in the Cook & Crisp™ Basket. Place the basket in the pot and close the Crisping Lid.
2. Press Dehydrate, set the temperature to 135°F (57°C), and set the time to 12 hours. Select Start/Stop to begin.
3. When dehydrating is complete, remove the basket from the pot and transfer the jerky to an airtight container.

Dehydrated Mango

Prep time: 5 minutes | Cook time: 8 hours | Serves 2

½ mango, peeled, pitted, and cut into ⅜-inch slices

1. Arrange the mango slices flat in a single layer in the Cook & Crisp™ Basket. Place in the pot and close the Crisping Lid.
2. Press Dehydrate, set the temperature to 135°F (57°C), and set the time to 8 hours. Select Start/Stop to begin.
3. When dehydrating is complete, remove the basket from the pot and transfer the mango slices to an airtight container.

Dried Beet Chips

Prep time: 5 minutes | Cook time: 8 hours | Makes ½ cup

½ beet, peeled and cut into ⅛-inch slices

1. Arrange the beet slices flat in a single layer in the Cook & Crisp™ Basket. Place in the pot and close the Crisping Lid.
2. Press Dehydrate, set the temperature to 135°F (57°C), and set the time to 8 hours. Select Start/Stop to begin.
3. When dehydrating is complete, remove the basket from the pot and transfer the beet chips to an airtight container.

Candied Maple Bacon

Prep time: 5 minutes | Cook time: 20 minutes | Makes 12 slices

½ cup maple syrup
¼ cup brown sugar
Nonstick cooking spray
1 pound (454 g) (454 g) thick-cut bacon

1. Place the Reversible Rack in the pot. Close the Crisping Lid. Preheat the unit by selecting Air Crisp, setting the temperature to 400°F (205°C), and setting the time to 5 minutes.
2. Meanwhile, in a small mixing bowl, mix together the maple syrup and brown sugar.
3. Once the Ninja Foodi has preheated, carefully line the Reversible Rack with aluminum foil. Spray the foil with cooking spray.
4. Arrange 4 to 6 slices of bacon on the rack in a single layer. Brush them with the maple syrup mixture.
5. Close the Crisping Lid. Select Air Crisp and set the temperature to 400°F (205°C). Set the time to 10 minutes, then select Start/Stop to begin.
6. After 10 minutes, flip the bacon and brush with more maple syrup mixture. Close the Crisping Lid, select Air Crisp, set the temperature to 400°F (205°C), and set the time to 10 minutes. Select Start/Stop to begin.
7. Cooking is complete when your desired crispiness is reached. Remove the bacon from the Reversible Rack and transfer to a cooling rack for 10 minutes. Repeat steps 4 through 6 with the remaining bacon.

Spicy Ranch Chicken Wings

Prep time: 10 minutes | Cook time: 20 minutes | Serves 4

½ cup water
½ cup hot pepper sauce
2 tablespoons unsalted butter, melted
1½ tablespoons apple cider vinegar
2 pounds (907 g) frozen chicken wings
½ (1-ounce / 28-g) envelope ranch salad dressing mix
½ teaspoon paprika
Nonstick cooking spray

1. Pour the water, hot pepper sauce, butter, and vinegar into the pot. Place the wings in the Cook & Crisp™ Basket and place the basket in the pot. Assemble the Pressure Lid, making sure the pressure release valve is in the Seal position.
2. Select Pressure and set to High. Set the time to 5 minutes. Select Start/Stop to begin.
3. When pressure cooking is complete, quick release the pressure by turning the pressure release valve to the Vent position. Carefully remove the lid when the unit has finished releasing pressure.
4. Sprinkle the chicken wings with the dressing mix and paprika. Coat with cooking spray.
5. Close the Crisping Lid. Select Air Crisp, set the temperature to 375°F (190°C), and set the time to 15 minutes. Select Start/Stop to begin.
6. After 7 minutes, open the Crisping Lid, then lift the basket and shake the wings. Coat with cooking spray. Lower the basket back into the pot and close the lid to resume cooking until the wings reach your desired crispiness.

Breaded Parmesan Arancini

Prep time: 10 minutes | Cook time: 28 minutes | Serves 6

½ cup extra-virgin olive oil, plus 1 tablespoon
1 small yellow onion, diced
2 garlic cloves, minced
5 cups chicken broth
½ cup white wine
2 cups arborio rice
1½ cups grated Parmesan cheese, plus more for garnish
1 cup frozen peas
1 teaspoon sea salt
1 teaspoon freshly ground black pepper
2 cups fresh bread crumbs
2 large eggs

1. Select Sear/Sauté and set to Medium High. Select Start/Stop to begin. Allow the pot to preheat for 5 minutes.
2. Add 1 tablespoon of oil and the onion to the preheated pot. Cook until soft and translucent, stirring occasionally. Add the garlic and cook for 1 minute.
3. Add the broth, wine, and rice to the pot; stir to incorporate. Assemble the Pressure Lid, making sure the pressure release valve is in the Seal position.
4. Select Pressure and set to High. Set the time to 7 minutes. Press Start/Stop to begin.
5. When pressure cooking is complete, allow pressure to naturally release for 10 minutes, then quick release any remaining pressure by turning the pressure release valve to the Vent position. Carefully remove the lid when the unit has finished releasing pressure.
6. Add the Parmesan cheese, frozen peas, salt, and pepper. Stir vigorously until the rice begins to thicken. Transfer the risotto to a large mixing bowl and let cool.
7. Meanwhile, clean the pot. In a medium mixing bowl, stir together the bread crumbs and the remaining ½ cup of olive oil. In a separate mixing bowl, lightly beat the eggs.
8. Divide the risotto into 12 equal portions and form each one into a ball. Dip each risotto ball in the beaten eggs, then coat in the bread crumb mixture.
9. Arrange half of the arancini in the Cook & Crisp™ Basket in a single layer.
10. Close the Crisping Lid. Select Air Crisp, set the temperature to 400°F (205°C), and set the time to 10 minutes. Select Start/Stop to begin.
11. Repeat steps 9 and 10 to cook the remaining arancini.

Chapter 12: Desserts and Breads

Classic Dinner Rolls

Prep time: 10 minutes | Cook time: 15 minutes | Serves 6

4 tablespoons plus 1 tablespoon cold unsalted butter, plus more at room temperature for greasing
3½ cups all-purpose flour
1 cup whole milk
1 tablespoon extra-virgin olive oil
1 tablespoon coconut oil
½ package active dry yeast
Nonstick cooking spray
¼ teaspoon sea salt

1. In a large mixing bowl, use a pastry cutter or two forks to cut the butter into the flour, breaking up the cold butter into little pieces, until the mixture resembles coarse cornmeal.
2. Put the milk, olive oil, and coconut oil in the pot. Select Sear/Sauté and set to Medium High. Select Start/Stop to begin. Bring to a gentle simmer, about 5 minutes, then press the Start/Stop button to turn off Sear/Sauté.
3. Pour the milk mixture into the flour mixture and stir in the yeast. Mix together until a dough forms.
4. Transfer the dough to a clean work surface dusted with flour and knead it by hand for about 5 minutes.
5. Wipe out the pot, then lightly grease it with butter. Place the kneaded dough in the pot. Cover the dough with plastic wrap and let it rise in a warm place until doubled in size, about 1 hour. Knead the dough again for about 5 minutes, then let it rise a second time for 30 minutes.
6. Turn the dough out onto a floured work surface and divide it evenly into 6 or 12 pieces. Shape each piece into a small ball and place in the Multi-Purpose Pan or an 8-inch baking pan greased with nonstick cooking spray. The rolls should be touching.
7. Close the Crisping Lid. Preheat the unit by selecting Bake/Roast, setting the temperature to 360°F (182°C), and setting the time to 5 minutes. Select Start/Stop to begin.
8. Place the pan on the Reversible Rack, making sure the rack is in the lower position. Place the rack with the pan in the preheated pot.
9. Sprinkle the rolls with the salt, then close the Crisping Lid. Select Bake/Roast, set the temperature to 360°F (182°C), and set the time to 15 minutes. Select Start/Stop to begin.
10. When cooking is complete, allow the rolls to cool, then pull apart and serve.

Garlicky Bread

Prep time: 5 minutes | Cook time: 8 minutes | Serves 8

2 eggs
¼ cup milk
½ French baguette, cut into 8 pieces
2 tablespoons extra-virgin olive oil
2 teaspoons garlic purée
1 teaspoon dried parsley

1. Place the Reversible Rack in the pot and close the Crisping Lid. Preheat the pot by selecting Air Crisp, setting the temperature to 375°F (190°C), and setting the time to 3 minutes. Press Start/Stop to begin.
2. Meanwhile, in a large mixing bowl, whisk together the eggs and milk. Place the bread in the egg mixture and coat each piece on both sides. In a small mixing bowl, mix together the olive oil, garlic purée, and parsley.
3. Place 4 pieces of bread on the preheated rack. Brush the top of each piece with the garlic mixture.
4. Close the Crisping Lid. Select Air Crisp, set the temperature to 375°F (190°C), and set the time to 2 minutes. Press Start/Stop to begin.
5. Open the lid and flip the bread. Brush with more of the garlic mixture. Close the lid and select Air Crisp, set the temperature to 375°F (190°C), and set the time to 2 minutes. Press Start/Stop to begin.
6. When cooking is complete, remove the garlic bread from the pot and transfer to a plate.
7. Repeat steps 3 through 6 with the remaining pieces of bread. Serve immediately while the garlic bread is warm.

Baked Zucchini Bread

Prep time: 10 minutes | Cook time: 40 minutes | Serves 6

2 eggs
8 tablespoons unsalted butter, melted
1⅓ cups sugar
1 teaspoon vanilla extract
1 teaspoon ground cinnamon
⅛ teaspoon ground nutmeg
½ teaspoon baking soda
¼ teaspoon baking powder
½ teaspoon sea salt
1½ cups all-purpose flour
1 cup grated zucchini
Nonstick cooking spray

1. Close the Crisping Lid. Preheat the unit by selecting Bake/Roast, setting the temperature to 325ºF (163ºC), and setting the time to 5 minutes. Select Start/Stop to begin.
2. Meanwhile, in a large mixing bowl, combine the eggs, butter, sugar, and vanilla. Add the cinnamon, nutmeg, baking soda, baking powder, and salt and stir to combine. Add the flour, a little at a time, stirring until combined.
3. Wring out the excess water from the zucchini and fold it into the batter.
4. Grease the Loaf Pan or another loaf pan with cooking spray and pour in the batter. Place the pan on the Reversible Rack, making sure the rack is in the lower position. Place the rack in the pot.
5. Close the Crisping Lid. Select Bake/Roast, set the temperature to 325ºF (163ºC), and set the time to 40 minutes. Select Start/Stop to begin.
6. When cooking is complete, remove the loaf pan from the pot and place it on a cooling rack. Allow the zucchini bread to cool for 30 minutes before slicing and serving.

Cinnamon-Sugar Dough Balls

Prep time: 10 minutes | Cook time: 10 minutes | Serves 4

⅓ cup all-purpose flour
⅓ cup whole-wheat flour
3 tablespoons sugar, divided
½ teaspoon baking powder
¼ teaspoon ground cinnamon, plus ½ tablespoon
¼ teaspoon sea salt
2 tablespoons cold unsalted butter, cut into small pieces
¼ cup plus 1½ tablespoons whole milk
Nonstick cooking spray

1. Mix together the all-purpose flour, whole-wheat flour, 1 tablespoon of sugar, the baking powder, ¼ teaspoon of cinnamon, and the salt in a medium mixing bowl.
2. Use a pastry cutter or two forks to cut in the butter, breaking it up into little pieces until the mixture resembles coarse cornmeal. Add the milk and continue to mix together until the dough forms a ball.
3. Place the dough on a floured work surface and knead it until a smooth ball forms, about 30 seconds. Divide the dough into 8 equal pieces and roll each piece into a ball.
4. Place the Cook & Crisp™ Basket in the pot. Close the Crisping Lid. Preheat the unit by selecting Air Crisp, setting the temperature to 350ºF (180ºC), and setting the time to 3 minutes. Press Start/Stop to begin.
5. Coat the preheated Cook & Crisp™ Basket with cooking spray. Place the dough balls in the basket, leaving room between each, and spray them with cooking spray.
6. Close the Crisping Lid. Select Air Crisp, set the temperature to 350ºF (180ºC), and set the time to 10 minutes. Press Start/Stop to begin.
7. In a medium mixing bowl, combine the remaining 2 tablespoons of sugar and ½ tablespoon of cinnamon.
8. When cooking is complete, toss the dough balls with the cinnamon sugar. Serve immediately.

Apple Pies

Prep time: 10 minutes | Cook time: 24 minutes | Serves 8

2 apples, peeled, cored, and diced
Juice of 1 lemon
3 tablespoons sugar
1 teaspoon vanilla extract
¼ teaspoon sea salt
1 teaspoon cornstarch
1 package refrigerated piecrusts, at room temperature
Nonstick cooking spray

1. In a large mixing bowl, combine the apples, lemon juice, sugar, vanilla, and salt. Let the mixture stand for 10 minutes, then drain, reserving 1 tablespoon of the liquid.
2. In a small mixing bowl or glass, whisk the cornstarch into the reserved 1 tablespoon of liquid. Stir this mixture into the apple mixture.
3. Place the Cook & Crisp™ Basket in the pot and close the Crisping Lid. Preheat the unit by selecting Air Crisp, setting the temperature to 350°F (180°C), and setting the time to 5 minutes. Press Start/Stop to begin.
4. Place the piecrusts on a lightly floured surface and cut them into 8 (4-inch-diameter) circles. Spoon 1 tablespoon of apple mixture into the center of each dough circle, leaving a ½-inch border. Brush the edges of the dough with water. Fold the dough over the filling and press the edges with a fork to seal.
5. Cut 3 small slits in the top of each pie. Coat each pie well with cooking spray and arrange 4 pies in the preheated Cook & Crisp™ Basket in a single layer.
6. Close the Crisping Lid. Select Air Crisp, set the temperature to 350°F (180°C), and set the time to 12 minutes. Press Start/Stop to begin. Once cooking is complete, check for your desired crispiness, then place the pies on a wire rack to cool.
7. Repeat steps 5 and 6 to cook the remaining hand pies.

Vanilla Icing Strawberry Toaster Pastries

Prep time: 5 minutes | Cook time: 20 minutes | Serves 4

1 refrigerated piecrust, at room temperature
¼ cup Simple Strawberry Jam
Nonstick cooking spray
Vanilla icing, for frosting
Rainbow sprinkles, for topping

1. Place the Cook & Crisp™ Basket in the pot and close the Crisping Lid. Preheat the unit by selecting Air Crisp, setting the temperature to 350°F (180°C), and setting the time to 5 minutes.
2. On a lightly floured surface, roll out the piecrust into a large rectangle. Cut the dough into 8 rectangles.
3. Spoon 1 tablespoon of strawberry jam into the center of each of 4 dough rectangles, leaving a ½-inch border. Brush the edges of the filled dough rectangles with water. Top each with one of the remaining 4 dough rectangles. Press the edges with a fork to seal.
4. Carefully place the pastries in the preheated basket. Coat each pastry well with cooking spray and arrange 2 pastries in the Cook & Crisp™ Basket in a single layer.
5. Close the Crisping Lid and select Air Crisp, set the temperature to 350°F (180°C), and set the time to 10 minutes. Press Start/Stop to begin. Once cooking is complete, check for your desired crispiness, then place the pastries on a wire rack to cool. Repeat steps 1 through 5 with the remaining 2 pastries.
6. Frost the pastries with vanilla icing, then top with sprinkles

S'Mores

Prep time: 5 minutes | Cook time: 4 minutes | Serves 4

4 graham crackers
4 marshmallows
2 (1½-ounce / 42.5-g) chocolate bars

1. Place the Cook & Crisp™ Basket in the pot and close the Crisping Lid. Preheat the unit by selecting Air Crisp, setting the temperature to 350°F (180°C), and setting the time to 5 minutes. Press Start/Stop to begin.
2. Break a graham cracker in half. Place half a chocolate bar on one half of the graham cracker. Add a marshmallow and top with the remaining graham cracker half to create a s'more. Repeat with the remaining ingredients to create 4 s'mores.
3. Using aluminum foil, wrap each s'more individually. Place all 4 foil-wrapped s'mores in the preheated Cook & Crisp™ Basket.
4. Close the Crisping Lid. Select Air Crisp, set the temperature to 350°F (180°C), and set the time to 4 minutes. Press Start/Stop to begin.
5. When cooking is complete, carefully unwrap the s'mores and serve.

Blackberry and Blueberry Crumble

Prep time: 10 minutes | Cook time: 20 minutes | Serves 6

1 (16-ounce / 454-g) package frozen blackberries

1 (16-ounce / 454-g) package frozen blueberries

2 tablespoons cornstarch

½ cup water, plus 1 tablespoon

1 teaspoon freshly squeezed lemon juice

5 tablespoons granulated sugar, divided

½ cup all-purpose flour

½ cup rolled oats

⅔ cup brown sugar

⅓ cup cold unsalted butter, cut into pieces

1 teaspoon ground cinnamon

1. Place the blackberries and blueberries in the Multi-Purpose Pan or a 1½-quart round ceramic baking dish.
2. In a small mixing bowl, stir together the cornstarch, 1 tablespoon of water, the lemon juice, and 3 tablespoons of granulated sugar. Pour this mixture over the fruit.
3. Place the pan on the Reversible Rack, making sure the rack is in the lower position. Cover the pan with aluminum foil. Pour the remaining ½ cup of water into the pot and add the rack with the pan to the pot. Assemble the Pressure Lid, making sure the pressure release valve is in the Seal position.
4. Select Pressure and set to High. Set the time to 10 minutes, then select Start/Stop to begin.
5. In a medium mixing bowl, combine the flour, oats, brown sugar, butter, cinnamon, and remaining 2 tablespoons of granulated sugar until a crumble forms.
6. When pressure cooking is complete, quick release the pressure by moving the pressure release valve to the Vent position. Carefully remove the lid when the pressure has finished releasing.
7. Remove the foil and stir the fruit mixture. Evenly spread the crumble topping over the fruit.
8. Close the Crisping Lid. Select Air Crisp, set the temperature to 400°F (205°C), and set the time to 10 minutes. Select Start/Stop to begin. Cook until the top is browned and the fruit is bubbling.
9. When cooking is complete, remove the rack with the pan from the pot and serve.

New York-Style Cheesecake

Prep time: 15 minutes | Cook time: 35 minutes | Serves 6

Nonstick cooking spray

1½ cups finely crushed graham crackers

4 tablespoons unsalted butter, melted

2 tablespoons granulated sugar

16 ounces (454 g) cream cheese, at room temperature

½ cup light brown sugar

¼ cup sour cream

1 tablespoon all-purpose flour

½ teaspoon sea salt

1½ teaspoons vanilla extract

2 eggs

1 cup water

1. Spray a 7-inch springform pan lightly with cooking spray. Cut a piece of parchment paper to fit the bottom of the pan and spray it with cooking spray. Cover the bottom of the pan tightly with aluminum foil so there are no air gaps.
2. In a medium mixing bowl, combine the graham cracker crumbs, butter, and granulated sugar. Press the mixture firmly into the bottom and up the side of the prepared pan.
3. Using a stand mixer or in a large bowl using an electric hand mixer, beat the cream cheese and brown sugar until combined. Add the sour cream and mix until smooth. Add the flour, salt, and vanilla, scraping down the side of the bowl as necessary.
4. Add the eggs and mix until smooth, being sure not to over-mix. Pour the cream cheese mixture into the prepared crust.
5. Pour the water into the pot. Place the springform pan on the Reversible Rack, making sure the rack is in the lower position. Place the rack in the pot.
6. Assemble the Pressure Lid, making sure the pressure release valve is in the Seal position. Select Pressure and set to High. Set the time to 35 minutes, then select Start/Stop to begin.
7. When pressure cooking is complete, allow the pressure to naturally release for 10 minutes, then quick release any remaining pressure by moving the pressure release valve to the Vent position. Carefully remove the lid when the pressure has finished releasing.
8. Remove the rack from the pot and let the cheesecake cool for 1 hour. Cover the cheesecake with foil and refrigerate to chill for at least 4 hours.

Chocolate Lava Cakes

Prep time: 10 minutes | Cook time: 20 minutes | Serves 4

Nonstick cooking spray
8 tablespoons (1 stick) unsalted butter, cut into pieces
¼ cup dark chocolate chips
¼ cup peanut butter chips
2 eggs
3 egg yolks
1¼ cups confectioners' sugar
1 teaspoon vanilla extract
½ cup all-purpose flour

1. Preheat the unit by selecting Bake/Roast, setting the temperature to 300°F (150°C), and setting the time to 5 minutes. Press Start/Stop to begin.
2. Meanwhile, grease 4 ramekins with cooking spray and set aside.
3. In a microwave-safe medium bowl, combine the butter, chocolate chips, and peanut butter chips. Microwave on high until melted, checking and stirring every 15 to 20 seconds.
4. Add the eggs, egg yolks, confectioners' sugar, and vanilla to the chocolate mixture and whisk until smooth. Stir in the flour a little at a time until combined and incorporated.
5. Divide the batter among the ramekins and wrap each with aluminum foil. Place the ramekins on the Reversible Rack, making sure the rack is in the lower position. Place the rack in the pot.
6. Close the Crisping Lid. Select Bake/Roast, set the temperature to 300°F (150°C), and set the time to 20 minutes. Select Start/Stop to begin.
7. When cooking is complete, remove the rack from the pot. Remove the foil and allow the ramekins to cool for 1 to 2 minutes.
8. Invert the lava cakes onto a plate and serve immediately.

Egg and Ham Pockets

Prep time: 10 minutes | Cook time: 29 minutes | Serves 4

5 large eggs, divided
1 tablespoon extra-virgin olive oil
Sea salt
Freshly ground black pepper
1 (8-ounce / 227-g) tube refrigerated crescent rolls
4 ounces (113 g) thinly sliced ham
1 cup shredded Cheddar cheese
Cooking spray

1. Select SEAR/SAUTÉ and set to MD:HI. Select START/STOP and let preheat for 5 minutes.
2. Lightly whisk 4 eggs in a medium bowl.
3. Once unit has preheated, add the oil and beaten eggs. Season with salt and pepper. Whisk the eggs until they just begin to set, cooking until soft and translucent, 3 to 5 minutes. Remove the eggs from the pot and set aside.
4. In a small bowl, whisk the remaining egg.
5. Remove the crescent rolls from the tube and divide them into 4 rectangles. Gently roll out each rectangle until it is 6-by-4 inches. Top one half of each rectangle with ham, cheese, and scrambled eggs, leaving about a ½-inch border.
6. Brush the edges of the filled dough with water. Fold over the rectangle and press firmly to seal. Brush the top of each pocket with the egg.
7. Place Cook & Crisp Basket in pot. Coat 2 pastries well on both sides with cooking spray and arrange them in the basket in a single layer. Close crisping lid.
8. Select AIR CRISP, set temperature to 375°F (191°C), and set time to 12 minutes. Select START/STOP to begin.
9. After 6 minutes, open lid, remove basket, and use silicone-tipped tongs to flip the breakfast pockets. Lower basket back into pot and close lid to continue cooking, until golden brown.
10. When cooking is complete, check for your desired crispiness. Place the pockets on a wire rack to cool. Repeat steps 7, 8, and 9 with the remaining 2 pastries.

Hazelnut and Chocolate Toaster Pastries

Prep time: 15 minutes | Cook time: 14 minutes | Serves 4

All-purpose flour
1 refrigerated piecrust, at room temperature
¼ cup chocolate hazelnut spread
Cooking spray
Vanilla icing, for frosting
Chocolate sprinkles, for topping

1. Place the Cook & Crisp Basket in the pot and close crisping lid. Select AIR CRISP, set temperature to 350°F (177°C), and set time to 5 minutes. Press START/STOP to preheat.
2. On a lightly floured surface, roll out the piecrust into a large rectangle. Cut the dough into 8 rectangles.
3. Spoon 1 tablespoon of chocolate hazelnut spread into the center of each of 4 dough rectangles, leaving a ½-inch border. Brush the edges of the filled dough rectangles with water. Top each with one of the remaining 4 dough rectangles. Press the edges with a fork to seal.
4. Once unit is preheated, carefully place two pastries in the basket in a single layer. Coat each pastry well with cooking spray. Close crisping lid.
5. Select AIR CRISP, set temperature to 350°F (177°C), and set time to 7 minutes. Select START/STOP to begin.
6. Once cooking is complete, check for your desired crispiness. Place the pastries on a wire rack to cool. Repeat steps 4 and 5 with the remaining 2 pastries.
7. Frost the pastries with vanilla icing, then top with sprinkles.

Simple Cinnamon Donuts

Prep time: 10 minutes | Cook time: 10 minutes | Serves 4

⅔ cup all-purpose flour, plus additional for dusting
3 tablespoons granulated sugar, divided
½ teaspoon baking powder
¼ teaspoon, plus ½ tablespoon cinnamon
¼ teaspoon sea salt
2 tablespoons cold unsalted butter, cut into small pieces
¼ cup plus 1½ tablespoons whole milk
Cooking spray

1. In a medium bowl, mix together the flour, 1 tablespoon of sugar, baking powder, ¼ teaspoon of cinnamon, and salt.
2. Use a pastry cutter or two forks to cut in the butter, breaking it up into little pieces until the mixture resembles coarse cornmeal. Add the milk and continue to mix together until the dough forms a ball.
3. Place the dough on a lightly floured work surface and knead it until a smooth ball forms, about 30 seconds. Divide the dough into 8 equal pieces and roll each piece into a ball.
4. Place the Cook & Crisp Basket in the pot. Close crisping lid. Select AIR CRISP, set temperature to 350°F (177°C), and set time to 3 minutes. Press START/STOP to begin.
5. Once preheated, coat the basket with cooking spray. Place the dough balls in the basket, leaving room between each. Spray them with cooking spray. Close crisping lid.
6. Select AIR CRISP, set temperature to 350°F (177°C), and set time to 10 minutes. Press START/STOP to begin.
7. In a medium bowl, combine the remaining 2 tablespoons of sugar and ½ tablespoon of cinnamon.
8. When cooking is complete, open lid. Place the dough balls in the bowl with the cinnamon sugar and toss to coat. Serve immediately.

Banana and Chocolate Bundt Cake

Prep time: 15 minutes | Cook time: 40 minutes | Serves 8

2 cups all-purpose flour
1 teaspoon baking soda
¼ teaspoon cinnamon
¼ teaspoon sea salt
1 stick (½ cup) unsalted butter, at room temperature
½ cup dark brown sugar
¼ cup granulated sugar
2 eggs, beaten
1 teaspoon vanilla extract
3 ripe bananas, mashed
1 cup semisweet chocolate chips
Cooking spray

1. Close crisping lid. Select BAKE/ROAST, set temperature to 325°F (163°C), and set time to 5 minutes. Select START/STOP to begin preheating.
2. In a medium bowl, stir together the flour, baking soda, cinnamon, and salt.
3. In a large bowl, beat together the butter, brown sugar, and granulated sugar. Stir in the eggs, vanilla, and bananas.
4. Slowly add the dry mixture to wet mixture, stirring until just combined. Fold in chocolate chips.
5. Use cooking spray to grease the Ninja Tube Pan or a 7-inch Bundt pan. Pour the batter into the pan.
6. Once preheated, place pan on the Reversible Rack in the lower position. Close crisping lid.
7. Select BAKE/ROAST, set temperature to 325°F (163°C), and set time to 40 minutes. Select START/STOP to begin.
8. After 30 minutes, open lid and check doneness by inserting a toothpick into the cake. If it comes out clean, it is done. If not, continue baking until done.
9. When cooking is complete, remove pan from pot and place on a cooling rack for 30 minutes before serving.

Breakfast Cinnamon Monkey Bread

Prep time: 5 minutes | Cook time: 20 minutes | Serves 8

¼ cup whole milk
1 teaspoon vanilla extract
½ teaspoon cinnamon
Cooking spray
2 (12½-ounce / 354-g) tubes refrigerated cinnamon rolls with icing, quartered

1. In a medium bowl, whisk together the eggs, milk, vanilla, and cinnamon.
2. Lightly coat the pot with cooking spray, then place the cinnamon roll pieces in the pot. Pour the egg mixture over the dough. Close crisping lid.
3. Select BAKE/ROAST, set temperature to 350°F (177°C), and set time to 20 minutes. Select START/STOP to begin.
4. When cooking is complete, remove pot from unit and place it on a heat-resistant surface. Remove lid. Let cool for 5 minutes, then top with the icing from the cinnamon rolls and serve.

Super Cheesy Pull Apart Bread

Prep time: 10 minutes | Cook time: 25 minutes | Serves 6

½ pound (227 g) store-bought pizza dough
3 tablespoons unsalted butter, melted
4 garlic cloves, minced
¼ cup shredded Parmesan cheese
¼ cup shredded Mozzarella cheese
¼ cup minced parsley
½ teaspoon kosher salt
½ teaspoon garlic powder
Cooking spray
Marinara sauce, for serving

1. Cut the pizza dough into 1-inch cubes. Roll each cube into a ball. Place the dough balls in a large bowl. Add the butter, garlic, Parmesan cheese, Mozzarella cheese, parsley, salt, and garlic powder. Toss, ensuring everything is evenly coated and mixed. Set aside.
2. Close crisping lid. Select BAKE/ROAST, set temperature to 325°F (163°C), and set time to 30 minutes. Select START/STOP to begin. Let preheat for 5 minutes.
3. Coat the Ninja Multi-Purpose Pan with cooking spray. Place the dough balls in the pan and place pan on Reversible Rack, making sure it is in the lower position.
4. Once unit has preheated, open lid and insert the rack in pot. Close lid and cook for 25 minutes.
5. Once cooking is complete, open lid and let the bread cool slightly. Serve with marinara sauce for dipping.

Cookie Pizza

Prep time: 10 minutes | Cook time: 35 minutes | Serves 6

22 ounces (624 g) premade sugar cookie dough
5 tablespoons unsalted butter, at room temperature
1 (8-ounce / 227-g) package cream cheese, at room temperature
2 cups confectioners' sugar
1 teaspoon vanilla extract

1. Select BAKE/ROAST, set temperature to 325°F (163°C), and set time to 40 minutes. Select START/STOP to begin. Let preheat for 5 minutes.
2. Press the cookie dough into the Ninja Multi-Purpose Pan in an even layer.
3. Once unit is preheated, place the pan on the Reversible Rack and place rack in the pot. Close crisping lid and cook for 35 minutes.
4. Once cooking is complete, remove the pan from the pot. Let cool in the refrigerator for 30 minutes.
5. In a large bowl, whisk together the butter, cream cheese, confectioners' sugar, and vanilla.
6. Once the cookie is chilled, carefully remove it from the pan. Using a spatula, spread the cream cheese mixture over cookie. Chill in the refrigerator for another 30 minutes.
7. Decorate with toppings of choice, such as sliced strawberries, raspberries, blueberries, blackberries, sliced kiwi, sliced mango, or sliced pineapple. Cut and serve.

Peanut Butter and Chocolate Bars

Prep time: 5 minutes | Cook time: 10 minutes | Serves 12

1 cup light corn syrup
1 cup granulated sugar
1 teaspoon vanilla extract
1 (10-ounce / 283-g) bag mini marshmallows
1 cup crunchy peanut butter
1 (9-ounce / 255-g) bag potato chips with ridges, slightly crushed
1 cup pretzels, slightly crushed
1 (10-ounce / 283-g) bag hard-shelled candy-coated chocolates

1. Select SEAR/SAUTÉ and set temperature to MD:HI. Select START/STOP to begin. Let preheat for 5 minutes.
2. Add the corn syrup, sugar, and vanilla and stir until the sugar is melted.
3. Add the marshmallows and peanut butter and stir until the marshmallows are melted.
4. Add the potato chips and pretzels and stir until everything is evenly coated in the marshmallow mixture.
5. Pour the mixture into a 9-by-13-inch pan and place the chocolate candies on top, slightly pressing them in. Let cool, then cut into squares and serve.

Arborio Rice and Coconut Milk Pudding

Prep time: 5 minutes | Cook time: 8 minutes | Serves 6

¾ cup arborio rice
1 (15-ounce / 425-g) can unsweetened full-fat coconut milk
1 cup milk
1 cup water
¾ cup granulated sugar
½ teaspoon vanilla extract

1. Rinse the rice under cold running water in a fine-mesh strainer.
2. Place the rice, coconut milk, milk, water, sugar, and vanilla in the pot and stir. Assemble pressure lid, making sure the pressure release valve is in the SEAL position.
3. Select PRESSURE and set to HI. Set time to 8 minutes. Select START/STOP to begin.
4. When pressure cooking is complete, allow pressure to naturally release for 10 minutes. After 10 minutes, quick release remaining pressure by moving the pressure release valve to the VENT position. Carefully remove lid when unit has finished releasing pressure.
5. Press a layer of plastic wrap directly on top of the rice (it should be touching) to prevent a skin from forming on top of the pudding. Let pudding cool to room temperature, then refrigerate overnight to set.

Cream Cheese Babka

Prep time: 25 minutes | Cook time: 30 minutes | Serves 8

For the Dough:
1 (31-ounce / 879-g) packet dry active yeast
¼ cup water, warmed to 110°F (43°C)
¼ cup, plus ¼ teaspoon granulated sugar, divided
2 cups all-purpose flour
2 large eggs, divided
½ teaspoon kosher salt
3 tablespoons unsalted butter, at room temperature
¼ cup milk

For the Filling:
8 ounces (227 g) cream cheese
¼ cup granulated sugar
1 tablespoon sour cream
1 tablespoon all-purpose flour
½ teaspoon vanilla extract
Zest of 1 lemon
Cooking spray
All-purpose flour, for dusting
3 tablespoons water

To Make the Dough

1. In a small bowl, combine the yeast, warm water, and ¼ teaspoon of sugar. Let sit 10 minutes until foamy.
2. Place the flour, yeast mixture, remaining ¼ cup of sugar, 1 egg, salt, butter, and milk into the bowl of stand mixer. Using the dough hook attachment, mix on medium-low speed until the dough is smooth and elastic, about 10 minutes.

To Make the Filling

3. In a medium bowl, whisk together all the filling ingredients until smooth.

To Make the Babka

4. Spray the cooking pot with the cooking spray. Place the dough in the pot. Cover the dough with plastic wrap and let it rise in a warm place until doubled in size, about 1 hour.
5. Spray the Ninja Multi-Purpose Pan or 8-inch baking pan with cooking spray.
6. Turn the dough out onto a floured work surface. Punch down the dough. Using a rolling pin, roll it out into a 10-by-12-inch rectangle. Spread the cheese filling evenly on top of the dough. From the longer edge of the dough, roll it up like a jelly roll.
7. Cut the roll evenly into 12 pieces. Place each piece cut-side up in the prepared pan. The rolls should be touching but with visible gaps in between.
8. Beat the remaining egg with 1 teaspoon of water. Gently brush the tops of the rolls with this egg wash.
9. Place the remaining 3 tablespoons of water in the pot. Place the pan on the Reversible Rack, making sure the rack is in the lower position. Then place the rack with pan in the pot.
10. Select SEAR/SAUTÉ and set to LO. Select START/STOP to begin.
11. After 5 minutes, select START/STOP to turn off the heat. Let the rolls rise for another 15 minutes in the warm pot.
12. Remove the rack and pan from the pot. Close crisping lid.
13. Select BAKE/ROAST, set temperature to 325°F (163°C), and set time to 30 minutes. Select START/STOP to begin. Let preheat for 5 minutes.
14. Place the rack with pan in the pot. Close lid and cook for 25 minutes.
15. Once cooking is complete, open lid and remove rack and pan. Let the babka completely cool before serving.

Coconut, Almond, and Chocolate Bars

Prep time: 8 minutes | Cook time: 20 minutes | Serves 8

1¼ cups all-purpose flour
6 tablespoons unsalted butter, melted
2 tablespoons granulated sugar
½ cup unsweetened shredded coconut, divided
½ cup chopped almonds, divided
Cooking spray
1 package instant vanilla pudding
1 cup milk
1 cup heavy (whipping) cream
4 tablespoons finely chopped dark chocolate, divided

1. Select BAKE/ROAST, set temperature to 375°F (191°C), and set time to 15 minutes. Select START/STOP to begin. Let preheat for 5 minutes.
2. To make the crust, combine the flour, butter, sugar, ¼ cup of coconut, and ¼ cup of almonds in a large bowl and stir until a crumbly dough forms.
3. Grease the Ninja Multi-Purpose Pan or an 8-inch round baking dish with cooking spray. Place the dough in the pan and press it into an even layer covering the bottom.
4. Once unit has preheated, place pan on Reversible Rack, making sure the rack is in the lower position. Open lid and place rack in pot. Close crisping lid. Reduce temperature to 325°F (163°C).
5. Place remaining ¼ cup each of almonds and coconut in a Ninja Loaf Pan or any small loaf pan and set aside.
6. When cooking is complete, remove rack with pan and let cool for 10 minutes.
7. Quickly place the loaf pan with coconut and almonds in the bottom of the pot. Close crisping lid.
8. Select AIR CRISP, set temperature to 350°F (177°C), and set time to 10 minutes. Select START/STOP to begin.
9. While the nuts and coconut toast, whisk together the instant pudding with the milk, cream, and 3 tablespoons of chocolate.
10. After 5 minutes, open lid and stir the coconut and almonds. Close lid and continue cooking for another 5 minutes.
11. When cooking is complete, open lid and remove pan from pot. Add the almonds and coconut to the pudding. Stir until fully incorporated. Pour this in a smooth, even layer on top of the crust.
12. Refrigerate for about 10 minutes. Garnish with the remaining 1 tablespoon of chocolate, cut into wedges, and serve.

Peach, Rhubarb, and Raspberry Cobbler

Prep time: 20 minutes | Cook time: 40 minutes | Serves 6

1 cup all-purpose flour, divided
¾ cup granulated sugar
½ teaspoon kosher salt, divided
2½ cups diced fresh rhubarb
2½ cups fresh raspberries
2½ cups fresh peaches, peeled and
    sliced into ¾-inch pieces
Cooking spray
¾ cup brown sugar
½ cup oat flakes (oatmeal)
1 teaspoon cinnamon
Pinch ground nutmeg
6 tablespoons unsalted butter, sliced,
    at room temperature
½ cup chopped pecans or walnuts

1. Select BAKE/ROAST, set temperature to 400°F (204°C), and set time to 30 minutes. Select START/STOP to begin. Let preheat for 5 minutes.
2. In a large bowl, whisk together ¼ cup of flour, granulated sugar, and ¼ teaspoon of salt. Add the rhubarb, raspberries, and peach and mix until evenly coated.
3. Grease a Ninja Multi-Purpose Pan or a 1½-quart round ceramic baking dish with cooking spray. Add the fruit mixture to the pan.
4. Place pan on Reversible Rack, making sure the rack is in the lower position. Cover pan with aluminum foil.
5. Once unit has preheated, place rack in pot. Close crisping lid and adjust temperature to 375°F (191°C). Cook for 25 minutes.
6. In a medium bowl, combine the remaining ¾ cup of flour, brown sugar, oat flakes, cinnamon, remaining ¼ teaspoon of salt, nutmeg, butter, and pecans. Mix well.
7. When cooking is complete, open lid. Remove the foil and stir the fruit. Spread the topping evenly over the fruit. Close crisping lid.
8. Select BAKE/ROAST, set temperature to 400°F (204°C), and set time to 15 minutes. Select START/STOP to begin. Cook until the topping is browned and the fruit is bubbling.
9. When cooking is complete, remove rack with pan from pot and serve.

Cinnamon Apple Crisp

Prep time: 15 minutes | Cook time: 20 minutes | Serves 8

4 to 5 Granny Smith apples, peeled
    and cut into 1-inch cubes
1 tablespoon cornstarch
½ cup, plus 1 tablespoon water
2 teaspoons cinnamon, divided
1 teaspoon freshly squeezed lemon
    juice
5 tablespoons granulated sugar,
    divided
½ cup all-purpose flour
½ cup rolled oats
⅔ cup brown sugar
⅓ cup unsalted butter, melted

1. Place the apples in the Ninja Multi-Purpose Pan or a 1½-quart round ceramic baking dish.
2. In a small bowl, stir together the cornstarch, 1 tablespoon of water, 1 teaspoon of cinnamon, lemon juice, and 3 tablespoons of granulated sugar. Pour this mixture over the apples.
3. Place pan on Reversible Rack, making sure the rack is in the lower position. Cover the pan with aluminum foil. Pour the remaining ½ cup of water into the pot. Insert rack with pan in pot. Assemble pressure lid, making sure the pressure release valve is in the SEAL position.
4. Select PRESSURE and set to HI. Set time to 0 minutes. Select START/STOP to begin.
5. In a medium bowl, combine the flour, oats, brown sugar, butter, remaining 1 teaspoon of cinnamon, and remaining 2 tablespoons of granulated sugar until a crumble forms.
6. When pressure cooking is complete, allow the pressure to naturally release for 10 minutes. After 10 minutes, quick release remaining pressure by moving the pressure release valve to the VENT position. Carefully remove lid when pressure has finished releasing.
7. Remove the foil and stir the fruit mixture. Evenly spread the crumble topping over the apples. Close crisping lid.
8. Select AIR CRISP, set temperature to 375°F (191°C), and set time to 10 minutes. Select START/STOP to begin.
9. Cooking is complete when the top is browned and the fruit is bubbling. Remove rack with the pan from the pot and serve.

Chapter 13: Staples

Air Crisp Bacon

Prep time: 2 minutes | Cook time: 25 minutes | Makes 1 pound bacon

1 pound (454 g) bacon

1. Place Cook & Crisp Basket in pot. Place the bacon in the basket. Close crisping lid.
2. Select AIR CRISP, set temperature to 390°F (199°C), and set time to 25 minutes. Select START/STOP to begin.
3. After 8 minutes, open lid and stir to separate the bacon slides. Close lid and continue cooking. After another 8 minutes, open lid and separate the bacon to ensure the strips are cooked evenly. Close lid and continue cooking.
4. When cooking is complete, open lid and remove bacon. Serve.

Boiled Eggs

Prep time: 2 minutes | Cook time: 15 minutes | Makes 2 to 12 eggs

1 cup water
2 to 12 eggs

1. Place Reversible Rack in pot, making sure it is in the lower position. Add the water to the pot. Arrange the eggs on the rack in a single layer. Assemble pressure lid, making sure the pressure release valve is in the SEAL position.
2. Select PRESSURE and set to LO. Set time to 8 minutes. Select START/STOP to begin.
3. Prepare a large bowl of ice water.
4. When pressure cooking is complete, quick release the pressure by moving the pressure release valve to the VENT position. Carefully remove lid when unit has finished releasing pressure.
5. Using a slotted spoon, immediately transfer the eggs to the ice water bath and let cool for 5 minutes.

Strawberry Jam

Prep time: 10 minutes | Cook time: 42 minutes | Makes 1½ cups

2 pounds (907 g) strawberries, hulled and halved
Juice of 2 lemons
1½ cups granulated sugar

1. Place ingredients in the pot. Using a silicone potato masher, mash together to begin to release the strawberry juices. Assemble pressure lid, making sure the pressure release valve is in the SEAL position.
2. Select PRESSURE and set to HI. Set time to 1 minute. Select START/STOP to begin.
3. When pressure cooking is complete, allow pressure to naturally release for 10 minutes. After 10 minutes, quick release remaining pressure by moving the pressure release valve to the VENT position. Cover the vent with a cloth in case of any spraying. Carefully remove lid when pressure has finished releasing.
4. Select SEAR/SAUTÉ and set to MD:HI. Select START/STOP to begin. Let the jam reduce for 10 to 20 minutes, stirring frequently, until it tightens.
5. When cooking is complete, mash the strawberries together using the silicone potato masher for a textured jam, or transfer the strawberry mixture to a food processor and purée for a smooth consistency. Let the jam cool, pour it into a glass jar with a tight-fitting lid, and refrigerate for up to 2 weeks.

Maple Applesauce

Prep time: 5 minutes | Cook time: 8 minutes | Serves 6

6 apples, peeled, cored, and chopped
2 tablespoons maple syrup
1 tablespoon brown sugar
¼ cup apple cider
½ teaspoon cinnamon

1. Place all the ingredients in the pot. Assemble pressure lid, making sure the pressure release valve is in the SEAL position.
2. Select PRESSURE and set to HI. Set time for 8 minutes. Select START/STOP to begin.
3. When pressure cooking is complete, quick release the pressure by moving the pressure release valve to the VENT position. Carefully remove lid when unit has finished releasing pressure.
4. Use a wooden spoon to stir and break any remaining chunks of apple into smaller pieces.
5. Serve warm or cool to room temperature. Store in an airtight container in the refrigerator.

Fluffy Quinoa

Prep time: 1 minutes | Cook time: 8 minutes | Serves 6

1 cup quinoa, rinsed
1½ cups water

1. Place the quinoa and water in the pot. Assemble pressure lid, making sure the pressure release valve is in the SEAL position.
2. Select PRESSURE and set to HI. Set time for 8 minutes. Select START/STOP to begin.
3. When pressure cooking is complete, quick release the pressure by moving the pressure release valve to the VENT position. Carefully remove lid when unit has finished releasing pressure.
4. Serve hot, or store in an airtight container in the refrigerator to use throughout the week.

Herbed Chicken Wing Stock

Prep time: 5 minutes | Cook time: 45 minutes | Makes 3 quarts

3 pounds (1.4 kg) chicken wings
1 carrot, peeled
2 ribs celery, halved
1 large onion, halved
1 head garlic, halved
4 sprigs fresh thyme
2 bay leaves
1 teaspoon black peppercorns
1 teaspoon kosher salt

1. Place all the ingredients in the pot. Cover with enough water to reach the max fill line. Assemble pressure lid, making sure the pressure release valve is in the SEAL position.
2. Select PRESSURE and set to HI. Set time for 45 minutes. Select START/STOP to begin.
3. When pressure cooking is complete, allow pressure to naturally release for 25 minutes. After 25 minutes, quick release any remaining pressure by moving the pressure release valve to the VENT position. Carefully remove lid when unit has finished releasing pressure.
4. Strain the chicken stock through a fine-mesh sieve and discard the solid pieces. Use a spoon to skim any remaining fat from surface and discard. Let cool, then transfer to airtight containers. The stock can last in the freezer for up to 3 months.

Barbecue Baked Three Beans with Bacon

Prep time: 15 minutes | Cook time: 25 minutes | Serves 8

5 bacon strips, thinly sliced
2 green bell peppers, chopped
1 white onion, chopped
2 cups barbecue sauce
½ cup molasses
½ cup dark brown sugar
½ cup apple cider vinegar
1 (15-ounce / 425-g) can kidney beans, rinsed and drained
2 (15-ounce / 425-g) cans cannellini beans, rinsed and drained
1 (15-ounce / 425-g) can black beans, rinsed and drained

1. Select SEAR/SAUTÉ and set to HI. Select START/STOP to begin. Let preheat for 5 minutes.
2. Add the bacon and cook for 5 minutes, stirring frequently. Add the bell peppers and onion and cook for an additional 5 minutes, stirring occasionally.
3. Add the barbecue sauce, molasses, brown sugar, vinegar, kidney beans, cannellini beans, and black beans and stir well. Assemble pressure lid, making sure the pressure release valve is in the SEAL position.
4. Select PRESSURE and set to LO. Set time to 15 minutes. Select START/STOP to begin.
5. When pressure cooking is complete, quick release the pressure by moving the pressure release valve to the VENT position. Carefully remove lid when unit has finished releasing pressure.
6. Serve.

Simple Cooked Black Beans

Prep time: 2 minutes | Cook time: 25 minutes | Makes 6 cups

2 cups dry black beans
6 cups water

1. Place the beans and water in the pot. Assemble pressure lid, making sure the pressure release valve is in the SEAL position.
2. Select PRESSURE and set to HI. Set time for 25 minutes. Select START/STOP to begin.
3. When pressure cooking is complete, allow pressure to naturally release for 20 minutes. After 20 minutes, quick release remaining pressure by moving the pressure release valve to the VENT position. Carefully remove lid when unit has finished releasing pressure.
4. Drain the beans and store them in an airtight container until ready to use.

Appendix 1 Measurement Conversion Chart

MEASUREMENT CONVERSION CHART

VOLUME EQUIVALENTS(DRY)

US STANDARD	METRIC (APPROXIMATE)
1/8 teaspoon	0.5 mL
1/4 teaspoon	1 mL
1/2 teaspoon	2 mL
3/4 teaspoon	4 mL
1 teaspoon	5 mL
1 tablespoon	15 mL
1/4 cup	59 mL
1/2 cup	118 mL
3/4 cup	177 mL
1 cup	235 mL
2 cups	475 mL
3 cups	700 mL
4 cups	1 L

VOLUME EQUIVALENTS(LIQUID)

US STANDARD	US STANDARD (OUNCES)	METRIC (APPROXIMATE)
2 tablespoons	1 fl.oz.	30 mL
1/4 cup	2 fl.oz.	60 mL
1/2 cup	4 fl.oz.	120 mL
1 cup	8 fl.oz.	240 mL
1 1/2 cup	12 fl.oz.	355 mL
2 cups or 1 pint	16 fl.oz.	475 mL
4 cups or 1 quart	32 fl.oz.	1 L
1 gallon	128 fl.oz.	4 L

TEMPERATURES EQUIVALENTS

FAHRENHEIT(F)	CELSIUS(C) (APPROXIMATE)
225 °F	107 °C
250 °F	120 °C
275 °F	135 °C
300 °F	150 °C
325 °F	160 °C
350 °F	180 °C
375 °F	190 °C
400 °F	205 °C
425 °F	220 °C
450 °F	235 °C
475 °F	245 °C
500 °F	260 °C

WEIGHT EQUIVALENTS

US STANDARD	METRIC (APPROXIMATE)
1 ounce	28 g
2 ounces	57 g
5 ounces	142 g
10 ounces	284 g
15 ounces	425 g
16 ounces (1 pound)	455 g
1.5 pounds	680 g
2 pounds	907 g

Appendix 2 Air Fryer Cooking Chart

Air Fryer Cooking Chart

Beef

Item	Temp (°F)	Time (mins)	Item	Temp (°F)	Time (mins)
Beef Eye Round Roast (4 lbs.)	400 °F	45 to 55	Meatballs (1-inch)	370 °F	7
Burger Patty (4 oz.)	370 °F	16 to 20	Meatballs (3-inch)	380 °F	10
Filet Mignon (8 oz.)	400 °F	18	Ribeye, bone-in (1-inch, 8 oz)	400 °F	10 to 15
Flank Steak (1.5 lbs.)	400 °F	12	Sirloin steaks (1-inch, 12 oz)	400 °F	9 to 14
Flank Steak (2 lbs.)	400 °F	20 to 28			

Chicken

Item	Temp (°F)	Time (mins)	Item	Temp (°F)	Time (mins)
Breasts, bone in (1 ¼ lb.)	370 °F	25	Legs, bone-in (1 ¾ lb.)	380 °F	30
Breasts, boneless (4 oz)	380 °F	12	Thighs, boneless (1 ½ lb.)	380 °F	18 to 20
Drumsticks (2 ½ lb.)	370 °F	20	Wings (2 lb.)	400 °F	12
Game Hen (halved 2 lb.)	390 °F	20	Whole Chicken	360 °F	75
Thighs, bone-in (2 lb.)	380 °F	22	Tenders	360 °F	8 to 10

Pork & Lamb

Item	Temp (°F)	Time (mins)	Item	Temp (°F)	Time (mins)
Bacon (regular)	400 °F	5 to 7	Pork Tenderloin	370 °F	15
Bacon (thick cut)	400 °F	6 to 10	Sausages	380 °F	15
Pork Loin (2 lb.)	360 °F	55	Lamb Loin Chops (1-inch thick)	400 °F	8 to 12
Pork Chops, bone in (1-inch, 6.5 oz)	400 °F	12	Rack of Lamb (1.5 – 2 lb.)	380 °F	22

Fish & Seafood

Item	Temp (°F)	Time (mins)	Item	Temp (°F)	Time (mins)
Calamari (8 oz)	400 °F	4	Tuna Steak	400 °F	7 to 10
Fish Fillet (1-inch, 8 oz)	400 °F	10	Scallops	400 °F	5 to 7
Salmon, fillet (6 oz)	380 °F	12	Shrimp	400 °F	5
Swordfish steak	400 °F	10			

Air Fryer Cooking Chart

Vegetables					
INGREDIENT	AMOUNT	PREPARATION	OIL	TEMP	COOK TIME
Asparagus	2 bunches	Cut in half, trim stems	2 Tbsp	420°F	12-15 mins
Beets	1½ lbs	Peel, cut in ½-inch cubes	1Tbsp	390°F	28-30 mins
Bell peppers (for roasting)	4 peppers	Cut in quarters, remove seeds	1Tbsp	400°F	15-20 mins
Broccoli	1 large head	Cut in 1-2-inch florets	1Tbsp	400°F	15-20 mins
Brussels sprouts	1lb	Cut in half, remove stems	1Tbsp	425°F	15-20 mins
Carrots	1lb	Peel, cut in ¼-inch rounds	1 Tbsp	425°F	10-15 mins
Cauliflower	1 head	Cut in 1-2-inch florets	2 Tbsp	400°F	20-22 mins
Corn on the cob	7 ears	Whole ears, remove husks	1 Tbps	400°F	14-17 mins
Green beans	1 bag (12 oz)	Trim	1 Tbps	420°F	18-20 mins
Kale (for chips)	4 oz	Tear into pieces,remove stems	None	325°F	5-8 mins
Mushrooms	16 oz	Rinse, slice thinly	1 Tbps	390°F	25-30 mins
Potatoes, russet	1½ lbs	Cut in 1-inch wedges	1 Tbps	390°F	25-30 mins
Potatoes, russet	1lb	Hand-cut fries, soak 30 mins in cold water, then pat dry	½ -3 Tbps	400°F	25-28 mins
Potatoes, sweet	1lb	Hand-cut fries, soak 30 mins in cold water, then pat dry	1 Tbps	400°F	25-28 mins
Zucchini	1lb	Cut in eighths lengthwise, then cut in half	1 Tbps	400°F	15-20 mins

Appendix 3: Index

Made in the USA
Monee, IL
05 November 2024

69313116R00083